T0033917

THE LEGENDARY HARRY CARAY

THE LEGENDARY HARRY CARAY

Baseball's Greatest Salesman

Don Zminda

ROWMAN & LITTLEFIELD
Lanham • Boulder • New York • London

Published by Rowman & Littlefield
An imprint of The Rowman & Littlefield Publishing Group, Inc.
4501 Forbes Boulevard, Suite 200, Lanham, Maryland 20706
www.rowman.com

Unit A, Whitacre Mews, 26-34 Stannary Street, London SE11 4AB

British Library Cataloguing in Publication Information Available

Library of Congress Cataloging-in-Publication Data

Names: Zminda, Don, author.
Title: The legendary Harry Caray : baseball's greatest salesman / Don Zminda.
Description: Lanham, Maryland : Rowman & Littlefield, [2019] | Includes bibliographical refer-
ences and index.
Identifiers: LCCN 2018034792 (print) | LCCN 2018060022 (ebook) | ISBN 9781538112953 (elec-
tronic) | ISBN 9781538112946 (cloth : alk. paper) | ISBN 9781538159071 (pbk : alk. paper)
Subjects: LCSH: Caray, Harry. | Sportscasters—United States—Biography.
Classification: LCC GV742.42.C37 (ebook) | LCC GV742.42.C37 Z65 2019 (print) | DDC
070.449796092 [B]—dc23
LC record available at https://lccn.loc.gov/2018034792

∞™ The paper used in this publication meets the minimum requirements of
American National Standard for Information Sciences Permanence of Paper
for Printed Library Materials, ANSI/NISO Z39.48-1992.

Printed in the United States of America

CONTENTS

ACKNOWLEDGMENTS

During the 20-plus years I spent working in broadcast support for STATS LLC, I often considered writing a book about Harry Caray, one of the preeminent sports broadcasters of all time. But it wasn't until I retired in 2016, and Christen Karniski of Rowman & Littlefield contacted me to inquire whether I was working on any book ideas, that I thought, "Hey, now I finally have the time to write that Caray book!" So, thanks first of all to Christen for helping to get me going and shepherding me through the process of producing this book. Thanks also to Andrew Yoder, my R&L production editor, for his great help in taking the book to completion.

Once I got into the work, I knew I wanted to interview people who knew Caray personally, including those who had worked with or written about him. Deb Segal, a personal friend who had worked in Chicago media for many years, helped me get in touch with Mike Leiderman, Rich King, and Al Lerner, who took time to share their thoughts about Harry. Thanks to Deb for laying the groundwork, and to Rich, Al, and, particularly, Mike, for providing their insights.

Mike Leiderman helped me get in touch with longtime Chicago sportswriter Rick Telander, whose thoughts about Caray were very illuminating, and Mark Liptak, a Chicago White Sox historian and the driving force behind the website flyingwhitesox.com. Along with sharing personal experiences with Caray dating back to his teenage years, Mark provided copies of his interviews with people from the Caray years that had appeared on the website.

I had known sportswriter and author Ron Rapoport since the 1980s—I was his postman during my pre-STATS days!—and when I learned Ron was now living near my Los Angeles home, I contacted him and asked if he could meet for lunch and talk about Harry. Ron not only gave me a helpful interview, but also suggested that I get in touch with Bob Verdi, who had collaborated with Caray on his 1989 autobiography, *Holy Cow!*, and Grant DePorter, CEO of Harry Caray's Restaurant Group. Bob and Grant were tremendously helpful to me, and through Grant I was able to arrange an interview with Dutchie Caray, Harry's remarkable widow. Ron Rapoport also helped me get in touch with David Israel, who had written about Harry dating back to the early 1970s and originally been slated to collaborate with Caray on *Holy Cow!* Thanks to David for a candid interview.

I have known Bob Vorwald, director of production for WGN-TV in Chicago, and Len Kasper, the Chicago Cubs' television voice since 2005, for more than a decade, and both were generous with their help. Thanks to Bob for his interview, and to Len for his e-mail about Harry, the Cubs, and WGN (thanks also to Bob for helping me get in touch with Chicago sports broadcast legend Jack Rosenberg). Through my past work in sports broadcast support, I was able to interview a number of people who had worked with Caray or had experience with him. Thanks to Bob Brenly, Thom Brennaman, Bill Brown, Pat Hughes, Jim Kaat, Wayne Larrivee, Ed Randall, and Dewayne Staats for granting me some time to talk about Harry. And big thanks to Tim McCarver, whose experiences with Caray stretched back to Tim's playing days with the St. Louis Cardinals.

I have been a member of the Society for American Baseball Research (SABR) for almost 40 years, and several SABR members were helpful to me on this project. Thanks to Bill Deane for explaining the nuances of the National Baseball Hall of Fame's Ford C. Frick Award; Steve Gietschier for guidance on the St. Louis part of Caray's career (along with getting me in touch with St. Louis sportswriter Rick Hummel); and Dan Schlossberg, who collaborated with Milo Hamilton on Milo's autobiography. Thanks also to Father John Smyth of Maryville Academy, a place that was important to Caray, for his time in talking about Harry's charity work.

Of the almost 30 people I interviewed for this book, three were particularly important. Bob Costas, who has written about Caray, worked on television documentaries with Harry, and eulogized Caray after his death, was kind enough to spend a few minutes talking about Caray (thanks also to Steve Horn for working to hook me up with Bob). Ned Colletti, whose long career in baseball included Caray's early years with the Cubs, spoke about not only Caray as a broadcaster, but also Caray as a personal friend. And Chip Caray, Harry's grandson and a noted broadcaster in his own right, could not have been more generous in sharing his personal thoughts about his grandfather. Many thanks to all.

Thanks to my longtime friend and former *Chicago Tribune* reporter John McCarron for sharing his documents on the White Sox stadium saga.

Thanks to my great STATS colleague and friend Meghan Sheehan for helping me contact people in broadcasting. And thanks to Meghan and my other friends and former coworkers for being in my corner during this work.

Finally, thanks to my personal support team for their help on this long (and sometimes tedious) project: my wife Sharon; my stepsons Steve and Mike; Mike's wife Nancy, and our grandsons, Matt and Sean.

Don Zminda
Los Angeles
June 2018

INTRODUCTION

Harry Caray was not your typical baseball announcer.

When Caray had serious medical issues at different points during his career, the president of the United States—one time a Republican, the other time a Democrat—called to check on his health.

One of those presidents, Ronald Reagan, called Harry on the air during a Chicago Cubs game to welcome him back after Caray had suffered a stroke. A year later, Reagan—a baseball broadcaster himself in his younger days—dropped in on Harry at Wrigley Field and helped him do a little play-by-play.

When Caray's friends put together a roast in Las Vegas to honor (and poke a little fun at) him, Frank Sinatra served as the honorary chairman.

When Caray was in Memphis to broadcast a basketball game, Elvis Presley called and sent a limo to take Harry to Graceland, where he and Elvis enjoyed some beer and barbecued ribs.

Caray, who became famous in his later years for his rousing version of "Take Me Out to the Ball Game" during the seventh-inning stretch, sang the song at a Cubs game with First Lady Hillary Clinton. He sang it at the Democratic National Convention. He sang it at Mrs. Clinton's 50th birthday party. He sang it with Robert Merrill of the New York Metropolitan Opera.

Along the way, Caray broadcast more than 8,000 major-league games. He also visited thousands of night spots, consumed hundreds of thousands of alcoholic beverages (according to estimates made by his friends), and personally interacted with probably a million or more baseball fans.

❖ ❖ ❖

No one ever broadcast a game like Harry Caray. "They sent me a tape of him and said, 'We want you to be like him,'" recalled his longtime St. Louis Cardinals broadcast partner, Jack Buck. "But there was no way I could. There's only one guy who could broadcast like him."[1] Some critics described Harry as a "homer"—a broadcaster who openly roots for the home team—but Caray was more accurately, as he liked to put it, a fan behind the mic. Like most fans, Caray rejoiced when his team did something good. His home run calls ("It might be . . . it could be . . . it is! . . . a home run!") were epic; his famous phrase—"Holy Cow!"—punctuated exceptional moments during a game; and his shouts of "Cubs win! Cubs win!" (or earlier, "Cardinals win!" or "A's win!" or "Sox win!") at the end of a victory reflected pure, unadulterated joy.

But like most fans, Caray was also unafraid to reflect his exasperation when a player or team was struggling. "Get him outta there!" he would sometimes groan when a pitcher was having a rough outing. He could use his voice and his power to zero in on a player's perceived shortcomings, and the results weren't always pleasant. Some players who became Caray targets—notably Ken Boyer with the Cardinals and Bill Melton with the White Sox—found themselves the objects of merciless booing. "I had to get out of Chicago," said Melton after the White Sox traded him. "People turned against me because of that man upstairs [Caray]. If I had to go back, I'd probably have quit baseball."[2]

Caray's feuds were legendary—and not just with players. He locked horns so frequently with St. Louis Cardinals manager Eddie Dyer that when Dyer held a press conference to announce his resignation, Cardinals management told Caray not to attend, lest a verbal or physical confrontation develop. When Caray was broadcasting games for the Chicago White Sox, he called the team's owner, John Allyn, a "stupid man." He called Bud Selig, owner of the Milwaukee Brewers and the future commissioner of baseball, a "jerk." His relationships with his fellow broadcasters sometimes turned frigid as well, for various reasons. As Bob Verdi, who collaborated with Caray on Harry's autobiography, *Holy Cow!*, put it, "Harry was not an angel."[3]

Caray was most famous for his work with the Chicago Cubs at the end of his career, and in some ways that is unfortunate. He broadcast until he was 83 years old, and after his 1987 stroke, he often struggled with names and at times had problems keeping up with the action. Comedians imitated him, playing his eccentricities for laughs. Caray didn't seem to mind, but many people lost sight of what a talented broadcaster Caray had been in his prime. Famed broadcaster Bob Costas insisted that Caray's greatest work had come decades earlier, when Harry was broadcasting for the St. Louis Cardinals. Said Costas,

> Most of America, because of the passage of time and because he had a very long run on a superstation, which reached the entire country when he was the voice of the Cubs, thinks of him as this lovable cartoon character. The truth is that the real Harry Caray was the voice of the Cardinals in the '50s and '60s. That Harry Caray had, yes, a bigger-than-life personality, yes he was bombastic and impossible to miss, but he was also an extraordinarily skillful baseball announcer. He understood the theater, especially the theater of the mind that is radio; most of those broadcasts were radio broadcasts, not television broadcasts. So the idea that he was just this crazy guy who mispronounced peoples' names or sang "Take Me Out to the Ball Game" and extolled the virtues of Budweiser, all of which was true, especially at the end of his career, short-shrifts his greatness as a baseball announcer. If he had retired in 1970 after the Cardinals let him go, he already would have earned a spot in the broadcasters' wing of the Baseball Hall of Fame. He was that good just on his pure merits.[4]

Caray broadcast for five teams, and with four of them his arrival coincided with a major upsurge in the popularity of the team. There was some good fortune involved. In St. Louis, Caray began working for the Cardinals as World War II was coming to an end, and the Cardinals were one of many teams that experienced a postwar boom. Caray's brief tenure describing games for St. Louis' other major-league team, the Browns, began one season after the Browns' only American League pennant in 1944. With the Chicago White Sox, Caray arrived just after a season in which the team lost 106 games and had drawn fewer than 500,000 fans; Harry's popularity gave the team an enormous boost, but so did a better product on the field. With the Chicago Cubs, his work became available to the entire country via the WGN-TV superstation when the Cubs were one of the few teams whose local broadcasts were available nationally. But if he arrived at the right time in each of those situations, he took advantage of his opportunities like few people could. He was the perfect salesman to take a hot product and make it seem even hotter.

During the course of a career that spanned more than four decades, Caray proved himself remarkably adept at promoting baseball on both radio and television. With the Cardinals, his radio broadcasts were so popular the team's multistate network of stations became the largest in baseball by far. When he shifted to primarily working on television with the White Sox in 1973, he helped make the team's broadcasts on a struggling UHF station competitive with the crosstown Cubs on mighty WGN. And with the superstation Cubs, Harry's enthusiastic game calls and seventh-inning stretch ritual of singing "Take Me Out to the Ball Game," beamed to the entire country, made Cubs (and Caray) fans of people who lived thousands of miles away. It looked like fun to be there singing along with him, and fans began flocking to "beautiful Wrigley Field" in record numbers.

✧ ✧ ✧

The public Caray was the ultimate people person: friendly, outgoing, partying late into the night and connecting with seemingly everyone he met. The private Caray was much more complicated. Born the year World War I started, he had a difficult childhood. He never knew his father, his mother died when he was an adolescent, and he was raised by an aunt who struggled to make ends meet. It left scars. Caray was married three times, was by his own admission not a good husband to his first two wives, and for most of his life had a distant relationship with his children and grandchildren. "He really had trouble being Dad," his grandson, Chip Caray—himself a successful baseball broadcaster— once said. "He had no trouble being Harry." As *Chicago Sun-Times* writer Rick Telander put it, "Harry Caray's story is like that of the smiling clown who dazzles crowds while crying on the inside."[5]

Yet, when it came to learning to relate to his actual—not just his baseball—family, Caray made great strides in his later years. His third marriage, to the former Dutchie Goldmann, was, by all accounts, a happy one. Through Dutchie, Chip Caray and others have said, Harry was better able to connect with his loved ones than at any point in his life. In 1998, Harry and Chip were scheduled to work together on Cubs broadcasts, something both men were eagerly anticipating. Unfortunately, Harry died just as the Cubs were about to begin spring training.

This is not a sad story, however. Harry wouldn't have it. Caray himself was a storyteller, and I found out in the course of my research that sometimes he took a good story and made it more dramatic, or took a sad story and made it a little sadder. We can grant him a storyteller's liberties, but I have corrected the historical record in the few cases where I found that Harry's stories did not gibe with the facts. Harry Caray lived an amazing life—no embellishments needed.

◦ ◦ ◦

Caray died in February 1998, and his seat in the Chicago Cubs' broadcast booth has been occupied since 2005 by Len Kasper. Len was kind enough to offer his personal thoughts on Harry's legacy, and particularly his impact on the Cubs.

> Cubs television history is unlike any other in sports in that it was way ahead of its time in broadcasting every game on WGN and in getting the games to a national audience at the dawn of the cable era. It is also a story dominated by two industry titans—Jack Brickhouse and Harry Caray. And while Jack started it all in the booth, it was Harry who elevated all of it—the station, the ballpark, day games, Budweiser, the must-see seventh-inning stretch—to another stratosphere.
>
> When I think of Harry's legacy, the first place I go is him *selling* the Wrigley Field, day game, party atmosphere experience. So many broadcasters from his era were of the "Call it down the middle" philosophy, but he let his proverbial hair down in front of the mic every day, which created a raucous, *fun*, unpredictable broadcast.
>
> The lesson Harry taught all broadcasters was that being yourself works and that baseball is supposed to be fun.
>
> When you think about his career, it's pretty stunning that he is largely remembered as the voice of the Cubs, even though he worked for the Cardinals and White Sox previously! That didn't matter to Cubs fans, who immediately welcomed him into their arms as he embraced the uniqueness of the Friendly Confines, day baseball, and a national TV audience.

Lastly, I have to give Steve Stone a lot of credit in that he counterbalanced Harry perfectly. He played the straight man as well as Bud Abbott did and always ceded the spotlight to Harry, while adding his baseball expertise to the broadcasts.[6]

One of Harry Caray's favorite phrases was, "You can't beat fun at the old ballpark." For many people, including myself, Harry made the ballpark a lot more fun.

I

THE MAN WHO WASN'T THERE

Well, a lot of things happened today and they were all great, and they were all thrilling, and they were all dramatic. Too bad we couldn't have had a victory that meant a pennant. But that will come. Sure as God made green apples, someday the Chicago Cubs are going to be in a World Series. And maybe sooner than we think.—Harry Caray, signing off on the final day of the 1991 season [1]

On October 14, 1908, the Chicago Cubs finished the Major League Baseball season in triumphant fashion: They defeated the Detroit Tigers, 2–0, behind right-handed pitcher Orval Overall, to win their second consecutive World Series. This was long before baseball games were broadcast on radio and television, and there was no live description of the final play—a little grounder in front of home plate, which Cubs catcher Johnny Kling picked up and threw to first baseman-manager Frank Chance for the final out. Cubs fans had to depend on the Chicago newspapers for details on the game. "When Orval shut out Detroit's Tigers 2 to 0 today in the fifth and final game of the 1908 World's Series," wrote I. E. Sanborn in the next morning's *Chicago Tribune*, "he drove the final nail into the greatest honors that ever fell to one baseball club—two-straight world's championship pennants flaunting on top of three-straight league championship emblems." [2] The Cubs were a dynasty, and more October celebrations seemed sure to come. They weren't just winning; they were *flaunting*.

But then the October celebrations stopped happening for the Cubs. For several decades they remained a powerful team, reaching the

World Series again in 1910, 1918, 1929, 1932, 1935, 1938, and 1945. Each time, however, it was the Cubs' opponents who did the celebrating. After World War II, the franchise began to struggle, and even after the club finally returned to at least occasional prominence during the era of divisional play, which began in 1969, the Cubs were unable to return to the World Series. Eventually, more than a century had passed since that 1908 triumph.

Finally, in 2016, the Cubs reached the World Series for the first time in 71 years. Their opponent was another club with a long championship drought: the Cleveland Indians (last World Series championship in 1948). But the Cubs were the sentimental favorites. The series went the seven-game limit, and Game 7 went into extra innings in front of a capacity crowd at Cleveland's Progressive Field and a national television audience of more than 40 million—the largest TV audience for a World Series game since 1991. The Cubs took the lead in the top of the 10th inning, and although the Indians battled back, the Cubs moved to within one out of that elusive title. On Chicago radio station WSCR, veteran Cubs broadcaster Pat Hughes had the call as Mike Montgomery pitched to Rajai Davis:

> A little bouncer slowly toward Bryant. He will glove it . . . throw to Rizzo. It's in time, and the Chicago Cubs win the World Series! The Cubs come pouring out of the dugout jumping up and down like a bunch of delirious 10-year-olds! The Cubs have done it! The longest drought in the history of American sports is over and the celebration begins![3]

The celebration, both in Chicago and by Cubs fans (and sympathizers) throughout the world, lasted for days. Even the Chicago Symphony Orchestra joined in: The night after Game 7, conductor James Levine included a rendition of "Take Me Out to the Ball Game" during the encore of that evening's Mahler/Berlioz presentation. When the city of Chicago staged a parade and rally to celebrate the victory on Friday, November 4, an estimated 5 million people were in attendance.

Yet, while the World Series triumph was sweet for Cubs fans everywhere, many were remembering people who had passed away too soon to take part in the celebrations. At the Cubs' celebratory rally in Grant Park, host Pat Hughes paid tribute to what he called the "Mount Rushmore of Cubs legends": Ernie Banks, the Hall of Fame shortstop (and the Cubs' first African American player), who had died in January 2015; Ron Santo, Hall of Fame third baseman and later a beloved Cubs radio broadcaster, who had died in December 2010; Jack Brickhouse, the team's longtime television broadcaster, who had died in August 1998; and Harry Caray, the man who succeeded Brickhouse in the team's broadcast booth, and who had died in February 1998.

Unlike Banks and Santo, Harry Caray never played a game for the Cubs, and his 16-year broadcast tenure with the team was less than half as long as Jack Brickhouse's 39 seasons behind the mic. Nonetheless, the absence of Caray from the Cubs' World Series celebration was particularly painful for many Cubs fans. Caray had been the primary broadcast voice of the team from 1982 through 1997—years in which the Cubs had reached new heights of nationwide popularity. During that time, the Cubs had often struggled, but the team had also won two division titles behind a group of charismatic players that included Ryne Sandberg, Greg Maddux, Mark Grace, and Sammy Sosa. Thanks to the combination of a colorful team, a beloved and historic home ballpark (Wrigley Field), the nationwide reach of the WGN television "superstation," and Caray's personal charisma, the Cubs had become more popular than ever during his years with the team. During Caray's tenure, Cubs home attendance surpassed the 2 million mark for the first time (in 1984); within a few years of his death, annual home attendances of 3 million-plus had become commonplace for the Cubs.

Caray was given much of the credit for the Cubs' increased popularity. "I grew up in the Chicago area," said longtime Major League Baseball executive Ned Colletti, who was part of the Cubs front office from 1982 to 1993, adding,

> and for most of the time before Harry came to the Cubs, the upper deck at Wrigley was not even open on many days . . . there just weren't enough fans. I think in 1982, the first year Harry was there, we had three or four sellouts all year. It was a very, very different environment than you see today, and I think Harry had a lot to do with the change. He had as much to do with it as anyone out of uniform, and maybe more than most of the people who *were* in uniform.[4]

Caray's fame was so great that in May 1987, when he returned to the Wrigley Field broadcast booth after suffering a stroke, President Ronald Reagan called Caray during the game to welcome him back. When Caray died in 1998, his funeral at Chicago's Holy Name Cathedral was described as one of the largest in the city's history. Some fans waited as long as seven hours to view the casket. At the Cubs' home opener in 1999, the team unveiled the first statue outside Wrigley Field honoring a person connected to the franchise: one depicting Harry Caray leading the crowd in his seventh-inning stretch rendition of "Take Me Out to the Ball Game." The Cubs would not honor one of their players with a statue until they unveiled one of Banks in 2008.

On November 4, the day of the Cubs' post–World Series celebration in downtown Chicago, a number of fans skipped the Grant Park parade to pay homage to Caray at his gravesite at All Saints Cemetery in suburban Des Plaines. In remembrance of Caray's 1991 vow that the Cubs would eventually reach the World Series "sure as God made green apples," many of the visitors left apples at the gravesite; others did the same at the foot of Caray's statue outside Wrigley Field. Caray's son-in-law, Coley Newell, not only brought four cases of apples to deposit at the gravesite, but also arranged for the cemetery groundskeeper to hook up a radio next to the grave to play the broadcast during every World Series game.

Many Cubs fans, however, yearned for something more: Much as they loved and respected Pat Hughes, they wished they could have heard Caray describing the moment the Cubs won the World Series. Anheuser-Busch, whose beers Caray had promoted for much of his career, found a way to simulate that moment. With the cooperation of the Caray estate and WGN, the brewery's marketing department assembled some of Caray's audio clips to put together a two-minute video in which Caray "announced" the final half-inning of Game 7. While the video showed anxious Cub fans standing outside Wrigley Field and watching the game from bars, Caray's voice narrated the action.

> The Cubs are three outs away from winning. Boy, if you've got a weak heart, turn the set off. The rest of you, stay with us. Now he's ready . . . the pitch. Bouncing ball . . . there's the throw . . . he is out! The Cubs win! Cubs win! The Cubs are the champions! Look at that mob scene! Holy cow! You talk about a mass of happy humanity! How about them Cubbies! Now our lives are complete! The impossible is possible! The unbelievable is believable! This is Harry Caray. So long, everybody![5]

The commercial would be voted by YouTube viewers as the 2016 ad "that goes straight to the heart." "Wasn't it amazing?" Caray's widow, Dutchie, said in an interview. "It really sounded just like Harry was there doing the game."[6] It was, of course, no substitute for Caray actually having been present for the Cubs' moment of triumph. But like the apples that were left at his gravesite and near his Wrigley Field statue, it was a sign of Harry's powerful connection to his fans, in good times and bad. Even 18 years after his death, Harry Caray—the man whose headstone bears the inscription "Forever dedicated to the fans of baseball"—hadn't lost his magic.

2

EARLY DAYS

A homecoming was celebrated by Harry Caray, when he was appointed sports editor of KXOK, St. Louis, as his entry in the big time also marked his return to the hometown, after serving his radio apprenticeship in Joliet, Ill., and Kalamazoo, Mich. Caray took over at KXOK, succeeding Jerry Burns, who entered the army at Jefferson Barracks, Mo. Harry is carrying on Burns's program, "Sports from a Different Angle," under the title of "Sports Extra," at the same time each evening, 10:45 CWT.—"On the Air Lanes," *Sporting News*, January 1944[1]

For a long time, pretty much all we knew for certain about Harry Caray's birth was that it took place in St. Louis, and that his birth name was Harry Christopher Carabina. As for the year, Harry's autobiography, *Holy Cow!*, which was written in 1989, doesn't say, and at various points in his broadcasting career, Caray frequently changed his story. "I can prove seven different ages," he laughingly told *Sporting News* in 1989. "As long as I'm alive and feeling good, what difference does it make?"[2] "He'd shave a couple years off his age every time he'd go to a new city," said Caray's son Skip.[3] The confusion was such that, when Caray died in 1998, the *Chicago Tribune* reported that Caray's birth year had been listed by various entities as 1920 (*New York Times*, *USA Today*, Cubs media guide), 1919 (*Chicago Tribune*), and 1914 (*Chicago Sun-Times*, *St. Louis Post-Dispatch*, *Sports Illustrated*).

Two decades after Caray's death, it is fairly certain that Caray's birthdate was March 1, 1914; that is the date listed in St. Louis health records, and that is also the date listed on his Social Security death record (available online at Ancestry.com and other genealogy websites). According to Caray's autobiography, he never met his father, Christopher Carabina; Caray wrote that his mother, the former Daisy Argint, remarried when Caray was about five or six but then died a couple of years later. The autobiography states that Caray's father's heritage was Italian and that his mother was Romanian; however, Caray's biography on the website for the State Historical Society of Missouri states that census records list both of Caray's parents as Albanian. (The 1920 census lists Harry's mother's birthplace as Albania but her native tongue as Romanian, which may account for the confusion.) The biography states that Caray's father was a waiter who served in the military in World War I and likely never rejoined his family after the war. According to Skip Caray, "His father had gone back to the old country, and when he heard [years later] that Dad had become successful, he wrote him a letter. Dad took the letter and threw it away unopened."[4]

Daisy Carabina, Harry's mother, worked as a seamstress, and times were difficult. After achieving fame in adulthood, Caray often talked about the day he graduated from grammar school. The boys were supposed to dress in white pants, but Harry couldn't afford a pair and had to wear his regular gray pants. "My classmates ridiculed me," he recalled. "I was very hurt and embarrassed. I was crying when I went to sleep that night, and I vowed that someday I would have enough money to buy 100 pairs of white pants."[5]

Daisy's second marriage took place not when Caray was five or six, but in 1926, when Harry was 12, to a man named Sam Capuran. Daisy died of pneumonia at the age of 37, on April 2, 1928, shortly after Harry's 14th birthday (copies of Daisy Argint's marriage and death certificates from the state of Missouri are available online). After his mother's death, Harry lived with his maternal uncle, John Argint, John's wife Doxie, and their four children, at 1909 LaSalle Avenue in St. Louis. Census records from 1930 list John Argint as a 37-year-old waiter, with Doxie listed as being 29 years old. Other household members according to the 1930 census were Olga Argint (10 years old), Elizabeth Argint (8), Nicholas Argint (7), Theodor Argint (5), and Harry Carabina, listed as being 15 years old.

In his autobiography, Caray wrote that John Argint either deserted his family or died, and that he was raised by Doxie. He did not die, as the 1940 census shows John Argint, Doxie, and the four Argint children (but not Harry) living on Selma Avenue in Webster Groves, a suburb southwest of St. Louis, where Caray's autobiography states that the family moved in 1930. It is, of course, entirely possible that John Argint left the family sometime between 1930 and 1940, and returned after Harry moved out, or that John's listed home address on the census forms was not his actual residence. When Doxie Argint died in 1959, in St. Louis, her obituary listed her children but not a husband. John Argint was living in Seattle when he died in 1963. John, Doxie, and the Argint children are buried at St. Matthew's Cemetery in St. Louis. I could find no other information about the family.

In an interview for the 2006 DVD *"Hello Again Everybody": The Harry Caray Story*, Harry's widow Dutchie said about Caray's adopted family: "He realized that he was living there, but he never felt that that was his family. . . . I guess he felt like there was no place for him, and he never really liked to talk about his childhood."[6]

Harry Carabina attended Webster Groves High School, graduating in 1932. The school yearbook for Harry's senior year lists him as a member of the school's baseball team for three years and the basketball team for two years, as well as one year as a member of the glee club. In baseball he was a middle infielder, a switch-hitter, and a good enough player to be offered a scholarship to the University of Alabama, according to his autobiography. Harry wrote that he turned down the offer because he could not afford the expenses for room and board, books, and travel. A 1978 *People* magazine article stated that Caray was a Golden Gloves boxing champion, a claim not mentioned in his autobiography (a list of St. Louis Golden Gloves champions on the boxing history website Boxrec.com does not contain the name Harry Carabina).

After high school, Harry played a little semipro ball and worked for a manufacturing company. In 1937, at age 23, he married Dorothy May Ganz; the marriage last 12 years and produced three children, one of whom was Harry Jr., who would win broadcasting fame of his own several decades later as Skip Caray. Throughout this time, Harry continued to follow baseball fervently, often attending Cardinals games at Sportsman's Park. "I'd go to the bleachers for 55 cents, and every time I was there, the game seemed really exciting to me," he told Richard

Dozer in 1972. "But then I'd listen on the radio the rest of the week, and the game seemed really dull."[7]

At that time, the Cardinals' and St. Louis Browns' main radio voice was France Laux. "In St. Louis, no one was more beloved in the 1930s and '40s than Laux," wrote sports broadcasting historian Ted Patterson. Laux's career had begun, accidentally, in 1927; a station in Tulsa, Oklahoma, had an emergency opening for someone to recreate that day's World Series game between the New York Yankees and Pittsburgh Pirates from telegraph transmissions, and someone suggested Laux. Arriving "with all of 90 seconds to spare," Laux broadcast the game, got good reviews, and a new career was born. By 1929, he had moved to KMOX in St. Louis, broadcasting games for both St. Louis teams.[8]

Laux's broadcasting style was plain and direct, and it appealed to baseball commissioner Kenesaw Mountain Landis, who would tell his announcers, "If you see men putting up a gallows in center field and then see them lead me out to it and hang me on it, describe it into the microphone but don't question the justice of the hanging."[9] With Landis making the assignments, Laux broadcast nine World Series and nine All-Star Games in the 1930s and 1940s. In 1937, he was selected the first winner of the Radio Announcer of the Year award given by *Sporting News*.

Laux was extremely popular in the 1920s and 1930s, but as St. Louis sportswriter Bob Broeg observed, "He always spoke in a flat, metallic southern type of accent. It was accepted in the 30s, but later on, when competition hit him in the war years . . . it was quite a drawback."[10] Harry Carabina had a similar assessment of Laux, and in 1940, he wrote a letter to Merrill Jones, the vice president and general manager of KMOX; it stated that he (Harry) could do a much better job of broadcasting. Jones was intrigued enough to give Carabina an audition and liked what he heard. He told Harry he would need some experience before breaking into the big time and helped him land a job as a "sports specialist" with WCLS in Joliet, Illinois. It was Bob Holt, the station manager of WCLS, who suggested that Harry change his last name from Carabina to Caray.

There were stumbles at first—long after he became famous, Caray loved to talk about his first awkward interview with a man who had bowled a 300 game—but Caray's work was solid enough for him to move to a bigger station, WKZO in Kalamazoo, Michigan, in 1941.

(WKZO's staff included another young broadcaster headed for fame: radio newsman Paul Harvey.) Among other assignments at WKZO, Caray got a chance to broadcast a semipro baseball tournament. It was at that tournament, Caray wrote, that he first used two of his signature phrases: "It might be . . . it could be . . . it is! . . . a home run!" after a homer, and his all-purpose expression of emotion, "Holy Cow!"[11]

Caray is sometimes credited with being the first broadcaster to use the term "Holy Cow" in a baseball broadcast, and he suggested as much in his autobiography, but that is not the case. Yankees shortstop-turned-broadcaster Phil Rizzuto, whose broadcasting career began in 1957, was also a frequent user of the phrase. Sports broadcasting historian Curt Smith gave Rizzuto credit for primacy of the term over Caray based on a story that Harry was in Sportsman's Park in St. Louis in 1942, and heard Rizzuto shout "Holy Cow!" to Yankees second baseman Gerry Priddy. That seems a stretch; among other things, Caray was working in Kalamazoo in 1942. In truth, neither man was the first to use or popularize the term in a baseball broadcast. Halsey Hall, who began broadcasting games for the minor-league Minneapolis Millers in 1934, "was using the phrase from the beginning," according to Hall's biographer, Stew Thornley; in fact, the title of Thornley's book is *Holy Cow!*[12] Lisa Winston of *USA Today*, who researched the term, wrote that Jack Holiday, who broadcast games for the New Orleans Pelicans of the minor-league Southern Association, was also using "Holy Cow!" as early as the 1930s. What may be true is that Caray was the first broadcaster to use the term in major-league games, and he almost certainly was the first to popularize the term for audiences listening to Major League Baseball. But that came later.

Caray's tenure in Kalamazoo came to an end in 1943. With World War II raging, his draft status was reclassified to 1-A, and he had to return to St. Louis for his induction physical. Caray flunked the physical due to poor eyesight, but fearful that his draft status might change, he remained in St. Louis and landed a job as a staff announcer at KXOK. In January 1944, he was appointed sports editor of the station, with his own nightly program. From the beginning, he worked to make himself stand out from the competition. "I started ripping everybody in sight," Caray said, reflecting on those days. "Everything that was accepted as popular I tried to make unpopular. Everything that was unpopular, well, I was on their bandwagon. It was a calculated thing to make people know you're there. And it worked."[13]

The 1944 season was a big one for St. Louis baseball. For the only time in their 52-year tenure in the city (1902–1953), the St. Louis Browns won the American League pennant. Their opponent in the World Series was the St. Louis Cardinals, who won their third straight National League pennant that year. (The Cardinals won the all-St. Louis World Series in six games.) Caray kept himself in the limelight. When the Browns returned from a road trip in August, *Sporting News* reported that Caray met the team at Union Station, and "by means of a portable recorder," transcribed interviews with Browns personnel for broadcast on his show the following night.[14] A photo in a December issue of the paper showed Caray seated alongside *Sporting News* publisher J. G. Taylor Spink, broadcasting reports from the annual major- and minor-league meetings.

Following the 1944 season, the Griesedieck Brothers brewery of St. Louis announced their intention to sponsor Cardinals and Browns broadcasts in 1945. In preparation for the move, the brewery hired Caray to handle hockey broadcasts for the St. Louis Flyers of the American Hockey League, as well as other sports, including college basketball, boxing, and wrestling. Caray was slated to be the number-three man for broadcasts of the major-league games in 1945, behind a still-to-be-named number-one broadcaster and analyst Gabby Street. The brewery was hoping to sign a nationally known play-by-play man like Mel Allen, Red Barber, or Bob Elson to handle the top spot. When those efforts failed, Caray decided to apply for the role.

He took his case directly to the president of the brewery, Edward J. Griesedieck, who told Caray of his admiration for the work of France Laux. When Caray asked why, Griesedieck said that he could read the newspaper and have a cup of coffee while listening to Laux without having his concentration disturbed. Caray countered that Griesedieck would be better served with a more animated broadcaster like himself, one who could keep the fan's attention focused on the game—and also on the sponsor's commercials. "Do you know how many thousands of dollars you're wasting on commercials while somebody's reading a newspaper?" Caray recalled saying to Griesedieck. "Wouldn't you rather have a guy who keeps the fan from reading the newspaper when you're paying to have him listen to your commercials?"[15] He got the job.

In the mid-1940s, it was commonplace for teams to broadcast live from the ballpark for their home games only; road games, if aired at all, were usually broadcast from the studio, with the announcers recreating the play-by-play based on telegraph reports from the road ballpark. It was also not uncommon for more than one station in a major-league city to broadcast a team's games. In 1945, Caray and Street broadcast the home games for both the Cardinals and the Browns. But they had competition: France Laux, who had not broadcast games in 1943–1944, returned to the airwaves to broadcast Cardinals and Browns games in 1945, with Johnny O'Hara as his partner.

Perhaps luckily, Caray and Street did not have to go head-to-head in 1945 against Dizzy Dean, former Cardinals pitching great, who had been broadcasting Cardinals and Browns games since 1941. Dean's broadcasts had been sponsored by the Falstaff Brewing Company, and the brewer had relinquished its option to broadcast games in 1945. Dean had been selected outstanding baseball broadcaster of the year by *Sporting News* in 1944, and his unique play-by-play calls ("swang and missed," "slud into third") drew so much attention that Dean would later receive a complaint from the English Teachers Association of Missouri, "on the ground that his grammar and syntax had a bad influence on their pupils."[16] In his article about Dean's 1944 broadcasting award, Spink wrote, "Dizzy became a terrific radio favorite in the St. Louis area last season—an accomplishment that was all the more remarkable because his broadcasts were carried over two stations of limited power."[17]

When Caray teamed up with Charles "Gabby" Street in 1945, wrote Stuart Shea, Street was the "star of the show; while Caray was well-liked, Street was a local hero."[18] Known as "Old Sarge"—he had served as a sergeant during World War I—Street had served as a Cardinals coach in the late 1920s, then became the team's manager in 1930 (after a one-game interim manager stint in 1929). In his first two seasons at the helm, Street led the Cardinals to the National League pennant, including an upset victory against the two-time defending champion Philadelphia Athletics in the 1931 World Series. Replaced as Cardinals skipper by Frankie Frisch in midseason 1933, Street returned to St. Louis for a one-year stint as manager of the Browns in 1938 (the team finished the year in seventh place). Street began his broadcasting career working with the Browns in 1940, then worked with Laux on Cardinals broadcasts.

As a major-league player with four teams from 1904 to 1912, Street had had a relatively undistinguished career—his lifetime batting average was only .208—but he was considered an excellent defensive catcher. In 1908, after Street had made several sensational catches of foul balls for the Washington Senators, sportswriter Preston Gibson insisted to another writer that Street was deft enough to catch a ball dropped from the top of the Washington Monument. After some goading from Gibson, Street agreed to it give a try. On the morning of August 20, Gibson climbed to the top of the monument and began dropping baseballs to the waiting Street from more than 500 feet high. On his 13th and final attempt, Street succeeded in catching one of the balls. Recalling the feat in 1947, Spink wrote, "Street's feat made him famous. Reports of his accomplishments, pictures, and mathematical computations circled the world."[19]

Street was 62 years old when the 1945 season began, but on May 24 of that year, he attempted to recreate his Washington Monument feat—this time from a tall building in St. Louis, with baseballs dropped by Harry Caray. As part of a war-bond drive, Caray originated his nightly *Sports Extra* show from the Civil Courts building in St. Louis. From the roof of the building—approximately 300 feet high—Caray dropped three balls to the waiting Street, who caught the first ball, missed the second, and caught the third. The rally netted more than $400,000 in bond sales, including $300,000 from the Griesedieck Brewery, which purchased the third ball. The next day, the *St. Louis Star-Times* featured a picture of Street standing poised to catch one of the balls, with the headline "Neat Feat, Street."[20] The stunt was part of a successful first season as a team for Street and Caray, the latter of whom commented on numerous occasions throughout the years about his respect and admiration for Street.

❧ ❧ ❧

The Caray–Street team returned for their second year in 1946, but this time they would be going head-to-head against Dizzy Dean, whose return to broadcasting games was promoted in large ads from his sponsor, Falstaff, in the St. Louis papers in April. ("Baseball ala 'Dizzy' Dean is not just another play by play. It's a riotous roundup of ribbing and rare, original Deanisms.")[21] As usual, Dean's work drew considerable attention. One example was a lengthy August *Sporting News* feature in which the baseball weekly went through a "typical Dean broadcast" from beginning to end.

The 1946 season was the first full year of baseball following the end of World War II, and it was a successful year for the Cardinals. The team returned to the World Series for the fourth time in five years, winning a best-of-three playoff series against the Brooklyn Dodgers after the clubs finished the regular season tied. In addition, the Cardinals had a home attendance of more than 1 million fans for the first time in franchise history. The club's home attendance of 1,061,807 was 79 percent higher than the 594,630 fans the club drew in 1945.

The local interest in the 1946 pennant race prompted Caray and Street's Griesedieck sponsors to add recreations of Cardinals road games to the broadcast schedule on dates on which the Browns were idle. The colorful, creative Caray, working from the St. Louis studios using wire reports, excelled at making the recreated games sound exciting and realistic; meanwhile Dizzy Dean often sounded bored when trying to recreate a game, at least according to Caray. "The people turned to me and Gabby," he wrote.[22]

On the night following the last game of the 1946 regular season, some friends of Cardinals star Stan Musial and rookie catcher Joe Garagiola threw a party for the team. Longtime St. Louis sportswriter Bob Broeg was one of the attendees. According to Broeg, another St. Louis writer, J. Roy Stockton, who was serving as toastmaster, made a speech attacking Cardinals owner Sam Breadon. The gist of the speech was that the Cardinals would have easily won the National League pennant—instead of having to face the Dodgers in a playoff—had Breadon not dealt away a number of veteran players. When Stockton was finished, Harry Caray was invited to speak. Caray came to Breadon's defense, offering several examples of Breadon's generosity to Cardinals players throughout the years. When Caray finished, Breadon thanked him and said he would never forget it.

          ✿ ✿ ✿

After winning the National League pennant, the Cardinals faced the Boston Red Sox in the 1946 World Series. Arch McDonald (Washington Senators) and Jim Britt (Boston Red Sox and Braves) were selected to work the national radio broadcasts for the series, in which St. Louis prevailed in seven games. *Sporting News* reported that after Game 1, numerous protests were phoned in to the Mutual outlet (KWK) broadcasting the game in St. Louis, "where fans had listened all season to the colorful descriptions of Dizzy Dean, Johnny O'Hara, Harry Caray, and Gabby Street."[23] A United Press article reported that acting St. Louis mayor Albert Schweitzer told the Gillette Safety Razor Company, sponsor of the broadcasts, that either Dean, O'Hara, Street, or Caray should be selected to work with Boston's Britt. Gillette did not honor the request, but it was a sign of the growing popularity of the Caray–Street team.

In November, Caray's work was given more tangible recognition: *Sporting News* selected him as the outstanding play-by-play announcer in the National League for 1946, with the Yankees' Mel Allen winning the honors for American League broadcasters. Wrote Spink,

> His versatility, frankness, enthusiasm, and thorough familiarity with the game have built up a wide following for Caray with his play-by-play broadcasts, in which he has the capable assistance of Gabby (Ol' Sarge) Street . . . who has an extensive inside knowledge and a wealth of historical information about the game.[24]

That winter, Breadon decided to capitalize on the increased interest in the Cardinals by broadcasting the team's complete schedule of games, both home and road, in 1947. Many of the road games would be recreated from wire reports, but the broadcasters would travel to some road sites and report the games from there. Both the Caray–Street crew's sponsor, Griesedieck Beer, and the Dean–O'Hara crew's sponsor, Falstaff, were interested in broadcasting the games. Along with Dean, the Falstaff crew had a bigger network and was willing to pay more money for the broadcast rights; however, Breadon awarded the contract to Griesedieck and the Caray–Street crew. When he gave the news to a surprised Caray, Breadon told him, "Young man, a few months ago at that testimonial dinner, I told you that I would never forget what you did. Well, consider this proof of that."[25] Beginning in 1947, Harry Caray would be the radio voice of the Cardinals—with no competitors.

3

VOICE OF THE CARDINALS

Catching on hereabouts is "Harry Caray Polka," featuring composer
Glenn Young and his band and a vocal group, the Base Hits. Sports
announcer Caray chimes in with his "Holy Cow" and "It Might Be,
Etc." As polkas go, this is as good as most.—"Popular Recordings,"
St. Louis Post-Dispatch, September 6, 1950[1]

The years immediately following World War II were boom times in
baseball. With the war raging, major-league attendance had dropped to
7,465,911 in 1943; that was the smallest number of fans to attend major-league games since 1935, when the country was in the midst of the
Great Depression (that year, the St. Louis Browns drew only 80,922
fans all season). Major League Baseball attendance rose to 8,772,746 in
1944, and then, with the war drawing to a close, to 10,841,123 in 1945.
That total was an all-time record and marked only the second time in
history that MLB attendance had surpassed the 10 million mark (the
other year was 1930).

More improvement was expected in 1946, but what happened surpassed the expectations of even the most optimistic MLB magnates. In
1946, 10 of the 16 major-league teams drew more than 1 million fans to
their home games; the New York Yankees became the first team to
surpass the 2 million mark in home attendance for a season; and a total
of 18,523,288 fans poured through the gates, almost 8 million more
than the record set the previous year. The upsurge continued in 1947,
when MLB attendance rose to 19.9 million, reaching the high-water
mark in 1948, when total attendance surpassed the 20 million mark for

the first time in major-league history (20,920,842). That number would not be surpassed until 1962, when there were four more major-league teams due to expansion. Although attendance began to drop off in 1949, with some observers blaming the increased availability of games on television, the total, even at its postwar low point (14.4 million in 1953), was far higher than at any point prior to the war.

Harry Caray's St. Louis Cardinals shared in the postwar attendance boom. After surpassing the million mark in home attendance for the first time in 1946, the Redbirds drew more than 1 million fans every year from 1947 through 1951, with home attendance peaking at 1,430,676 in 1949, a year in which the Cardinals battled the Brooklyn Dodgers for the National League pennant down to the last day (Brooklyn took the flag by a one-game margin). That remained a club record until 1966, the season the Cardinals moved into the second Busch Stadium.

Was Caray's popularity a major factor in the Cardinals' postwar attendance increase? Testimonial evidence from the time says yes. In 1949, Bill DeWitt, president of the St. Louis Browns, the Cardinals' Sportsman's Park landlords, specifically singled out Caray and Gabby Street for helping draw 14,500 fans for a weekday afternoon game between the Cardinals and Boston Braves. "I believe the tremendous radio play announcers Harry Caray and Gabby Street have been giving the club was greatly responsible for this turnout," said DeWitt.[2] Two years later, Sporting News wrote of Caray, "His broadcasts helped the Cardinals top the 1,000,000 mark for the sixth year in a row, and his popularity was attested by a crowd of nearly 30,000, which turned out for Radio Appreciation Day at St. Louis, August 5."[3] And in 1952, Sporting News reported that a review of license plates from cars parked outside Sportsman's Park for a Cardinals–Dodgers game revealed that fans from 38 states, Canada, and Mexico had attended the contest. "The widespread representation of the August 24 crowd," the paper wrote, "was due in part to the broadcasts of Harry Caray, who . . . is heard over an extensive Cardinal network that reaches into many states."[4]

However, one should be cautious about giving Caray too much credit for the Cardinals' postwar attendance increase, as the phrase "a rising tide lifts all boats" applies well to what was happening in St. Louis. Table 3.1 compares the team's annual finish in the National League standings with its National League rank in home attendance from 1945 to 1953, Caray's first nine years broadcasting Cardinals' games.

During that nine-year period, the Cardinals were consistently one of the league's stronger teams, posting a winning record each year and finishing either first, second, or third in the standings in all but one season (1950, when they finished fifth). Yet, in this same period, the Cardinals never ranked higher than third in the league in attendance. It is fair to point out that the St. Louis area was not (and never has been) one of MLB's bigger markets; according to 1950 census data, the St. Louis metropolitan area ranked seventh in population among the 10 metropolitan areas that had at least one major-league team at the time. Nonetheless, the St. Louis area had a higher population (1.67 million) in 1950 than metropolitan Cleveland (1.45 million)—but the Indians had a home attendance of at least 1 million in every season from 1946 to 1955, drew more than 1.5 million fans each year from 1947 to 1951, and topped the 2 million mark twice, including 2.6 million in the Indians' World Series championship season of 1948. (Cleveland did have the advantage of a playing in a home stadium with a much larger seating capacity than the Cardinals' Sportsman's Park.)

Another way to look at this is by comparing the Cardinals' annual home attendance to that of the National League as a whole. During the years in which each league had eight teams, an average club's home attendance would provide 12.5 percent of the league total. From 1945

Table 3.1. Cardinals, Rank in National League Standings versus Rank in National League Attendance, 1945–1953

Year	Won–Lost	Rank in NL Standings	Attendance	Rank in NL Attendance
1945	95–59	second	594,630	fifth
1946	98–58	first	1,061,807	fourth
1947	89–65	second	1,247,913	sixth
1948	85–69	second	1,111,440	sixth
1949	96–58	second	1,430,676	third
1950	78–75	fifth	1,093,411	fifth
1951	81–73	third	1,013,429	third
1952	88–66	third	913,113	fourth
1953	83–71	third	880,242	third

to 1948, the Cardinals' home attendance contributed less than 12.5 percent to the league's total each year, despite having excellent teams. The figure then rose to more than 12.5 percent each year from 1949 to 1952, with a high of 15.1 percent in 1949; that seems like a trend, but if it was, it didn't last. From 1953 to 1961, the last nine seasons of the National League's eight-team era, Cardinals' home games provided more than 12.5 percent of the league total only twice, in 1954 and 1957. In truth, the Cardinals franchise's attendance boom didn't begin until their move into the second Busch Stadium in May 1966. In 1967, the team's first full season in Busch II, the Cardinals drew more than 2 million fans to their home games for the first time in team history and led the National League in attendance for the first time since 1901. By then, Harry Caray's long tenure in the Cardinals radio booth was almost at its end.

❁ ❁ ❁

Although Caray's work was not necessarily a major factor in the Cardinals' postwar attendance increase, his ability to attract radio listeners has solid statistical backing. Each April during Caray's tenure with the Cardinals, *Sporting News* would produce a log listing the radio stations that were carrying each team's broadcasts. In 1947, the first season that Caray and Street had exclusive rights to the Cardinals' broadcasts, the log listed a total of 17 stations that were broadcasting the Redbirds' games, all of them in either Missouri, Illinois, or Arkansas. In 1948, the number rose to 41 stations, most in the majors (the Detroit Tigers were second, with 22 stations). The network grew to 53 stations in 1949, 64 in 1950, 71 in 1951, 73 in 1952, 75 in 1953, and 91 in 1954. The team with the second-largest network in 1954, the Milwaukee Braves, had only 43 stations on board. The number of stations in the Cardinals' network leveled off after that, but this was most likely due to the fact that the team's St. Louis flagship station, beginning in 1955, was powerful 50,000-watt KMOX, whose broadcasts could be heard in numerous states far from Missouri.

Impressive as they are, these numbers likely *underestimate* the number of stations that were broadcasting Caray's games; they were published in the spring, and it was not uncommon for stations to join a club's radio network after the season started. For example, the Cardinals' spring total of 75 stations in 1953 was reported to have grown to 87 by the end of the year, according to *Sporting News*. At its peak, the Cardinals' radio network consisted of stations in as many as 12 states.

The growth of the Cardinals' radio network was seen in many circles as a credit to Caray. Interestingly, longtime St. Louis sportswriter Bob Broeg told Curt Smith that in St. Louis proper, public opinion about Caray was roughly divided 50–50, compared with previous Cardinals broadcasters like France Laux and Dizzy Dean. But in the smaller towns that comprised the huge Cardinals' radio network, Broeg thought listeners approved of Caray by something like a 95-to-5 margin. "Harry was a god," Broeg said about Caray's popularity in the hinterlands.[5]

Stan Musial, the Cardinals' greatest star during the 1940s and 1950s, commented to Rich Wolfe and George Castle,

> Harry made a lot of great Cardinal fans back in those days, because after the war there weren't many cars around and people didn't travel. Harry made all these fans in Arkansas, down in Tennessee, all the Southern states, Kansas, and other places. We were the team for the West. We had all those fans. But Harry made them great fans through listening to him and Cardinals baseball.[6]

In July 1949, Caray was the subject of a *St. Louis Star-Times* profile written by Bill Fleischman. The article summarized Caray's career and included a couple of pictures, one of them showing Harry at the microphone with his nine-year-old son "Skippy" (the "number-one rooter") seated in his lap. "Although some people find that Caray and his unending enthusiasm over the Cardinals sound better when the ears are plugged with cotton," wrote Fleischman, "most of his listeners don't. He receives 1,500 letters a week during the baseball season, approximately 900 of them from out of town."[7]

So great was Caray's pull that, on one occasion, he even helped a Cardinals fan from out of town find a babysitter. In 1948, a Redbirds fan named Ed Rak from Jefferson City, Missouri, wrote Caray that he was unable to attend games at Sportsman's Park because he needed to care for his two-year-old son. Caray read Rak's letter over the air and received more than a dozen calls from listeners offering to care for the child while he attended a game.

By 1950, Caray was cashing in on his popularity with the Cardinals radio network by producing a weekly column for newspapers in the team's broadcast area. *Sporting News* reported that a total of 65 papers were carrying the column. Its title? "Holy Cow," of course. (The next spring, the paper reported that Caray had gone to the U.S. Patent Office to trademark the term "Holy Cow" for use in his newspaper columns.)

✿ ✿ ✿

In those early years with the Cardinals, an important factor in Caray's success was his skill in re-creating broadcasts from wire reports. In 1947, the first year Caray and Street broadcast both Cardinals home and road games, they were working live from the road site only when the team was visiting either Chicago or Cincinnati; all other road games were broadcast from the St. Louis studios using wire reports. (It wasn't until the early 1950s that the Cardinals broadcast crew began traveling to every National League road site.) Caray's ability to make the re-creations sound realistic drew praise from *Sporting News*:

> So realistic are the play-by-play of Cardinals' out-of-town games, as constructed by Harry Caray over WTMV, that the fans find it difficult to distinguish between them and the direct-from-the-park accounts when the Redbirds are at home. As a result, the station and newspapers have been compelled to answer many queries as to whether it is a ticker game, or the original, and wagers have been placed on the question.[8]

In his book *Cardinals Journal*, John Snyder described Caray's meticulous system for making the re-creations sound realistic: "He and Street placed a photograph of the out-of-town park in front of them that showed the park's size and dimensions along with the location of the grandstands and bleachers. As each play came in on the ticker, in code, the Western Union operator interpreted the message, who passed it in to Caray, who then reconstructed the scene as if he were actually present. Sound effects and crowd noises were added."[9]

The re-creations could be challenging for Caray and his broadcast crew. A 1948 *Sporting News* article about a "three-hour-and-28-minute marathon" between the Cardinals and Brooklyn Dodgers at Ebbets Field stated that the wire-service operator "wore a blister on his fingers" decoding the wire reports and had to finish the game using his left hand. The re-creation was briefly disrupted when a cleaning crew, thinking the game was over, walked into the studio "with a vacuum cleaner going full blast." And Gabby Street "used up his full quota of six cigars and said good-night in sign language, his vocal capacity being exhausted." The article concluded with a note that Street needed to have his dentures recapped the next day.[10]

✿ ✿ ✿

As his fame increased, Caray was earning national, as well as regional, recognition. *Sporting News*, which had named him the National League's top radio play-by-play broadcaster in 1946, gave Caray the same award in 1948, 1949, and 1951. In his article about the 1948 broadcasting awards, *Sporting News* publisher J. G. Taylor Spink wrote,

> Caray's versatility, enthusiasm, and thorough familiarity with the game have built up a wide following. Among the factors scoring heavily in his favor for the National League award is the wealth of background information which he presents on his play-by-play broadcasts. This information not only includes statistics about the team and individual performances of the Cardinals and opposing clubs, but also human-interest material about the performers.[11]

Even in the years when he was winning broadcasting awards and helping grow the Cardinals radio network, Caray had his share of critics. One of them was *St. Louis Post-Dispatch* sports editor J. Roy Stockton, the man whose putdown of Cardinals owner Sam Breadon at a team banquet in 1946 had brought an immediate, and vigorous, response from Caray. Stockton even downplayed Caray's role in the growth of the team's radio network, saying, "You could have put Mother Goose on as the Cardinals' voice, and the sticks would have loved her."[12]

Stockton may have had a personal axe to grind with Caray; however, there were also critics who missed Dizzy Dean, who had been relegated to St. Louis Browns broadcasts when the Cardinals chose the Caray–Street team as the clubs' exclusive radio crew in 1947. In an article about Dean in September 1947, *Washington Post* writer John Crosby wrote that the fact that Dean "should be calling the games of the team that occupies the cellar position of the American League is a triumph of commerce over art." Crosby went on to compare Caray unfavorably to Dean, even deriding Caray's vaunted re-creations.

> The contrast between Caray and Dean is violent. Caray is a hysterical, rabidly pro-Cardinal announcer, who shouts himself into exhaustion over any play larger than a foul tip. "It looks like . . . it might be . . . it IS—a HOME RUN," he screams. His broadcasts of telegraph games are little horrors of fakery. He uses recordings of crowd noises and invents endless phony details . . . that are obviously not carried on the wire, and almost goes out of his mind when any Cardinal gets as far as first. [13]

In St. Louis, letters to the local sports columnists could be passionate on both sides of the fence in critiquing Caray's work. Typical was a series of letters to Bill Fleischman's "Voice from the Sidelines" column in the *St. Louis Star-Times* in October 1949. It began with a letter from a traveling salesman named H. Cooper, who claimed he visited all the major-league cities during the course of a year, giving him a chance to listen to numerous major-league broadcasts. "The poorest announcer of all," Cooper wrote, "is Harry Caray. He doesn't give the visiting team a break, 50 percent of his statistics are boring, and he doesn't give a true picture of a situation." In the next two weeks, Fleischman's column was full of letters either agreeing with the salesman ("It was indeed a great treat to hear a couple of really good broadcasters [Mel Allen and Red Barber] describe the World Series in a concise manner without the screaming to which we are accustomed from Caray") or passionately coming to Caray's defense ("If the Cardinals didn't have Caray their attendance would be about 300,000"). [14]

Caray could be controversial, even in the small towns Bob Broeg thought were 95 percent in his favor. A 1952 edition of the *Alton (Illinois) Evening Telegraph* included a blistering letter to sports editor Lee Baker from a "Cardinal fan who would go thirsty rather than buy a bottle of GB [Griesedieck Beer] and help pay Mr. Caray's salary." Wrote the fan, "If the now-famous Liars' Club ever forms a subsidiary of Second Guessers, Mr. Caray will retire the traveling trophy in record time, I suspect." A week later, however, Baker's column featured letters from fans springing to Caray's defense. [15]

The topper, however, was undoubtedly the listener who so disliked Caray that the FBI needed to be summoned to a Cardinals–Philadelphia Phillies game in July 1949.

> An unsigned letter reportedly threatening to blow up Sportsman's Park, the St. Louis Cardinals, and radio sportscaster Harry Caray is being investigated by the Federal Bureau of Investigation. . . . [Cardinals president Fred] Saigh would only state that the letter was from a "crank" who "threatened to throw a tear gas bomb at Caray."[16]

Fortunately for everyone, the letter writer (who suggested that the Cardinals "get someone else to broadcast your games") never materialized. But the FBI took the threat seriously enough to assign officers to police the stands and keep the broadcast booth under surveillance during the Cardinals' subsequent three-game series against the Brooklyn Dodgers.

In Caray's autobiography, he put this incident in 1948, with the letter writer a racist threatening to kill Caray and bomb Sportsman's Park during a Dodgers–Cardinals game if Jackie Robinson, who the previous year had become the first African American player in the 20th century to appear in a major-league game, was allowed to play in St. Louis again.[17] Caray's story appears to be an embellishment, but the incident apparently did help him get a raise. At the time, he was negotiating a new contract with Oscar Zahner of Griesedieck Brothers and trying to get the same sort of money Dizzy Dean was receiving to broadcast St. Louis Browns games; Zahner countered by saying Dean was worth more money because he received more publicity.

But the bomb-threat story was page-one news in St. Louis, with "this big headline like war had been declared," according to Caray. Seeing this as an opportunity, Caray grabbed a paper, took it to Zahner, and said, "You SOB. Dizzy Dean never got publicity like this."

"I got my raise," said Caray. "I was a cocky kid in those days."[18]

4

CHANGING TIMES

The Caray–Street combination is the best in baseball—the best I ever hear, at any level, and I hear several. Ninety-nine out of every 100 who would disagree with this statement are so strongly anti-Cardinals that they just won't give credit where credit is due.—Merle Jones, *(Carbondale, Illinois) Southern Illinoisan*, July 1950[1]

Harry Caray's early years broadcasting St. Louis Cardinals games were always eventful. There was seldom a dull moment, either for Caray, the Cardinals, or Major League Baseball.

Even on their way to a World Series championship in 1946, the Cardinals had to deal with two major roster shakeups—one of them not of their choosing. Before the season started, team owner Sam Breadon, who was always concerned with the bottom line, sold off several veteran mainstays from the team's wartime champions (Jimmy Brown, Walker Cooper, Johnny Hopp, Ray Sanders) to other National League clubs. Then in late May, three more Cardinals—Lou Klein, Max Lanier, and Freddie Martin—left the team to play ball in the Mexican League. The three Cardinals were among a group of 18 major leaguers who abandoned their teams to join the Mexican League, which was offering generous salaries and bonuses to American players in a bid to become a third major league. The players quickly grew tired of the conditions in Mexico, and many never received all of the money they had been promised. All were suspended for five years by MLB but were allowed to return in 1949, after some of the players sued to be reinstated.

The sale of Johnny Hopp and Ray Sanders in early 1946 opened up playing time in the Cardinals lineup for rookie Dick Sisler, the son of St. Louis Browns Hall of Famer George Sisler. While he would ultimately have a fine career, Dick Sisler was not his dad, and at one point late in the season, Cardinals fans loudly booed when the young Sisler was sent up to pinch-hit. Caray, who would soon become known for being ultra-critical of struggling players, vigorously came to Sisler's defense. "That even such a small minority could be so unfair, so unjust, as to even think of booing this likable kid, seemed to me inconceivable," Caray told listeners to his KXOK radio show. "This kid has to pay the price because his name is Sisler. The unfair comparison between father and son will ever be present."[2]

There was more upheaval in baseball in 1947, when Jackie Robinson broke baseball's color line with the Brooklyn Dodgers. There had been no known African American players in the major leagues since the 1880s, and Robinson, although welcomed by many, was also greeted in major-league circles with responses that varied from unease to outright hostility. That was definitely the case in St. Louis, a city with strong Southern traditions. Scott Ferkovich of the Society for American Baseball Research has pointed out that Sportsman's Park in St. Louis was the last stadium in MLB with a Jim Crow section. "Until the 1944 season," wrote Ferkovich, "black patrons could sit only in the right-field pavilion."[3] It has also been noted by Caray and others that the 1947 Cardinals team included a number of players from the South, most with rural backgrounds. The Cardinals would be one of the slower MLB teams to integrate, not adding their first black player, Tom Alston, until 1954.

In 1947, the Cardinals had their first meeting with Robinson and the Dodgers in Brooklyn on May 6, 7, and 8. The next day, May 9, Stanley Woodward of the *New York Herald Tribune* wrote a story that garnered nationwide attention (and later earned Woodward the E. P. Dutton Award for best sports reporting of the year). The gist of Woodward's story was that a group of Cardinals had tried to organize a strike with other National League players against Robinson, with the players refusing to take the field against him. After hearing about the strike threat, Woodward wrote that National League president Ford Frick confronted the Cardinals players:

Frick addressed the players, in effect, as follows: "If you do this, you will be suspended from the league. You will find that the friends you think you have in the press box will not support you, that you will be outcasts. I do not care if half the league strikes. Those who do will encounter swift retribution. And will be suspended, and I don't care if it wrecks the National League for five years. This is the United States of America, and one citizen has as much right to play as another.[4]

The story generated a great deal of positive publicity for Woodward and Frick, and condemnation of the Cardinals and other National League players who had supposedly planned the strike; however, there is reason to believe that the strike threat never took place. Warren Corbett, who wrote about the subject in the Spring 2017 edition of the Society for American Baseball Research's *Baseball Research Journal*, concluded that the strike plot was based only on rumors reported to Frick by Sam Breadon, that Cardinals players had assured Breadon that the "strike talk was only talk," and that Frick's stern address to the Cardinals players never happened. St. Louis sportswriter Bob Broeg, who was close to the team, referred to Woodward's story as "barnyard vulgarism," and even *Pittsburgh Courier* writer Wendell Smith, a confidant of Robinson, wrote that the strike story was "greatly exaggerated and made a better newspaper story than anything else."[5]

In his autobiography, Caray wrote about the strike story: "While all this was going on, I was neither a crusader nor a commentator. I was a baseball announcer."[6] But he went on to praise Robinson's character and ability as a ballplayer, and wrote that although he was not afraid to criticize Robinson on the air, he strove to be fair and often received hate mail for making positive comments when Jackie made a good play. Caray felt that he was popular with African American listeners, with a willingness to visit taverns in black neighborhoods to promote his sponsor, Griesedieck beer.

The 1947 season included an important milestone for Caray: his first television broadcasts, with he and Street working simulcasts (with the same audio going to both the radio and television audience) for a limited number of games. The Cardinals would telecast as many as 48 games a year during their early years using the new medium but steadily decreased the number due to the team's fear of its impact on attendance. Most of the telecasts were road games. Caray, who would later become a national celebrity due to his popularity broadcasting baseball on tele-vision, struggled at first when broadcasting exclusively for a TV audi-ence. "They told me, 'Everyone will be watching the picture, so don't talk as much,'" he later recalled. "The first few days I hardly said a word, just pointed things out when they happened. Then the mail started coming in. 'What's wrong with Harry Caray? Is he sick? He's not broadcasting like he does on radio.'"[7]

There was one more notable event for the Cardinals in 1947: In November, Sam Breadon, who had owned the club since 1920 but was in ill health (he would die of cancer in May 1949), sold his majority share of the Cardinals to a syndicate headed by Robert Hannegan and Fred Saigh. At the time, Hannegan was serving as U.S. postmaster general under Harry Truman (he resigned that position after the sale). Hannegan had grown up in St. Louis, sold peanuts at Cardinals home games as a teenager, and had been a football star at St. Louis University. He had also served as chairman of the Democratic National Com-mittee. He was much more famous in St. Louis than Saigh, so it prob-ably made sense that Hannegan became team president, even though Saigh owned more stock. But although he was only 44 years old in 1947, Hannegan suffered from hypertension, and in January 1949, he sold his share of the team to Saigh. Hannegan died in October 1949.

The Saigh regime (his name was pronounced "sigh"), which lasted until 1953, was a contentious period in Cardinals history, and one that saw the team begin to decline from the two-plus decades in which it annually contended for the National League pennant. Described by the *New York Times* as a "small, dapper man with an eye for business deals," Saigh was a tax and corporate attorney, who, according to the *Times*, "freely expressed his opinions about the team, though he knew little about baseball."[8] Although he paid his players generously, money could be a problem. One example: To buy out Hannegan, Saigh agreed to the sale of Murry Dickson, a valuable pitcher whose major-league career lasted until 1959, and who helped deny the Cardinals the 1949 National League pennant by defeating St. Louis five times.

According to Bob Broeg, Saigh "operated the team as a 90-day won-der, a financial wizard completely contemptuous of baseball front office operation."[9] During his tenure, Saigh announced a plan for a new 47,000-seat stadium in St. Louis (nothing ever came of it), hired inexpe-rienced managers (Marty Marion and Eddie Stanky) in consecutive years, helped lead the ouster of baseball commissioner Happy Chandler (who was replaced by Ford Frick), and got into income tax trouble that eventually led to a prison term (which prompted Frick to force Saigh to sell the team). Perhaps most damaging to the team's ability to compete with other National League powers was Saigh's refusal to sign black players. Wrote longtime Cardinal executive Bing Devine, "When Fred Saigh owned the club, they wouldn't sign blacks. So they missed the top black prospect from St. Louis, [future American League Most Valuable Player] Elston Howard."[10]

Saigh also became involved in a feud between Eddie Dyer, the Cardinals' manager from 1946 through 1950, and Harry Caray. Speaking of Caray, Saigh told Peter Golenbock,

> I fired him about three times. Harry was a great second-guesser, and our manager, Eddie Dyer, would come to me and threaten, "Either Caray or me!" So I'd fire Caray for a day or two, and they'd kiss and make up, and we'd hire him back. Dyer was very touchy about second-guessing. The players didn't like it, either. Very few baseball players had a good word for Harry.[11]

In truth, Saigh didn't really have the power to fire Caray, whose employer was Griesedieck beer—not that he didn't try. According to Caray, Saigh became incensed at one point after hearing Harry praise Jim Hearn, a pitcher who Saigh's Cardinals had sold to the New York Giants on waivers; he demanded that the brewery invoke a one-week clause in Caray's contract that allowed it to terminate him. Saigh only backed off after the brewery, which greatly valued Caray's talents as a salesman for their beer, told Saigh that if he forced them to fire Caray, they would place a two-page ad in the St. Louis papers explaining their position. That put an end to the discussion.

Whether or not Saigh had the power to fire Caray, the feud between Harry and Eddie Dyer was real and not pleasant. When Dyer resigned as Cardinals manager at the end of the 1950 season, club management specifically told Caray not to be present when Dyer made his announcement to the press. According to *Sporting News*, "Caray was told the ballclub feared an 'incident' between the radio announcer and Dyer, who was in no mood to see him. Dyer frequently has labeled second-guessing by Caray during his five years as 'vicious.'"[12]

Caray was unapologetic about his criticism of Dyer, saying, "Everybody second-guesses the manager. Not once this year did the Sportsman's Park fans boo the players. The only guy they ever booed was Dyer." As for being requested not to attend Dyer's resignation announcement, Caray said, "Well, I didn't go because I was told it might stir up trouble if I did. Anyway, I've been thrown out of better places than that."[13]

The feud with Eddie Dyer was not the only difficulty Caray faced during the Fred Saigh years. In November 1949, Caray's first marriage ended in divorce after almost 12 years. In the 1940s, divorces usually required the petitioner to provide a cause, and Dorothy May Caray described her husband as "cold and indifferent," telling the judge that he seldom spoke to her, and when he did "it was always about his broadcasting."[14] Mrs. Caray was awarded custody of their three children, including 10-year-old Skip, who unfortunately learned about his parents' divorce from a headline in one of the St. Louis papers while on his way to school. "It was the longest walk of my life," Skip would recall, adding that after learning about the divorce, people at school "stared at you like you had two heads." Although he lamented the fact he was often separated from his father for long periods after the divorce, Skip said in later years that "we always had a great father–son relationship"; he added that "our only difficulty was we never saw each other."[15] Harry Caray would marry for a second time in January 1952, to the former Marian Binkin. This marriage, which produced two daughters, would end in divorce in 1974.

Caray was dealt another major blow in February 1951, when his beloved broadcast partner, Gabby Street, died of pancreatic cancer at age 67. Caray paid tribute to Street on his radio show, saying, "I was associated with Gabby going onto seven years, but we didn't *work* a single day together. We just laughed, lived, and argued."[16]

Seeking a successor to Street, the Ruthrauff and Ryan Advertising Agency of St. Louis put an ad in *Sporting News*, stating that the opportunity "is open only to a 'Big-Name' baseball man," specifically an "ex-Major League Baseball player, umpire, or other baseball figure."[17] The agency auditioned applicants to work with Caray, ultimately settling on another former catcher with St. Louis ties, Gus Mancuso. "From this point on," wrote Stuart Shea, "the Cardinals were Harry Caray's show on both TV and radio. Caray answered to nobody, and his future second and third bananas would not be allowed to threaten him in any way."[18] The Caray–Mancuso tandem lasted until the end of the 1953 season, when the Cardinals reassigned Mancuso to a scouting role.

※ ※ ※

In June 1951, a group headed by colorful—and sometimes controversial—baseball magnate Bill Veeck announced plans to acquire ownership of the St. Louis Browns; however, Bill and Charlie DeWitt, the Browns' majority owners, controlled only 56 percent of the team's stock, with the remainder divided among 1,400-plus stockholders. The deal was contingent on Veeck's group being able to acquire enough of the remaining stock so that they controlled at least 75 percent of the club. Veeck offered the stockholders seven dollars per share for stock that had been purchased for three dollars a share, so reaching the goal seemed assured. But then the drive to acquire the outstanding stock hit a roadblock. "It was at this point," wrote Veeck in his autobiography, "that Harry Caray, on his own nightly sports show, began to implore the stockholders not to sell their stock to this well-known capital-gains hustler, this con man"—meaning Veeck.[19]

In his autobiography, Caray denied Veeck's charge, saying he had merely stated on the air that he hoped a personal friend who owned Browns stock might be able to make some money on the deal. It is difficult to determine who is correct here, but in truth, the main object of Veeck's ire wasn't Caray; it was Fred Saigh, who, he wrote, "put his announcer Caray to work on me" in an effort to keep Veeck from acquiring the Browns. Ultimately, Veeck's group met its goal with room to spare, winding up with 79.9 percent of the Browns' stock.

The stock controversy marked the beginning of a feud between Saigh and Veeck, who—improbable as this may sound—had hopes of driving Saigh and the Cardinals out of St. Louis once he acquired control of the Browns. Although he understood that the Redbirds had long been the city's dominant team, he felt that the Cardinals "were on the downgrade on the field, and, just as important from my point of view, they were weak in the front office. . . . Saigh didn't have the foggiest notion of what he was doing."[20]

During the next two years, Veeck attempted a number of maneuvers designed to make Saigh look bad. These included signing a number of former Cardinals to contracts with the Browns and even bringing back Dizzy Dean to broadcast the team's games. For a time, Veeck's moves seemed to be paying off: In 1952, Browns attendance increased by more than 200,000, while Cardinals attendance was dropping by 100,000 (they still easily outdrew the Browns, 913,113 to 518,796).

To no one's surprise, Caray did not stay neutral during the battle for St. Louis supremacy. When Veeck fired manager Rogers Hornsby— one of the many former Cardinals he had hired to work for the Browns—in midseason 1952, Caray invited the Hall of Fame second baseman to be a guest on his radio show. He told Hornsby, whose firing had been publicly applauded by a number of Browns players, "I think it's unfortunate that you should be subjected to the humiliation and embarrassment of some of those quotes by individual ballplayers."[21] Caray also ridiculed Veeck's numerous player deals, telling *Sporting News*, "Frankly, I'm confused with what Veeck was doing."[22]

In Caray's autobiography, he claimed that Veeck used to say that if he could get rid of Harry Caray, he could get rid of the Cardinals; however, Veeck's autobiography made it clear that his main target in the battle for St. Louis supremacy was Fred Saigh and stated that he "would have run the Cardinals out of St. Louis" had Saigh not run into problems with the Internal Revenue Service. In April 1952, Saigh was indicted on charges of evading $49,206 in federal income taxes. In January 1953, he pleaded no contest to two counts of underpaying his taxes and was sentenced to 15 months in prison (he was released after serving six months). Pressured by Ford Frick, Saigh sold the Cardinals in February 1953. According to Saigh, the highest bids were from groups interested in moving the Cardinals to another city (Milwaukee or Houston), which would have meant the realization of Veeck's improbable dream. Instead he sold the club to a local St. Louis ownership group for a reported $3.75 million.

The new owner was the Anheuser-Busch Brewery, headed by August A. (Gussie) Busch Jr.—a man Veeck knew would be impossible to run out of St. Louis. Having failed to get approval from the American League to move the team himself, Veeck sold the Browns after the 1953 season to an ownership group that moved the team to Baltimore (the club changed its name to the Orioles). Veeck and Harry Caray would hook up again in Chicago, more than 20 years later, in much more pleasant circumstances for both.

In the meantime, Caray began a long relationship with Gussie Busch—and Budweiser.

5

NEW PARTNERS

Due to the uncertainty of the retention of Harry Caray as play-by-play broadcaster of the Cardinals' games for 1954, some 40 broadcasters from all parts of the country have applied for the job. Caray has handled the Cardinal play-by-play broadcasts since 1945 for the Griesedieck Bros. Brewing Company. With Anheuser-Busch now owning the club and Griesedieck's contract having expired this fall, Busch is taking over most of the radio broadcasting and televising of the games for next year. One applicant, to show his versatility, volunteered to broadcast the games, help Eddie Stanky manage the team, and even sweep out the clubhouse afterward.—*Sporting News*, October 1953[1]

Born in St. Louis on March 28, 1899, August Anheuser "Gussie" Busch Jr. was the second son of August A. Busch Sr. and the grandson of Adolphus Busch, cofounder of the Anheuser-Busch Brewery. After the death of his older brother Adolphus in 1946 (August A. Busch Sr. had died in 1934), Gussie became president of the brewery. Prior to the brewery's purchase of the Cardinals in February 1953, Busch had never been directly involved with sports and was not considered much of a baseball fan. In fact, the brewery only got involved in negotiations to purchase the Cardinals when "it became clear that no serious offers were being made by any St. Louis group which have any chance of assuring the Cardinals remaining here," according to the St. Louis bank executives who represented Anheuser-Busch in the negotiations with Fred Saigh.[2]

Somewhat awkwardly for Busch and Budweiser, the club's radio broadcasts had been sponsored by one of the brewery's biggest rivals, the Griesedieck Bros. Brewery, since 1945, with a contract that continued through the 1953 season. Asked about this conflict when the purchase of the team was announced, Busch said, "I don't think that makes a great deal of difference. I am going at this from a sports angle and not as a sales weapon for Budweiser beer."[3] Privately, however, Busch was telling the Anheuser-Busch board of directors, "Development of the Cardinals will have untold value for our company. This is one of the finest moves in the history of Anheuser-Busch."[4] Within two months of purchasing the Cardinals, Busch had negotiated with Bill Veeck to buy Sportsman's Park from the Browns and announced plans to change the name of the park to Budweiser Stadium. After protests from temperance groups and Busch's fellow National League owners about naming the park after an alcoholic beverage, he reversed course and changed the park's name to Busch Stadium. (The next year, the brewery introduced a new product, Busch Bavarian beer.)

Harry Caray, of course, had been associated with the Griesedieck brewery for as long as it had been sponsoring Cardinals games, and as he wrote in his autobiography, "It didn't seem likely that Anheuser-Busch would retain a broadcaster who had, for so long, been so closely identified with their competitor."[5] According to Caray, such big names as Mel Allen, Red Barber, and Bill Stern were being mentioned. *Sporting News* reported that several candidates had been auditioned by an advertising agency.

During the 1953 season, Caray met with Gussie Busch personally and received verbal assurance that he would be brought back to broadcast the team's games; however, the Cardinals did not immediately make a public announcement, and according to Caray, many in the Anheuser-Busch organization were still lobbying for a big-name broadcaster. It wasn't until the brewery had surveyed beer wholesalers in the states that broadcast Cardinal games, and found strong support for Caray, that the team announced in early November that Harry had been signed to a two-year contract to broadcast Cardinals games; he was also hired to broadcast other sporting events, including St. Louis University basketball games. In a break with Fred Saigh's reluctance to broadcast Cardinals games on television, the club announced plans to televise many of the team's road contests. Ultimately, the Cardinals opted to telecast the club's entire 77-game road schedule—but no home games—in 1954. Broadcasting only road games would become a long-standing Cardinals tradition under Gussie Busch. "Once Busch became owner," wrote Stuart Shea, "the Cards stopped televising home games entirely. After 1952, the club did not allow a home telecast until 1982."[6]

Like Fred Saigh, Gussie Busch did not know much about baseball. And like Saigh, he did not let that deter him from becoming heavily involved in the day-to-day operation of the club. Busch often went to Caray for advice, particularly during his early years owning the team. The two bonded quickly, in good part because they had similar personalities. "Gussie Busch was my kind of guy, what I call a booze-and-broads man," Caray wrote in his autobiography.[7] Both were outgoing and enjoyed a drink, a card game, a party, and the company of women. Busch would be married four times, Caray three. "We became very good friends," Caray told Richard Dozer. "I tried to avoid baseball conversations with him, but he insisted. Our relationship was more than just an announcer and a multimillionaire owner of a brewery. It was friends."[8] During their years together, Busch involved Caray in discussions regarding the hiring of Cardinals managers and general managers, and at one point even offered the general manager's job to Caray himself (he turned it down).

Busch was anxious to win, and he could be meddlesome with the baseball people he hired. He changed managers and general managers frequently, and often impulsively, sometimes to the detriment of the team. But unlike Fred Saigh, he had money to spend, and he used it both to upgrade the club's aging ballpark and rebuild its talent base. (An early attempt by Busch to strengthen the team by purchasing National League stars like Ernie Banks and Gil Hodges from their current clubs went nowhere.) And unlike Saigh, Busch welcomed the addition of black players to the club's roster. In 1954, Tom Alston became the Cardinals' first African American player, and during the next decade St. Louis was among the most aggressive major-league teams in signing and trading for black players. Several of these players became part of the core of the Cardinals championship clubs of the 1960s, notably Bob Gibson, Lou Brock, Bill White, and Curt Flood. Under Busch, after complaints from the club's African American leaders, the Cardinals became one of the first major-league teams to integrate their Florida spring training facilities.

At the same time, Busch could make moves that frustrated the team's African American players, for example, the hiring of Solly Hemus—a man regarded as racially insensitive by some of the team's black stars—as manager of the Cardinals (see chapter 7). Ultimately, the Cardinals regained their place as one of the National League's dominant teams under Busch's ownership, but they did not win their first pennant during his tenure until 1964—the 12th season of his regime.

✲ ✲ ✲

With Gus Mancuso no longer part of the Cardinals broadcast crew, Caray had two new partners in the broadcast booth in 1954: Milo Hamilton and Jack Buck. Both would go on to win the National Baseball Hall of Fame's Ford C. Frick Award for broadcasting excellence. When Hamilton left after the 1954 season, the Cardinals replaced him with another future winner of the Frick Award, former Redbirds catcher Joe Garagiola. Caray would have complicated relationships with all three.

Born in 1927, in Fairfield, Iowa, Milo Hamilton was only 26 years old when the 1954 season began. He had begun his broadcasting career while serving as a U.S. Navy Seabee at the end of World War II, then worked college football and basketball games at the University of Iowa before graduating in 1950. By 1953, Hamilton was serving as sports director for WTVI, a television station in the St. Louis area; part of his job included broadcasting St. Louis Browns games on both TV and radio as a fill-in for Dizzy Dean and Buddy Blattner. When the baseball season ended, Hamilton broadcast St. Louis University basketball games, which were sponsored by Anheuser-Busch, and prior to the 1954 season the Cardinals hired him to provide color commentary for the team's road games, along with handling commercials.

Hamilton traveled on the road with Caray for the first half of the 1954 season, and the relationship was uncomfortable from the beginning, to say the least. "I'll never forget how that 1954 season started," Hamilton wrote in his 2006 autobiography, *Making Airwaves*. "At his introduction to me, [Caray] looked me right in the face and said, 'Kid, don't worry about your mic being on because *I* am the announcer here.'"[9] That was one of a number of encounters with Caray in which Hamilton felt Harry was putting him down, and he held negative feelings toward Caray for the remainder of his life. Hamilton devoted many pages of *Making Airwaves* to expressing those feelings, even referring to Caray by the derisive nickname "The Canary." The Cardinals did not renew Hamilton's contract after the 1954 season; he moved on to Chicago to broadcast Cubs games (the first of two tenures with the Cubs for Hamilton, who also broadcast games for the White Sox, Braves, Pirates, and Astros). Hamilton and Caray would hook up again almost three decades later, once more with much unpleasantry.

Caray would have a longer and more positive relationship with the other broadcaster who joined the Cardinals crew in 1954: Jack Buck. Born in 1924, in Holyoke, Massachusetts, Buck was a Boston Red Sox fan as a child but switched his allegiance to the Cleveland Indians when his family moved to Cleveland in 1939. Drafted into the U.S. Army after graduating high school, Buck served in the European Theater in World War II and received a Purple Heart after being wounded in battle. When the war ended, he entered Ohio State University and began his sports broadcasting career working Ohio State basketball games. After graduating in December 1949, he broadcast minor-league games for the Columbus Red Birds, a Cardinals farm team. In 1953, he became the radio voice of another Cardinals farm club, the Rochester Red Wings, and that year he auditioned to become one of Caray's partners for 1954.

He got the job, but as was the case with the Caray–Hamilton partnership, things did not start smoothly. To begin with, Buck was not Caray's choice to get the job: Harry wanted the team to hire Chick Hearn, at the time a broadcaster in Peoria, Illinois, and later the legendary voice of the Los Angeles Lakers basketball team. On top of that, Cardinals vice president Bill Walsingham had sent Buck a tape of a Caray broadcast with a note saying, "This is the way we want you to broadcast." When he got that note, Buck wrote, "I knew I was in trouble. I could no more broadcast a game in Caray's style than I could any other announcer's. . . . If the people in St. Louis didn't like my style, I'd have to go elsewhere."[10]

In 1954, Buck's role was similar to Hamilton's: He worked road games with Caray during the second half of the season, but his main job was to give score updates and read commercials. It helped Buck that 1954 was the first season Anheuser-Busch owned the Cardinals; he had done Budweiser commercials while working for the team's Rochester farm club in 1953, while Caray was coming off a decade in which he had done commercials for the rival Griesedieck brewery. Buck worked with the brewery's advertising agency in crafting the commercials and even attended classes at the brewery to witness the details of making and packaging beer. As for baseball play-by-play, Buck, like Hamilton, was strictly secondary to Caray; the duo, he wrote, "didn't have a lot to do because the broadcasts were definitely Harry's. I did a couple of innings a game, and that was it."[11] He did, at least, get to appear on television; with the Cardinals televising their entire road schedule in St. Louis, Buck got some on-air time with the radio–TV simulcasts of the club's games.

"When my dad started, Harry Caray was the main man, and he kind of let my dad know in no uncertain terms that he was the main man," Jack Buck's son Joe—himself a famous broadcaster—told *Sports Illustrated* in 2014. "If there was something big going on in a Cardinals game, he'd tap my dad on the shoulder, and Harry would sit down and [call] it."[12] The relationship would develop a little more balance as Buck got more experience. He also embellished his reputation by working network television broadcasts, including game-of-the-week baseball games, Big Ten basketball, and American Football League games for ABC, as well as National Football League games on both television and radio for CBS. For several seasons, Buck was the television voice of one of the NFL's most popular teams, the Dallas Cowboys.

On the baseball side, Buck would remain a Cardinals broadcaster for the rest of his life after 1954, except for a couple of short stints, and his pairing with Caray is still remembered fondly. "Harry Caray and Jack Buck were one of the greatest duos ever. They were so dynamic," said Bob Costas, the 2018 winner of the Ford C. Frick Award. "They're two of the greatest baseball announcers ever, with distinctly different styles in the same booth and the same time at or near the peak of their powers."[13] The duo wasn't afraid to push the boundaries of good taste from time to time. "Some of things that Harry said and some of the things that I said trying to be funny—if I said them now, it would be on the front page of every paper in the country . . . I would get fired," Buck said in 2001.[14]

In a 1975 interview with Roy Holliman of *Florida Today*, Buck compared his style with Caray's.

I could never broadcast a game like Harry. Oh, maybe for a few innings or even for one game. But for 162 games a season? Never. Look, when a team is behind by seven runs in the seventh inning, they've lost the game, right? It's just a matter of getting it over with. And that's the way I look at things. Now Harry, if the team is down by seven in the seventh, he thinks the Cardinals are sure to score eight to pull it out.

Oh, but wait. Harry couldn't broadcast a game like me, either. I think it takes talent to do what Harry does, but I also think it takes talent to do what I do.[15]

Ultimately, Buck would become a broadcasting legend comparable to Caray, and he would receive the Frick Award in 1987, two years prior to Caray. But Buck would not come into his own as the definitive voice of the Cardinals until Caray left the team after the 1969 season. "When I was working with Harry Caray, he was so dominant that I was really the number-two announcer on that team. And happy to be so at that time," Buck told Steve Nidetz in 1990. "I never thought I'd wind up staying in St. Louis. I thought I'd go elsewhere and Harry'd continue to hold forth."[16] Happily for Buck, he eventually got the opportunity to shine on his own.

Before the Cardinals added Buck and Hamilton to work with Caray in 1954, they came close to hiring Joe Garagiola, a St. Louis native and former Redbirds catcher who was still an active player with the Chicago Cubs. Garagiola had played for the Cardinals from 1946 to 1951, and he was an old friend of Caray's. "Back in 1949, when I was catching for the Cardinals and Harry was doing the play-by-play," Garagiola told Herb Heft in 1955, "he'd be down on the bench during practice and we'd exchange wisecracks and comments. 'Joe,' he said, 'with all your gab, you're in the wrong racket. You ought to be up in that booth with me instead of behind the plate.'"[17]

According to Caray, "We had had an eye on Joe for some time. He's a natural for radio. Gabby Street and I used to plan that Joe would take over when Gabby stepped down. Unfortunately, Gabby's death upset this plan."[18] At the time of Street's death, Garagiola was only 25 years old and wanted to keep playing, so Gus Mancuso became Caray's partner in 1951–1953. When the team decided not to bring back Mancuso in 1954, and Garagiola's team, the Chicago Cubs, offered him a contract with a $2,500 pay cut, Garagiola expressed interest in becoming Mancuso's successor; however, the Cubs got wind of this and revised their offer to Garagiola to one with a slight raise. So, he opted to play another year. But shortly after the 1954 season ended, Garagiola announced he was retiring from baseball to work in broadcasting—as a new partner for Harry Caray.

The first work for the Caray–Garagiola tandem came not on baseball broadcasts, but on college football; Caray was doing play-by-play for University of Missouri football games, and Garagiola was assigned the pregame show. The duo also worked some Notre Dame football contests. "Hear the Notre Dame–U.S.C. Football Game as only HARRY CARAY can describe it—Thrills—Excitement," said an ad in the *St. Louis Post-Dispatch* from November 26, 1954. It featured a large photo of Caray, along with a blurb saying, "Listen to 'Pre-Game Warmup'— Joe Garagiola, 12:45 p.m." Caray, Garagiola, and Jack Buck also teamed up to work St. Louis University basketball games that winter. In January 1955, the Cardinals officially announced Garagiola would be one of the team's radio–TV broadcasters, with the schedule again including the telecasting of all 77 Cardinal road games.

When he began working with Caray and Buck in 1955, Garagiola was already well-known in the St. Louis area. Born in St. Louis in 1926, in an Italian American area known as the "Hill," Garagiola was a childhood friend of future Hall of Famer Yogi Berra, whose offbeat observations (known as "Yogi-isms") would be a featured part of Garagiola's commentary for as long as he worked in broadcasting. Signed by the Cardinals shortly before his 16th birthday in 1942, Garagiola made his major-league debut four years later and played an important role in the team's World Series championship that fall; he played in five of the seven games against the Boston Red Sox and batted a solid .316. That was probably the high point of a nine-year major-league career in which Garagiola batted .257. Although he often made light of his baseball skills, Garagiola admitted that he was an average major-league player. He added, "I don't mind saying that I think average for a major leaguer is pretty good."[19]

From the start, Garagiola was a hit with the broadcast audience, particularly when paired with Caray. He had a folksy, everyman style, saying players were "runnin' and throwin'" rather than "running and throwing." When a listener complained, he responded, "Ma'am, if I start saying he's *running* or he's *throwing* or he's *hitting*, I ain't gonna be *working*." [20] What did seem to work was Garagiola's chemistry with Caray. Wrote Herb Heft,

> Caray and Garagiola make up a highly articulate, listenable team in which there is little attempt to speak textbook English. Caray has a sure, fast delivery of excitable range. Garagiola's delivery is a bit slower, and his voice stays a pretty level tenor. In his occasional shots at play-by-play he has done extremely well.
>
> "Harry has brought me along slowly and wisely," said Garagiola in a statement unusual because so many mic sidekicks try to kick each other when they're off the air. "He puts me on for a half-inning of play-by-play here, another half-inning there, and has given me a lot of valuable tips. He's a very enthusiastic fan. I hope I can emulate him in that respect. You ought to see how wrung-out he is after a ballgame." [21]

When the pair started working together, Garagiola was very deferential toward Caray and quick to credit Harry for helping him develop as a broadcaster. "He was first mate to Captain Harry Caray of the Redbird broadcasting brigade," wrote Robert L. Burnes in *Sporting News*. [22] At one point during the 1955 season, Garagiola even wrote a letter to *Sporting News*, complaining about a story that referred to Milwaukee Braves announcer Earl Gillespie laying claim to Caray's pet term, "Holy Cow." "We may not be ahead of the Braves in the standings," wrote Garagiola, "but please don't let them move ahead of us in the 'Holy Cow' League." [23]

The duo even inspired verse. In 1956, *Sporting News* published a seven-stanza poem entitled "Harry and Joe," written by Dr. Julius S. Bischof, a St. Louis dentist. The third stanza read, "And when there's a lull on the playing field/Never to silence do these two yield—/They inject fine banter so pleasing to hear/And throw in a plug for Budweiser beer." [24]

"When the Cardinals are ahead, there's no funnier duo in the game than Caray and Garagiola. And if you think that [Pittsburgh Pirates broadcaster] Bob Prince blows a gasket each game, you should hear this Caray fellow!" wrote Al Abrams of the *Pittsburgh Post-Gazette* in 1957. "Caray, a personable, friendly guy, gives the regular account of the game, while Jolly Joe pitches in with expert comment. This makes for excellent coverage." [25]

But the Caray–Garagiola relationship began to change as Garagiola's fame—both as a broadcaster and a celebrity—began to grow. An entertaining public speaker, he soon became a nationally known figure. "Making public speeches for the [Anheuser-Busch] brewery," wrote Warren Corbett, "he graduated from church-basement suppers and Rotary and Kiwanis luncheons to marquee sports banquets all over the country. The comedian Jack Paar, who knew nothing about baseball, invited Garagiola to his *Tonight* show because he heard that the ex-player was funny."[26]

Impressed by Garagiola's television appearances, J. B. Lippincott Publishing Company approached Garagiola about putting together a book featuring some of Garagiola's favorite anecdotes and funny stories. The book, *Baseball Is a Funny Game*, was a sensation, spending eight weeks on the *New York Times* best-seller list during the summer of 1960—the first sports book ever to hit the best-seller lists, according to *Sporting News*. The book's success led to more national TV work for Garagiola, including stints on NBC's *Today* show, work on national baseball broadcasts, and more *Tonight* show appearances.

Garagiola's growing fame did not sit well with Caray, a man who, like Garagiola, had a sizable ego (veteran broadcaster Lindsay Nelson once called Garagiola the "single most ambitious man I ever met").[27] Jack Buck wrote that Caray "resented the fact that Joe was getting all of that attention and never mentioned Harry. . . . When you're dealing with egos, a broadcast booth can become quite cramped."[28] According to Buck, Caray's relationship with Garagiola deteriorated to the point that the two stopped being friends.

The strain in the Caray–Garagiola relationship was noticed by listeners. "The outspoken Caray also has ruffled the feathers of some of his cohorts in the radio booth," wrote sports columnist Jimmy Claus in 1961. "For part of last season, at least, there was a notable coolness between Caray and Joe Garagiola."[29] With Garagiola holding ambitions for expanding the scope of his work, it was no major surprise when he left the Cardinals broadcast crew following the 1962 season. Caray spoke about the rift in a 1975 interview.

> Garagiola's a guy I fought to hire when I was with the Cardinals on KMOX. . . . I'm the only guy who saw in Joe Garagiola—a lousy catcher and a horrible hitter—the potential as an entertainer. But once he becomes successful, I see him at the World Series walking

across the field. He says, "Hi, how are ya, nice to see ya," and walks by. I thought, "Is this the Frankenstein monster I created? The guy I treated better than my own son?"[30]

Garagiola found plenty of work after leaving KMOX. In baseball, he broadcast the NBC Game of the Week (1961–1964); was part of the New York Yankees broadcast team (1965–1967); covered national broadcasts and numerous baseball postseasons for NBC television (1977–1988); and later broadcast local games for the California Angels and Arizona Diamondbacks. His NBC pregame show, *The Baseball World of Joe Garagiola*, won a Peabody Award in 1973. He was awarded the National Baseball Hall of Fame's Ford C. Frick Award in 1991. Garagiola also hosted his own PGA Tour golf tournament, the Joe Garagiola Tucson Open, and even served as the TV host of the annual Westminster Kennel Club Dog Show, a role that was spoofed in the Christopher Guest film *Best in Show*. ("Still a champion even though she was sent off in disgrace," said Fred Willard, who was lampooning Garagiola, about a dog who was disqualified during the competition. "Like Shoeless Joe Jackson.") "I did not think it was funny," said Garagiola about the parody.[31]

Garagiola's nonsports work was equally extensive. He had two stints as host of the NBC *Today* show, served as a guest host of the *Tonight* show (where he once interviewed John Lennon and Paul McCartney of the Beatles), and hosted such quiz shows as *To Tell the Truth* and *He Said, She Said*. In 2013, the Baseball Hall of Fame honored Garagiola with the Buck O'Neil Lifetime Achievement Award for his contributions to the game. He died in 2016, at age 90.

Despite the well-documented friction in his relationship with Garagiola, Caray managed to write some positive words about his longtime partner in his 1989 autobiography, *Holy Cow!* "To this day," Caray wrote, "Joe is one of the best color men in the business."[32]

6

KMOX

There's seldom an in-between when it comes to an opinion on sportscaster Harry Caray. You either love him like the rich uncle who just paid off the mortgage on the old homestead or you consider him several notches below the guy who smashed the fender on your new Rolls Royce.—Bill Fleischman, *St. Louis Globe-Democrat*, November 1961[1]

On the field, the 1955 season was the worst in many years for the St. Louis Cardinals. The club won only 65 games, the fewest for the franchise in 31 years, and finished seventh in the eight-team National League, its worst finish in the standings since 1919. But there was one bit of good news for the Redbirds *off* the field: for the first time in 15 years, the club's broadcasts returned to one of the nation's most powerful radio stations, KMOX.

Founded as a 5,000-watt station in 1925, KMOX had begun broadcasting Cardinals games in 1926, the year the team won its first World Series. In 1929, the popular France Laux began broadcasting Cardinals and Browns games on KMOX. A year later KMOX became one of the few radio stations in the country designated as a 50,000-watt clear channel station, meaning that no other station in the country could use the same frequency. KMOX's signal was so powerful that on a good night, it could be heard in 44 states, and reportedly listeners as far away as East Africa and Guam could listen to the station. (Joe Buck wrote that his father Jack received letters from listeners in Africa on a regular basis.) In the early days more than one St. Louis station was permitted to broadcast Cardinals games, but the Laux broadcasts on KMOX were by far the most popular. However, KMOX stopped broadcasting Cardinals games in 1941, with Laux moving to another St. Louis station, KXOK. Now, in 1955, the Redbirds were back on KMOX—with Harry Caray, Joe Garagiola, and Jack Buck at the mic.

As noted in Chapter 3, the Cardinals' multi-state network of radio stations had been a key factor in helping expand Caray's reach and popularity. But now, with KMOX's signal booming across the nation and even into other countries, his popularity expanded even more. Bob Costas, who grew up on Long Island (and whose own voice would later be heard on KMOX), described how he would try to pick up Cardinals broadcasts for his father, a gambler who often had a betting interest in the games: "I would sit there twisting that dial, kind of calibrating it like a safecracker, at 10 or 11 years old. If the atmospheric conditions were right, sometimes clearly and sometimes crackling with static, you could pick up Harry Caray and Jack Buck doing the Cardinals." Costas would describe KMOX as "truly like the *New York Times* of St. Louis and the region."[2]

Famed baseball writer and sabermetrician Bill James, who grew up in Kansas, was another KMOX listener. In the 1985 edition of his *Baseball Abstract*, James wrote about listening to Caray's broadcasts as a child.

> I realize with a sense of shock how much of my own attitude about the game and about my profession, which I thought I had found by myself, I may in fact have picked up from hundreds of hours of listening to Harry Caray as a child.
>
> Or perhaps it is false pride. I love Harry Caray. You have to understand what Harry Caray was to the Midwest of my childhood. In the years when baseball stopped at the Mississippi, KMOX radio built a network of stations across the Midwest and into the Far West that brought Major League Baseball into every little burb across the landscape. Harry's remarkable talents and enthusiasm were the spearhead of their efforts, and forged a link between the Cardinals and the Midwest that remains to this day; even now, some of my neighbors are Cardinal fans.[3]

Another KMOX—and Caray—fan was future president Bill Clinton, who remembered listening to Caray as a child growing up in Arkansas.

"He made those games come alive," Clinton told *Chicago Tribune* writer Ed Sherman.[4]

Not only presidents listened to Caray and KMOX, but also kings—at least a king of a sort. One day in the mid-1960s, when Caray was in Memphis, Tennessee, to broadcast a St. Louis Hawks basketball game, Caray got a call to his hotel room. "Harry," the caller said, "this is Elvis Presley. I grew up in Tupelo, Mississippi, listening to you call the Cardinal games on KMOX. I think you're the greatest. I'm sending a car over right now to bring you to Graceland." According to Caray, he stayed up until the wee hours of the morning with the King of Rock and Roll, eating barbecue, drinking beer, and talking baseball.[5]

KMOX had a special significance for future Cardinals great Lou Brock, who grew up in the 1940s and 1950s in the segregated town of Collinston, Louisiana. In his Hall of Fame acceptance speech in 1985, Brock spoke about the impact of listening to the Cardinals on KMOX.

> One summer night, while searching the dial of our old Philco radio, I came across a baseball game between the Brooklyn Dodgers and the St. Louis Cardinals. This game was being broadcast by two sportscasters, Harry Caray and Jack Buck. I was so overwhelmed by this game that I thought I had tuned into another world, a world of genuine expression of feeling, in which life had no façade, and that hurt and loneliness were not the natural price for being alive. Such a world was in total contrast to my surroundings . . . for you see, Jim Crow had excluded me from the mainstream of society; therefore, I was free from pressure to pretend, free of self-consciousness, which creates a false persona. I could not allow these things to stand in the way of my pursuit of excellence. Through KMOX sports, baseball fed my fantasy about what life offered. Baseball could arouse and comfort me, because in identifying with it, I felt free and alive, just like anyone else.[6]

In the opinion of many observers, the Caray of the KMOX years was at the pinnacle of his broadcasting powers. In 1998, Skip Bayless of the *Chicago Tribune* paid tribute to the "St. Louis Harry."

> The St. Louis Harry took me out to the ballgame via radio, and I never wanted to miss the eighth and ninth. That Harry was so good he ruined the first big-league game I saw in St. Louis. It didn't quite

measure up to the ones Harry had brought to Technicolor life for me as I lay in bed with the lights out.

That Harry was known and cherished by millions from North Dakota to south Texas. That Harry did games for 50,000-watt KMOX out of St. Louis, along with affiliate stations from here to Petticoat Junction.

Some nights, Harry so electrified games that he probably interrupted signals up and down the dial. Oh did I love hearing him say something as trivial as "two-two." Harry hit the "ts" so hard that he made "two-two" sound more dramatic than "Four score and seven years ago."[7]

Bob Costas echoed similar sentiments, saying that Caray's "best work came in St. Louis as voice of the Cardinals."

Back in the '50s and '60s, when baseball was the unquestioned national pastime and when radio, where baseball plays best, was still the primary outlet, Harry was at the peak of his powers. His outsized personality, his authentic passion for the game, and the distinctiveness of his style all combined with extraordinary broadcasting skills. What came out of radios all over St. Louis and the Midwest was so compelling that many clear-thinking people still contend that a Caray broadcast could be more vivid and exciting than attending the game.[8]

Author Jerry Lansche called the Caray–Jack Buck combo the "greatest broadcasting team of all time." He reserved special praise for Caray, writing,

If you were a Cardinal fan, Harry Caray just monopolized your interest. Harry'd do the first three innings, and Jack did the next three, and Harry finished up. But those first three innings with Harry were draining. Harry was such a good broadcaster that you were in the game every inch of the way. You felt like you were there.[9]

Cardinals star Tim McCarver, who made his major-league debut with the Redbirds in 1959, at age 17, before going on to his own distinguished career as a broadcaster, grew up in Memphis listening to Caray broadcasts. McCarver and his friends used to play a three-man game called "corkball," featuring a hitter, pitcher, and fielder. "How well we played the game," McCarver wrote, "wasn't as important as who sounded the most like Harry Caray. And I did." Summing up Caray's impact, McCarver wrote,

> Harry Caray's popularity in St. Louis was extraordinary. When I went to St. Louis after signing with the Cardinals right out of high school, I thought Harry was larger than life. There is a saying in our [sports broadcasting] business that people don't tune in to hear a broadcaster. If anyone came close to defying that, it was Harry. [10]

❈ ❈ ❈

The Caray of the KMOX years was confident enough to bring his broadcasts into the dugout, the bleachers—and even an airplane. In July 1957, rather than conduct an interview with an individual Cardinals player, coach, or official, Caray decided to host his daily pregame show right from the team's dugout—despite the nearby presence of numerous St. Louis players and coaches. "Boys, this is a live program," he warned them. "Please be careful as to what you say."

The players did behave themselves in terms of their words, but not their actions. First, pitcher Herm Wehmeier removed Caray's glasses while Harry was interviewing Cardinals coach Stan Hack. "Hey! Give me back my glasses. I can't see!" Caray pleaded.

He got the glasses back, but not before Cardinals players Eddie Kasko and Joe Cunningham mussed up Caray's hair and Wehmeier twisted his ear. Then someone dropped ice cubes down Caray's back.

Caray pressed on with his interview, but meanwhile players were rolling up his trousers and yanking the hairs on his legs, producing screams of "Ouch!" Next, Caray suddenly jumped while interviewing outfielder Wally Moon; pitcher Sam Jones had given Harry a hotfoot.

The finale of the players' escapade came when Cunningham said, "Let's have a striptease"; with that, the players began unbuttoning Caray's shirt and removing his trousers. Caray finally gave up and ended the interview show. A photo in *Sporting News* showed him after the high jinks had ended, grinning broadly and holding his glasses with his shirt still unbuttoned. (Caray wasn't the only victim of the Cardinals' playfulness: Catcher Dick Rand of the opposing Pittsburgh Pirates, who was watching the show from the Cardinals dugout, took off after discovering the Cardinals were putting lit cigarettes in his hip pocket.)[11]

❋ ❋ ❋

In 1958, MLB became a coast-to-coast enterprise for the first time, with the Brooklyn Dodgers moving to Los Angeles and the New York Giants to San Francisco. One result for Caray and the Cardinals was that, facing increased line charges for televising games from the West Coast, the team continued to reduce its total of televised games, which had dropped from 77 in 1954 and 1955, to 65 and 53 the next two years, respectively. In 1958, the Redbirds televised only 31 games—all of them road games, per Gussie Busch custom. The addition of teams playing on the West Coast also meant the increased use of air travel for National League teams. The Cardinals' first trip to California in 1958, came on a flight from Chicago, where the team had been playing the Cubs, to San Francisco.

The trip, on a chartered American Airlines DC-7, took six hours and 40 minutes to cover the 1,856 air miles. Some of the 48-member Cardinals party played hearts, gin rummy, or pinochle. Stan Musial read the *Wall Street Journal*. As for Caray, he recorded his daily *Sports Digest* KMOX program from the plane, dubbing it a "cloud by cloud" broadcast. Cardinals trainer Bob Bowman told Caray, "None of the boys required special air-sickness pills," but not everyone had a great flight. Pitcher Sam Jones told Caray, "Smooth or not, I'd rather be on the back end of a slow-moving train than the front end of a fast-flying plane."[12]

The Cardinals would take air travel to another level in October and November 1958, making a 22-game postseason trip to Hawaii, Korea, and Japan. A number of the games were broadcast on a delayed basis by KMOX, with Joe Garagiola doing the play-by-play. Caray did not make the trip.

❋ ❋ ❋

On June 7, 1958, Caray did something that would soon become a staple of his broadcasting work: He reported that day's Cardinals–Philadelphia Phillies game from the left-center field bleachers of Busch Stadium. Responding to the pleas of the crowd, Caray and Jack Buck removed their shirts; Joe Garagiola did not. During a break, Caray ordered five buckets of beer for the bleacher fans.

Although he was far from most of the action, Caray enjoyed the vantage point and direct interaction with the bleacher fans. "Stan's swing looks even more graceful from out there," he said about watching Musial swing the bat. "You see the bat coming right out at you and watch the ball going over the fence [Musial homered during the game]. It's terrific."

The broadcast was not without its challenges. At one point, Cardinals center fielder Curt Flood made a long run to track down a fly ball near the left-center field wall. The crowd roared, and Caray described the catch as "one of the finest catches he'd seen in some time." There was one problem, which Caray did not share with his listeners: From Harry's vantage point, Flood was out of his line of sight when he made the catch.[13]

* * *

Caray was never a person who shied away from controversy, and during the KMOX years he occasionally played a featured role in issues involving players and executives from other teams—and in one case, he played referee in a verbal spat between a manager and an umpire—with serious repercussions for both combatants. The first case involved future Hall of Famer Duke Snider and his Los Angeles Dodgers general manager, Buzzie Bavasi. In May 1958, Caray was interviewing Bavasi during a rain delay when he asked Bavasi about Snider, who was struggling in the Dodgers' first season in Los Angeles. Bavasi went into a tirade about several issues involving Snider, finishing with, "He seems more interested in his avocado ranch than in his job with the Dodgers."

"Your charm is exceeded only by your frankness," said Caray. The Bavasi–Snider feud became a page-one story in *Sporting News*, including denials from Bavasi that he was attempting to trade Snider, a complaint from Snider about Bavasi's comments, and another story reporting a truce between the two.[14]

In May 1961, volatile Cardinals manager Solly Hemus, speaking at a fans' luncheon in Pittsburgh along with Pirates manager Danny Murtaugh, blasted National League umpires Frank Secory and Frank Dascoli, saying "Secory and Dascoli are the most arrogant umpires, and they don't even give 100 percent." Murtaugh also complained about the umpiring in the previous day's Cardinals–Pirates game, but more diplomatically.

Hearing about Hemus's blast, Dascoli came looking for Hemus prior to that night's game. Before that could happen, Caray grabbed Dascoli and suggested that the umpire and manager air their grievances on Caray's pregame show; Dascoli and Hemus both agreed. The result was a long, heated debate, with Hemus repeating his "arrogant" charge and Dascoli saying, "I think Hemus has enough problems with the Cardinals—never mind the umpires." The discussion lasted several minutes. When it was over, Caray asked the combatants to shake hands, but both refused.

National League president Warren Giles was not pleased when he heard about the on-air debate, saying that he was "convinced that both parties used bad judgment in agreeing to participate in this type of program." Perhaps not coincidentally, the Cardinals fired Hemus in July 1961, on orders from Gussie Busch; a month later, Giles fired Dascoli in one of the rare cases of an umpire being dismissed in the middle of a season. But the "sensational, blow-by-blow account . . . made possible by Harry Caray, the Cardinals' voice" was certainly entertaining listening for fans on the KMOX network.[15]

The night after the Hemus–Dascoli debate, a Caray interview produced more headlines. This time, Caray's pregame guest was Pirates slugger Dick Stuart, who complained of being platooned by Murtaugh with another first baseman, Rocky Nelson, and suggested that the Pirates trade him if they weren't going to play him regularly. "There's no money sitting on the bench," he told Caray. According to Les Biederman in *Sporting News*, "Caray almost fell over when Stuart blithely indicated he'd prefer to be playing some place other than on the world's champions if he had to ride the bench."[16] This time, the issue ended much more positively for Caray's guest; coincidentally or not, Stuart began playing more regularly shortly after the interview and wound up leading the Pirates with 35 home runs that season.

One more installment of "Tell It All to Harry" occurred in July 1962. This time, Caray's guest was Houston Colt .45s pitcher Dick (Turk) Farrell, who confessed to Caray on the Cardinals pregame show that he had thrown a spitball—an illegal pitch—to Stan Musial the previous night "and couldn't get him out." Caray, seeing the significance of the confessed, asked Farrell, "Do you mean you throw a spitball?" Farrell replied, "Oh everyone loads them up once in a while. Everyone does, I think. I know [Braves pitcher Lew] Burdette does all the time, so if I throw one in nine innings, it looks like it oughta be okay." When reporters began questioning him about his statement to Caray, Farrell said, "If I had known it would cause all this, I wouldn't have gone over for the interview." The issue eventually blew over with no damage to Farrell; Colt .45s publicity chief Bill Giles reported Farrell's confession to the National League president, who happened to be his father, and said that Warren Giles "indicated there was nothing illegal about a man admitting he'd thrown a spitter."[17] But once more Harry Caray was in the middle of the action—to the benefit of his listeners on powerhouse KMOX.

7

UP AND DOWNS

After talking before several service clubs in Jefferson City, Mo., the other day, General Manager Frank Lane and Tony Buford of the Cardinals, accompanied by Gov. Phil Donnelly, visited the state penitentiary to discuss baseball with some of the inmates. As a general rule, the convicts admitted they like the Cardinals and enjoyed the broadcasts of the games. But there was one dissenter. "I like the Cardinals, but I don't like their broadcaster, Harry Caray, and as soon as I get out of here, I'm going to tell him so," the chap informed Lane. "That's a good idea," said Lane. "How much longer do you have to serve?" "Twenty-two years," was the sheepish reply.—Oscar Ruhl, *Sporting News*, December 1955[1]

When Anheuser-Busch purchased the Cardinals in 1953, the team solved a major problem that had existed under Fred Saigh: the lack of financial resources to compete with the National League's top teams. With the Cardinals no longer reluctant to add black players to their roster, the team was also now free to compete for this important source of baseball talent. The Browns' move to Baltimore in 1954 made the Redbirds the sole major-league team in St. Louis for the first time since the early 1900s. And the Cardinals' games were being reported by a popular broadcast team (Caray, Buck, and Garagiola) on an expanded network of stations (headed by KMOX), which could help enlarge the club's fan base. But despite these new advantages, the team made only sporadic progress in its quest to once again become one of the National League's dominant teams.

For the Cardinals franchise, the first decade of Gussie Busch's regime was marked by inconsistency, with short bursts of success followed almost immediately by setbacks. After winning 83 games and finishing in third place in the National League in Busch's first year, 1953, the club won only 72 games in 1954, and dropped to seventh place, with just 68 wins in 1955. After a slight improvement with a 76–78 record in 1956, the team won 87 games in 1957, mounting a challenge to the pennant-winning Milwaukee Braves before finishing in second place, eight games back. But then the club dropped back into the second division, with 72 wins in 1958, and 71—with another seventh-place finish—in 1959. The 1960 season saw the Redbirds on the upswing again, with 86 victories and third place in the standings. But the team regressed again, finishing in the National League's second division in both 1961 and 1962, although the club managed to finish slightly above .500 (80–74 and 84–78, respectively) both years.

The ups and downs of running a baseball team were maddening to Busch, who was used to consistent success in his other endeavors. In a 1957 *Sports Illustrated* profile, Busch was incredulous when St. Louis mayor Raymond Tucker told him he had gone to bed when the previous night's Cardinals game went into extra innings.

> "Went to bed?" cried Gussie. "I stayed with it until the finish. Why, I couldn't go to bed not knowing how it turned out." He shuddered. "I hate close ballgames. The only time I enjoy a game is when they're winning about 12 to nothing. That ninth inning was terrible to take. I died."
>
> "I was never," Gussie said as he flipped off the car radio, "what you'd call a baseball fan until the brewery bought the Cardinals. I used to go duck hunting with Stan Musial and Red Schoendienst before we took over the club. But I never got too excited about the game, and I guess I couldn't understand why other people did. But I've discovered that you can't get close to a team and not get involved. Now I'm hooked and hooked good."[2]

Busch was not known for his patience, and he frequently changed managers and front-office personnel during this period. Eddie Stanky, the manager he inherited from the Fred Saigh regime, was dismissed in May 1955; he was replaced by Harry "The Hat" Walker, who finished out the year but wasn't brought back in 1956. The next Cardinals manager, Fred Hutchinson, lasted almost three full seasons, including a second-place finish in 1957, but he was fired in the latter stages of the 1958 season on orders from Busch. Hutchinson would become the manager of the Cincinnati Reds in midseason 1959, and lead the Reds to the National League pennant two years later.

Busch's next full-time manager, Solly Hemus, was a former Cardinals player who became a Busch favorite after writing Gussie a letter saying how much he had loved playing for the Redbirds and Busch. Hemus, who was a member of the Cardinals' active roster for the first two-plus months of the 1959 season, quickly alienated the team's African American players. During a game against the Pittsburgh Pirates on May 3, Hemus started a brawl after being hit in the leg by a pitch from the Pirates' Bennie Daniels, an African American. According to Curt Flood, who was one of the Cardinals' four black players at that time, Hemus called a team meeting the next day and told the squad that he had called Daniels a "black son-of-a-bitch." Flood wrote that the black players "sat with our jaws open, eyeing each other. We had been wondering how the manager really felt about us, and now we knew. Black sons-of-bitches." After that Flood was permanently alienated from Hemus, who, he wrote, "acted as if I smelled bad."[3]

Despite his issues with the team's African American players, Hemus had some success as a Cardinals manager, finishing in third place in 1960 (after a seventh-place finish in 1959). But when the team struggled at the start of the 1961 campaign, Hemus was replaced midseason by Johnny Keane, a longtime member of the Cardinals' franchise as a minor-league manager and major-league coach. Keane had managed many of the club's players in the minors, and he bonded well with the African American members of the team. He would ultimately lead the Cardinals to their first World Series championship under Busch in 1964—but Keane, who was aware Busch had come close to replacing him with Leo Durocher during the 1964 season, resigned when the Series was over to take the helm of the club that the Cardinals had just defeated, the New York Yankees.

✻ ✻ ✻

The Cardinals' front office under Busch was just as chaotic. After serving as his own general manager in 1953, with input from manager

Eddie Stanky, Gussie assigned Dick Meyer, a brewery executive whose main qualification for the job appeared to be that he had played some amateur baseball, to the position. When Meyer said he wanted to return to the brewery after two years, the Cardinals had a ready-made candidate, Bing Devine, in their farm system. Meyer even brought Devine to St. Louis to groom him to take over the job. But before Devine could be promoted, friends of Busch persuaded him to instead hire Frank Lane, who had had success as the general manager of the Chicago White Sox.

Frank Lane's nickname was "Trader," and for good reason; David Halberstam wrote, "Lane was a man who traded not so much to build a better team, but almost out of psychological need, an irresistible impulse driving him to move players around." It was said of Lane that he always had three teams: one on the field, one coming, one going. After becoming general manager of the Cardinals, Lane improved the product on the field, and the club finished in second place in his second season at the helm, 1957. But he also made so many deals that, as Halberstam put it, "It appeared likely that, given the chance, he would continue to trade as an end in itself, thereby inevitably destabilizing his own team."[4] In his first year with the Cardinals, Lane traded away longtime St. Louis favorite Red Schoendienst. He was also about to trade Stan Musial to the Phillies (for star pitcher Robin Roberts) until Gussie Busch, who was alerted to the proposed deal by Musial's business partner, put a stop to it. By the spring of 1957, Lane had so alienated Busch that Gussie publicly announced that if the Cardinals did not win the National League pennant in 1957, Lane would be gone. And he was, despite the team's second-place finish. After the season, the Cardinals gave Lane permission to talk to the Cleveland Indians about becoming the Tribe's general manager and did not stand in his way when Lane chose to move on to Cleveland.

Lane's resignation resulted in the promotion of Bing Devine to general manager. Devine held the job for almost seven years and built the team that won the World Series championship for Busch in 1964; however, Devine's path to success was anything but smooth. Along with being forced by Busch to hire Solly Hemus as manager in 1959, Devine had to contend with the club's 1962 hiring of 80-year-old Branch Rickey as a "special advisor" reporting directly to Busch. Devine was ultimately able to assert his authority over Rickey (who, wrote Bob Broeg, "regarded Bing as his glorified office boy"),[5] but he was not around to celebrate the Cardinals' 1964 World Series championship; with the team playing well but still in fifth place, nine games behind the first-place Philadelphia Phillies, in August 1964, Busch fired him. When the Cardinals rallied to win the National League pennant and World Series, *Sporting News* named Devine its Major League Executive of the Year for the second-straight season—even though Devine was no longer working for the Cardinals.

※ ※ ※

Harry Caray, of course, was broadcasting Cardinals games throughout this period. At times, he found himself involved in the palace intrigue; at other times, he was merely a commentator. But as always, Harry was never one to shy away from the action. "Some of your announcers today," Caray told John Smith in 1975, "could care less about the game. Hell, they'd rather be out playing golf or something. But me, I'm hated and loved. My style is that of the fan—my voice shows the disappointment when a guy strikes out, but it also shows the joy when someone gets a base hit."[6]

When the Cardinals were struggling under manager Eddie Stanky in the 1950s, Caray was not reluctant to express his displeasure on the air. According to Milo Hamilton, Harry told his listeners, "You know, we've got [minor-league manager] Harry Walker leading by five games in Rochester. Dixie Walker's leading by seven in Columbus. And Johnny Keane's got his club playing well in Omaha. And here we are with Eddie Stanky wallowing in fifth place."[7] Caray's questioning of Stanky's managerial strategy was so well-known that at an offseason luncheon prior to the 1955 season, attended by both Caray and Stanky, *St. Louis Post-Dispatch* sports editor J. Roy Stockton kiddingly asked Stanky, "Eddie, who do you think will give you the most help in strategy this season? Harry Caray or Joe Garagiola?" Caray reddened at the remark and told Stanky, "All three of us [including Stockton] will do all right for you, Eddie."[8]

"Stanky was very unpopular with the fans," Caray told Myron Cope in 1968. He added sarcastically, "And the reason he was unpopular was me. . . . He'd step onto the field and there would be a loud boo. The thinking was that there was something I could do to keep that boo from being so audible over the mic."[9]

Caray's constant criticism of Stanky drew the ire of Anheuser-Busch public relations director Al Fleischman, a frequent critic of Harry's work. Fleischman wrote to general manager Dick Meyer that Caray's accounts of Cardinals games were "becoming a serious problem." Cardinals public relations director Jim Toomey also voiced concerns about Caray, objecting to Harry's "continual criticism of Cardinal trades" and "general denunciation" of the team's player development program.[10]

Yet, Caray remained unafraid to speak his mind—even if it meant disagreeing with Gussie Busch. When Frank Lane left the team after the 1957 season, Caray and his second wife, Marian, attended a formal dinner party at Busch's Grant's Farm home. During the party, Busch kept trying to get Caray to express an opinion about the club's willingness to let Lane take the Cleveland Indians general manager's position. Busch suggested that the Cardinals were better off without Lane. According to Myron Cope,

> Caray sidestepped Busch's questions, but Busch persisted into dinner. "All right," said Caray finally, "if you're forcing me to, I think Frank Lane would have been great, just perfect, if there weren't so many stumbling blocks thrown into his path. Hell, are you kidding?" he roared at Busch. "Who the hell do you have who can carry Frank Lane's briefcase?"[11]

Caray's response stunned the crowd, but after an awkward few minutes, Busch shrugged it off and even complimented Caray for his honesty.

In 1964, Caray became involved with Busch's romancing of Leo Durocher as a possible replacement for Johnny Keane. The Cardinals were struggling in August when Caray happened to interview Durocher, who at the time was a coach for the Los Angeles Dodgers, on his pregame show. During the interview, Durocher, who had won three National League pennants in the 1940s and 1950s but hadn't managed a major-league team since 1955, told Caray that he was ready to return to managing—and that he'd love the chance to manage a talented team like the Redbirds. The interview intrigued Busch, and he told Caray to bring Durocher out to Gussie's home at Grant's Farm to discuss the possibility of replacing Keane; however, Busch felt that he needed permission from Walter O'Malley, the Dodgers' owner, before offering the St. Louis manager's job to Durocher, and O'Malley was out of the country on an African safari.

In the meantime, the Cardinals began winning, so Busch held off on making a change. Ultimately, Busch's well-publicized dalliance with Durocher blew up in his face; when the Cardinals—thanks in large part to a total collapse by the first-place Philadelphia Phillies—pulled off a miracle finish and won the National League pennant and then the World Series, Keane, who was upset by Busch's lack of support, chose to resign as manager.

✿ ✿ ✿

While Caray enjoyed a good relationship with Busch during most of the time they worked together, his relationships with Cardinals players, and members of the St. Louis sports media, were often strained. Caray had a long-running feud with *St. Louis Post-Dispatch* sports editor J. Roy Stockton that dated back to the 1940s. His relationship with Stockton's successor, Bob Broeg, was so contentious that on a couple of occasions, people had to pull Broeg and Caray apart. "I found that his exaggerations of the game were one thing, but he was difficult to have a drink with in those days," Broeg told Rich Wolfe and George Castle. "You'd say black was black and he'd say it was white. All of a sudden, his eyes squinting behind those thick glasses, he'd say something derogatory." The two finally agreed to stay out of each other's way.[12]

In May 1960, both Broeg and Bob Burnes of the *St. Louis Globe-Democrat* wrote columns criticizing Cardinals manager Solly Hemus for his treatment of Stan Musial, who was often being benched or pulled out of the lineup by Hemus; Broeg wrote that the Cardinals appeared to be trying to embarrass Musial. Caray vigorously defended Hemus on his nightly sports program. "If in order to prove one's friendship you have to carelessly indict an entire organization and brutally crucify a young manager whose name or stature, granted, will never approach Musial's," Caray told his listeners, "then it is a sad commentary indeed for what is termed the power of the press."[13]

A more recent *Post-Dispatch* writer, Rick Hummel, reported a mostly positive experience with Caray in an e-mail to the author. But Hummel also mentioned the wariness that Cardinals players and management felt around Caray.

Harry and I became pretty good friends after he got with the Cubs. But I grew up listening to him on KMOX and marveled how exciting he made every play and at how much beer he must have sold as a huckster. When I went to my first game, there weren't as many exciting plays made as he had suggested on radio, but he made the game fun. Not much fun, however, for players like Ken Boyer, who paid a heavy price for turning down an interview with Caray one time. Caray did not hesitate to get all over Boyer if he failed in a particular key at-bat and made sure he always played second fiddle to Stan Musial.

But, again, I liked Caray the person very much. He bought my future wife and me lunch at his restaurant after we got our wedding license in Chicago. And he always would buy me dinner or drinks when I came in while I was covering the Cardinals in Chicago. I think Cardinals players and front-office types always were wary of Caray because he had as much clout as any broadcaster outside the major markets and, maybe including the major markets.[14]

When it came to Cardinals players, Caray could often be enthusiastic with his praise. He could also be helpful to players with postcareer ambitions. In his book *Uppity*, Cardinals first baseman Bill White related how, in 1961, he encountered Caray in the Cardinals dugout before the game and needled him for having an "easy job" compared to playing baseball. Caray responded, "If you think what I do is so easy, you should put that bat down and try it sometime. It's not as easy as you think." Taking up the dare, White agreed to make an audition tape for KMOX general manager Bob Hyland, who liked what he heard well enough to invite White to spend time in the KMOX studios learning the ins and outs of the broadcasting business. By 1965, White was hosting his own pregame show, and after his playing career he became a successful play-by-play broadcaster.[15] In the foreword of his book, he thanked Caray and Hyland for giving him his start in broadcasting.[16]

At the same time, Caray could be brutal with struggling players. Among Cardinals players, Caray's criticisms of third baseman Ken Boyer were so well-known that they became food for parody—and some bitterness. In *October 1964*, David Halberstam wrote that Boyer's teammates felt Caray had turned on Boyer after Harry asked him for an interview during a game Caray was broadcasting from field level at Los Angeles Memorial Coliseum. Boyer had said no, and the two exchanged harsh words. After that, it was said, Caray berated Boyer often, and with venom. Cardinals reserve catcher Bob Uecker, who would later go on to his own successful career as both a broadcaster and a comedian, used to regale his teammates with an imitation of Caray sticking it to Boyer:

> "Well, here's the Captain, Ken Boyer [Uecker would say]. Boyer haaaasn't had an RBI in his last 52 games. . . . I don't understand why they continue to boo him here at Busch Stadium. . . . Striiiike one, he doesn't eeeeven take the bat off his shoulder . . . here's striiiike two . . . and striiiiike three . . . he nevvvver even took the bat offfff his shoulder. I don't know why they're booing him."[17]

Caray became notorious for this description of a Boyer at-bat: "It's the last of the ninth. The Cardinals have the tying run on second. Two out. Boyer's the hitter. We'll be back in one minute with the wrap-up."[18]

In a 2018 interview, former Cardinals star (and 2012 winner of the National Baseball Hall of Fame's Ford C. Frick Award for broadcasting excellence) Tim McCarver told the author, "Harry was tough on players. There was a fear factor there; you didn't want to make Harry mad. I don't think it affected players' play on the field, though; I mean, we won three pennants and two World Series during the 1960s. But there was a healthy amount of respect for him."[19]

In his autobiography *The Way It Is*, former Cardinals outfielder Curt Flood wrote,

> Most of us liked [Caray] personally, because he was a convivial companion, but his rabble-rousing descriptions of ballgames made our flesh crawl. His specialty was enthusiasm for the Cardinals as an institution, tempered with harsh objectivity toward the individual player's performance.

Flood went on to describe how Caray would express deep disappointment when a Cardinals player failed in the clutch, punctuating his narration with an "Oh, no!" Caray's descriptions, Flood felt, could turn Cardinals fans against a player. "By affecting public opinion," he wrote, "he affected our livelihood. So we kept tabs on his broadcasts. . . . Whoever among our pitchers was not working on a particular day was sure to be in the clubhouse, listening to Harry's spiel."[20]

In 1960, *The Long Season*, a book written by Cincinnati Reds—and former Cardinals—pitcher Jim Brosnan, was published. The book, one of the first of its kind, was Brosnan's candid diary of his experiences during the 1959 baseball season. Brosnan had spent the first two months of the season as a member of the Cardinals (he also pitched for St. Louis in 1958), and the book contains several passages about Caray. In one of them, Brosnan and Cardinals reliever Phil Clark talked about Caray, who had recently been critical of both Brosnan and Redbirds pitcher Bill Smith. "Caray should keep his remarks to himself," Brosnan said to Clark. "He blasted Smitty last night when he relieved you. There was no call for that. Here is the kid's first appearance of the year, and Caray has given up on him. What's more, his opinion encourages everybody within 200 miles of St. Louis." Brosnan continued,

> Caray, in solemn vocal tears after [Milwaukee Braves third baseman Eddie] Mathews had greeted Smith with a single to drive in the ninth run in a 9–3 loss, had said, "How can anyone expect Solly Hemus to produce with material like this?" One dozen ill-chosen words, and Smith was skewered on the barb of public opinion. . . . To suggest that Smith was a symbol of Hemus's failure so far as a manager was to undermine Smitty's chances of keeping his job. Publicity, especially bad publicity, attaches itself like mold to a ballplayer's name.[21]

In other parts of the book, Brosnan referred to Caray as "Old Blabbermouth" and "Tomato Face," and told his wife, "I guess [Caray] thinks I'm letting the Cardinals down, and he's taking it as a personal insult."[22] Brosnan's wife suggested that her husband spit tobacco juice on Caray's shoes when the two met again; Brosnan wrote he was tempted to do so—but held off—when he encountered Caray later in the season, after Brosnan had been traded to Cincinnati.

About a year after his trade to the Reds, Brosnan and his wife encountered Caray in a Cincinnati restaurant. When Caray offered to buy the Brosnans a drink, Jim's wife said, "I wouldn't take a drink from you if you were the last man on earth." Caray was taken aback and sat down with the Brosnans for a discussion that wound up lasting two and a half hours. Brosnan, who said he never resented Caray's criticism as much as his wife did, still wondered, "Why did he have to do it that way? Red Barber doesn't do it, Vin Scully doesn't do it."

Harry said, "I'm the fan. I talk like a fan."

I said, "Neither Red Barber nor Vin Scully talks like a fan. They talk like poets."

He said, "That's true. I ain't no poet." [23]

8

GLORY DAYS

Even before the [1968] World Series got under way Wednesday, it was shudderingly clear that one result was as predictable as bunting on the commissioner's box: Millions of television and radio listeners, whose eardrums may have healed in the year since the Cardinals–Red Sox Series, are once again going to be exposed to a feverish clamor coming from a Cardinals delegate to the NBC broadcasting team. It was equally certain that across America the baseball public would then divide into two camps—those who exclaimed that by God! Harry Caray was almost as exciting as being in the park, and those who prayed he would be silenced by an immediate attack of laryngitis.—Myron Cope, October 1968[1]

When the 1963 baseball season began, the St. Louis Cardinals had stability in the front office, with Bing Devine beginning his sixth season as the team's general manager. They had a respected manager, Johnny Keane, who was starting his second full year at the helm. The roster included a mixture of emerging stars (including Bob Gibson, Tim McCarver, and Curt Flood) and solid veterans (Ken Boyer, Dick Groat, and Bill White). Even 42-year-old Stan Musial was coming off a season in which he had batted .330, third best in the National League. The Cardinals infield of Bill White, Julian Javier, Dick Groat, and Ken Boyer was so talented that at the All-Star Game in Cleveland on July 9, the starting infield for the National League consisted of the four Redbirds (Javier was replacing Bill Mazeroski of the Pittsburgh Pirates, who was injured). The Cardinals seemed ready at last to become serious contenders for the National League pennant—both in 1963, and in the years to come.

The club made a strong move to take the flag in 1963. After lagging behind the Los Angeles Dodgers for most of the season, the Cardinals got everything together in late August, winning 19 games in a 20-game stretch from August 30 to September 15. When the Dodgers arrived in St. Louis for a three-game series beginning on September 16, they were only one game ahead of the Cardinals. Unfortunately for the Cardinals, the Dodgers took the first two games of the series. In the series finale on September 18, the Cardinals led, 5–1, entering the eighth inning, but the Dodgers scored three times to pull within a run. In the ninth, Dodgers rookie Dick Nen homered over Busch Stadium's right-field roof to tie the score with his first major-league home run. The Dodgers ultimately won the game in the 13th inning and went on to take the pennant by a six-game margin over the Cardinals. (When a reporter wrote that Harry Caray had described the Nen home run by saying, "Oh my God, it's over the roof!" Caray wrote a letter to *Sporting News*, stating that he had listened to a tape of the broadcast and, "I did not say, 'my God,' nor did I use the Lord's name at all.")[2]

Despite the disappointing finish, it was a good season for the Cardinals, and a good year for Harry Caray. In April, Harry's son Skip joined the broadcasting crew of the Tulsa Oilers, the Cardinals' Texas League farm team. It was believed to be the first time in history that a father and son were broadcasting games in organized baseball at the same time. Although he was only 23 years old, Skip already had worked with Harry for several years describing University of Missouri football games.

In August 1963, Stan Musial announced he would be retiring at the end of the season. Caray had been announcing Cardinals games since 1945, early in Musial's career, and he had witnessed—and described—the vast majority of Stan the Man's major league at-bats. Caray would (of course) be at the mic for Musial's last major league at-bat on September 29, at Busch Stadium. Here is Caray's description, the audio of which is available on YouTube:

> Here's Musial. Listen to the crowd again. A base hit would give the Cardinals the lead. . . . Take a good look, fans. Take a good look. This might be the last at-bat in the major leagues. . . . Remember the stance. And the swing. You're not likely to see his likes again. . . . A

hot shot on the ground to right field! A base hit! The Cardinals lead, 1–0. Listen to the crowd! Listen to the crowd! (Musial is removed for a pinch-runner.) They'll tear the joint apart when he trots off the field. There he goes! The end of a great career. A standing ovation for Musial! Here's the way he racks it up: 3,026 games, 10,973 at-bats, 1,949 runs scored, 3,630 hits, 725 doubles, 177 triples, 475 home runs, 1,950 runs batted in.[3]

After the strong season in 1963, the Cardinals were expected to contend for the National League pennant in 1964. But as noted in chapter 7, the Redbirds played mediocre ball for much of the season, resulting in Gussie Busch's dismissal of general manager Bing Devine in mid-August, as well as his flirtation with Leo Durocher as a possible replacement for manager Johnny Keane. Despite playing better ball, the Cardinals were still six and a half games behind the first-place Philadelphia Phillies on the morning of September 21, with only 13 games left to play (the Phillies had 12 games remaining). It took an epic collapse by the Phillies—10 straight losses—combined with a hot streak by the Cardinals, for St. Louis to close the gap. The Cincinnati Reds were also gaining ground on the Phillies.

Entering the final games of the regular season on October 4, the Cardinals and Reds were tied for the league lead, with the Phillies one game back. The Reds were hosting the Phillies, while the Cardinals were at home against the last-place New York Mets, who had defeated the Redbirds both Friday and Saturday. All kinds of scenarios were possible, including an unprecedented three-way tie. But the Phillies routed Cincinnati, 10–0, and the Cardinals entered the ninth inning of their game against the Mets with an 11–4 lead. Gussie Busch's—and Harry Caray's—first National League pennant was at hand.

With the Cardinals three outs away from clinching the flag, Caray found a way to ensure he was both at the KMOX microphone to do the play-by-play and available for postgame interviews on the field: He broadcast the inning from Busch's box next to the field. His call of the final out featured some impromptu comments in the background from Busch.

(Busch shouts, "One more strike. Come on!") If you've never heard Mr. Gussie Busch excited, you just heard him over my shoulder. . . . Johnny Keane about to bring the Redbirds their first pennant since

1946. . . . Listen to this crowd! (Busch shouts, "Come on! Let's go! Get him out!"). . . . Everybody's standing up! A high pop foul; McCarver's there! The Cardinals win the pennant! The Cardinals win the pennant! The Cardinals win the pennant! Everybody out! Everybody congratulating everybody! The Cardinals have just won the pennant! Mayhem on the field![4]

In the World Series, the Cardinals faced the New York Yankees, the fifth time these longtime rivals were meeting in the Series (but the first time since 1943). NBC carried the nationwide broadcast of the World Series on both radio and television in the 1960s, and its format in 1964 was to use local broadcasters from the Series opponents to help report the games. As a result, Caray worked the NBC television broadcasts with Curt Gowdy for Games 1, 2, 6, and 7, and Games 3 through 5 with Gowdy on radio. Gowdy and Caray alternated TV-radio assignments with Joe Garagiola—by then a national broadcaster with NBC—and Phil Rizzuto, a member of the Yankees crew.

For Caray, it was a rare opportunity to showcase his work for a national audience. Unlike his Cardinals partner, Jack Buck, who frequently worked baseball *Game of the Week* and AFL and NFL football games, which were broadcast nationally, Caray's coast-to-coast work had been limited to one MLB All-Star Game and some Cotton Bowl and Notre Dame football games. Caray's television work in the Series— in which the Cardinals defeated the Yankees in seven games—drew some harsh criticism. Vince Leonard of the *Pittsburgh Press* wrote,

> The audio portion featured Curt Gowdy and regular Cardinal 'caster Harry Caray, who roots more for the Redbirds than [longtime Pittsburgh Pirates broadcaster] Rosey Rowswell ever did for the Pirates.
>
> Caray was recruited from the radio ranks for the game and kept forgetting that he was not on audio. He was an irritating chatterbox, not only calling every obvious play but making predictions on the outcome of things.
>
> His funniest prediction, on a ball that held up, was, "You can see the wind on that one." Sixth-grade science books tell us the wind is invisible. It seems that every time Harry Caray takes to the air, he commits himself (ouch!).[5]

Don Page of the *Los Angeles Times* was more succinct. "Oh yes, a word about Series announcer Harry Caray: ludicrous."[6]

❋ ❋ ❋

After their World Series championship in 1964, the Cardinals regressed under new manager Red Schoendienst in 1965, finishing in seventh place, with an 80–81 record. But while the team had a disappointing year, Caray's 1965 season featured a personal highlight. On May 29, he was in Houston to broadcast the Cardinals game against the Houston Astros, who were scheduled to host the Milwaukee Braves the next day. The Braves had already announced that they were moving to Atlanta in 1966, and their games were being broadcast back to Atlanta, with Mel Allen the primary radio voice. Allen was unavailable for the May 30 broadcast, so the Atlanta crew asked 25-year-old Skip Caray to fill in for him. Skip, who had arrived in Houston a day early, appeared briefly on Harry's television broadcast of the Cardinals–Braves game on May 29. It was believed to be the first time the son of a major-league broadcaster had aired a MLB game, and naturally also the first time a father and son had broadcast a game together.

At the time, Skip was the radio voice for the home games of the Atlanta Crackers of the International League, in addition to teaming up with Harry for University of Missouri football broadcasts and Jack Buck for St. Louis University basketball games. "Chances are that I wouldn't have gotten a job to begin with if I hadn't been Harry Caray's son," Skip told *Sporting News*. "But I feel that if I do become a major-league announcer, it will have to be because I'm good." Overall Skip thought being the son of a famous broadcaster "has helped me more than it has hurt me," but he admitted he had once thought of changing his name.[7]

After several more years of working college and minor-league games, Skip Caray moved up to the "majors" in 1968, becoming the lead broadcaster for the Atlanta Hawks of the National Basketball Association. He joined the Atlanta Braves broadcast crew in 1976, a position he would hold until his death in 2008. Like his father, Skip was unafraid to criticize the players and teams whose performance he was describing, He also had a playful sense of humor. "During a dull or hopelessly lopsided game," wrote Bruce Weber of the *New York Times* in his 2008 Skip Caray obituary, "he sometimes would give his viewers or listeners permission to turn off the broadcast as long as they promised to patronize its sponsors; or lament, when the Braves' pitchers had walked too many, that not only were bases loaded, 'but I wish I was, too.'"[8]

∗ ∗ ∗

The 1966 season was another so-so year for the Cardinals; the team finished in sixth place in the 10-team National League with an 83–79 record; however, the club was a hit at the box office. On May 12, after almost five decades at Sportsman's Park, which had been renamed Busch Stadium in 1953, the Cardinals moved into a new Busch Stadium, a round, multipurpose park in downtown St. Louis that the Redbirds would share with the city's NFL franchise, also known as the Cardinals. Although multipurpose stadiums would fall out of favor by the 1990s, Busch II was an immediate hit, with a St. Louis baseball-record 46,048 fans filling the park for the opening game against the Atlanta Braves. For the year, the Cardinals' home attendance of 1,712,980 was a franchise record by almost a half-million fans.

The July 2, 1966, issue of *Sporting News* featured a story about Harry Caray as part of the baseball weekly's profiles of major-league broadcasters (Milo Hamilton, then in his first year with the Atlanta Braves, had been profiled several weeks earlier). "A man who speaks his mind," wrote author Dick Kaegel, "the colorful aircaster has survived storms of controversy and changes of club ownership and sponsors to last 22 years with his beloved Redbirds."

"My whole philosophy is to broadcast the way a fan would broadcast," Caray told Kaegel. "I'm a bit of a paradox. Some people think I'm always favorable to the Cardinals, and some people think I'm always so critical of them. I guess it comes down to your style of broadcasting." According to Kaegel, "Harry's style is enthusiastic and emotional, and veteran listeners believe they can detect his feelings—his dejection or elation—by the inflection of his voice. Tune in to Harry, they say, and you can tell who is winning without hearing the score."[9]

∗ ∗ ∗

If 1965 and 1966 were years of dejection for Caray and the Cardinals— at least in terms of how the team performed on the field—the 1967 season was one of elation. The Cardinals won their first six games, took the National League lead for good on June 19 (they were tied for first place with other teams on a couple of occasions), and won the National League pennant by 10 and a half games over the second-place San Francisco Giants. The team's 101 victories were the most for a Cardinals team since 1944. Led by 1966 trade acquisition Orlando Cepeda, a native of Puerto Rico and a unanimous choice as the 1967 National League Most Valuable Player, the team took on the colorful nickname of "El Birdos." Cardinals fans filled the new Busch Stadium throughout the season; the club led the National League in home attendance for the first time since 1901, surpassing the 2 million mark for the first time in franchise history. The team's home attendance of 2,090,145 would remain a franchise record until 1982.

For Harry Caray, it was a season of satisfying play-by-play calls; Caray began counting off the Cardinals' "magic number"—the combination of St. Louis wins and/or opponent losses needed for the Redbirds to clinch the pennant—for his listeners when the number was 42. But as usual with Caray, his work had both supporters and detractors. In a letter to the "Voice of the Fan" section of *Sporting News* in the September 16 issue, a resident of St. Louis named Al Flint criticized Caray for his long-standing habit of mentioning the hometowns of fans who had written notes to Harry, saying that they were attending or listening to the game. "What can possibly be done to get Harry Caray to stop broadcasting names of all the towns in the U.S. and Canada represented in crowds at Cardinal games?" Flint wrote. But two weeks later, "Voice of the Fan" featured a letter from Bob Laurie, a resident of Niagara Falls, New York, who wrote, "To a fan in far off Niagara Falls, you feel like a member of a pennant-winning family."[10]

The Cardinals faced the American League champion Boston Red Sox in the World Series. With NBC again broadcasting the games on television and radio, Caray was paired with Curt Gowdy on TV for Games 3, 4, and 5, and on radio with Pee Wee Reese and Jim Simpson for Games 1, 2, 6, and 7. With Caray about to begin his television gig for Game 3, Don Page of the *Los Angeles Times* praised the work of Boston Red Sox broadcaster Ken Coleman in Games 1 and 2. But he warned his readers about Caray.

> By contrast you are about to experience the histrionics of the National League's foremost flag-waver, Harry Caray. He is the St. Louis

broadcaster and makes Harry Wismer [a radio broadcaster known for hyperbole] sound like Everett Dirksen [a notably taciturn U.S. senator]. Hopefully, Caray will realize he's the guest of a national audience and will suppress his flaming partisanship during the next three games. [11]

The 1967 World Series went the seven-game limit, with the Cardinals winning the finale behind future Hall of Famer Bob Gibson. Caray, who was part of the NBC radio crew for the finale, wasn't behind the mic when Gibson struck out Boston's George Scott for the final out; he was in the Cardinals clubhouse to interview members of the winning team and broadcast the World Series trophy presentation.

* * *

The 1968 season was another great one for the Cardinals; the Redbirds took the National League lead for good on June 1, winning the National League pennant by nine games over the second-place San Francisco Giants. The team was led by Bob Gibson, who won both the Cy Young and National League Most Valuable Player awards, while winning 22 games and posting a 1.12 earned run average. But the Cardinals lost the World Series in seven games to the Detroit Tigers when Gibson, who had won Game 7 for the Cardinals in both 1964 and 1967, lost the finale to Mickey Lolich and the Tigers.

Once again, Caray was part of the NBC World Series broadcast crew, paired with Curt Gowdy for Games 1, 2, 6, and 7; however, this time he was not part of the radio crew for Games 3, 4, or 5; instead, NBC's Jim Simpson broadcast the games with Caray's St. Louis partner, Jack Buck. This was likely a sign of Buck's growing prominence as a broadcaster on the national stage.

As for Caray, his World Series work again drew considerable criticism. Once again, the leader of the anti-Caray chorus was Don Page of the *Los Angeles Times*, who began his October 5 column by paraphrasing Simon and Garfunkel's "Mrs. Robinson," but using the name of Dodger broadcaster Vin Scully.

Where have you gone Vin Scully? Our nation turns its lonely ears to you.

❖ ❖ ❖

> Curt Gowdy threw out the first cliché, Harry Caray bobbled his
> syntax, and the verbal linescore in the 1968 World Series thus far
> reads: Gowdy—bad puns, no hits, and no errors. Caray—nothing
> across. . . .
>
> In our sophisticated and overly critical pueblo, the fans demand a
> winner, and Scully spoils them.
>
> Gowdy and Caray are adequate, and they labor under the same
> handicap as most baseball announcers. They address their audience
> as if it were comprised of simpletons. They are masters of the obvi-
> ous, regents of redundancies. [12]

Another Caray critic was Vince Leonard, TV-radio editor for the
Pittsburgh Press. Leonard referred to Harry as "Rooter Caray" and
wrote, "Caray clichés came torrentially: 'I'm intrigued by the style of
McLain.' . . . 'Mayo Smith and Red Schoendienst prove that nice guys
win; they're two wonderful guys.' . . . 'There he goes,' on a Lou Brock
steal attempt. . . . 'They're trying to fatten up the gap.' . . . 'Some lucky
fan has a souvenir.' . . . 'Sky-high,' on a popup. [13]

The opinions of Bettelou Peterson, TV-radio writer for the *Detroit
Free Press*, might perhaps be accused of bias, as her hometown Tigers
were the Cardinals' World Series opponents. But like Leonard, Peterson criticized Caray for use of clichés. She also wrote,

> What a grand relief it was to hear loud-mouth Harry Caray shut up
> and act a little like a grown-up reporter instead of a howling 10-year-
> old. Enthusiasm is fine, but it's about as unprofessional as you can
> get. The bias shown by Harry is understandable. Harry's the Cards'
> announcer, and he's an emotional guy. In St. Louis people like his
> style. But NBC shouldn't inflict him on a nationwide audience. [14]

Throughout his career, Caray was the subject of both great praise
and—at times—intense criticism. But the reviews of his work in the
1964, 1967, and 1968 World Series seemed unusually harsh. It might be
that on a national stage, Caray's style—usually told to a local audience
by someone who liked to describe himself as a fan (of the local team)
with a microphone—simply didn't transfer well to calling games for a
coast-to-coast audience, a setting where the broadcaster was expected
to be more unbiased. Whether that is true, Caray's immense popularity

throughout his career in the cities where he broadcast games locally make it difficult to suggest he should have ever changed his style.

9

END OF AN ERA

The St. Louis Cardinals without Harry Caray would be like toast without butter, like California without smog, like Joe Namath without girls.

The Cardinals can get rid of Red Schoendienst and Bing Devine, for all I care. Curt Flood, too. And Tim McCarver. Even Mike Shannon. I won't fret.

The Cardinals without Harry Caray, though, would be like a boat without a rudder, like a man without a woman, like watermelon without seeds.—Bob Fallstrom, *Decatur Herald*, September 1969[1]

On November 2, 1968, Harry Caray was in Columbia, Missouri, to broadcast the University of Missouri's 42–7 victory against Oklahoma State. After the game, Caray drove back to St. Louis, which is about 125 miles away. Once there, he decided to catch some of the hockey game between the St. Louis Blues and Minnesota North Stars at the St. Louis Arena, leaving after the first period to meet a female friend for dinner. After that, Caray and his companion headed to the Chase-Plaza Hotel, where they planned to have a nightcap. It was now around 1:30 a.m. It was a rainy night, and after parking his car near the hotel, Caray stepped out to cross the street, Kingshighway. He apparently did not see the car that was coming down the road. Caray described what happened in a 1978 *Chicago Tribune* feature story.

I get out of the car and start to cross Kingshighway. My friend is looking in the rearview mirror, primping her hair. Suddenly she sees

a body—my body—flying 50 feet in the air. I swear to God, she tells
me she screamed, "Holy Cow!" This was 1 a.m. Sunday morning. A
young kid who'd just gotten back from Vietnam that morning and
who'd gotten engaged and had been drinking ever since. He was
dead drunk, driving without a license, without insurance, in a driving
rain, and he'd hit me head-on.[2]

Caray's injuries included a broken and dislocated shoulder, facial cuts,
and compound fractures of both legs. According to Caray, rainwater
and blood congested his lungs, and he almost died on the street. He
stated he was lying in the street with the rain pouring down until the
driver of a Goodwill truck stopped, put Caray in the back, covered him
with burlap bags to protect him from the rain, and took him to the
hospital. He said he did not wake up until the following Thursday.

Some of the more dramatic details from Caray's account of the accident are not corroborated by contemporary sources. With the help of
Jessica Luna, Sunshine law coordinator for the St. Louis Police Department, I was able to obtain a copy of the four-page police report from
Caray's 1968 accident. According to the report, Detective James Rob-
ertson of the Ninth District was sitting in his police vehicle at 206 N.
Kingshighway, close to the hotel, when he observed Caray get out of his
car and attempt to cross the six-lane highway. As he stepped into the
center northbound lane, Caray walked into the path of a 1959 Chevrolet; he was struck by the right front fender of the car and his body was
"thrown approximately 35 feet." The driver stopped to render assis-
tance, and another police vehicle was summoned. St. Louis Police Car
99-a, not a Goodwill driver, took Caray to City Hospital (he was trans-
ferred to Barnes Hospital later that night).

The driver of the Chevrolet told police he immediately applied his
brakes when he saw Caray and attempted to swerve left to avoid hitting
him "but knew he couldn't stop in time, so he attempted to swerve to
his left, west side of street, to miss Caray, but this was unsuccessful, as
Caray moved in this direction, and he struck Caray with the right front
of his vehicle." The driver of the Chevrolet was indeed a 21-year-old
U.S. Marine, but as far as "being dead drunk," there is nothing in the
police report that would corroborate this. The driver was not adminis-
tered an intoximeter test, the "Had Been Drinking" box was not
checked under "Contributing Circumstances Indicated," and he was
allowed to drive his vehicle away after being interviewed by the police.

While the "charges" box was redacted in the police report I was able to review, press stories the day after the accident stated only that the driver of the vehicle was given a citation for failure to display a driver's license; Caray, meanwhile, was ticketed for crossing a street outside a crosswalk.[3]

Caray's statement that he "did not wake up until the following Thursday" is also not supported by contemporary sources. An Associated Press story on Tuesday, November 5, said that Caray's condition, originally listed as critical, had been upgraded to fair on Monday morning, and a hospital spokesman said Caray was "conscious and alert after spending a quiet night."[4]

✿ ✿ ✿

Whatever the exact circumstances of the accident, the resilient Caray was soon on the way to recovery. By the weekend following the accident, Bob Hyland, general manager of KMOX and a frequent visitor to the hospital, was telling reporters Caray was "full of spirit and already tired of being in the hospital. He's been pestering the doctors to go back to work."[5] Caray had numerous other visitors to the hospital, and in the evenings his friends would have food and even martinis sent in from a nearby restaurant; he compared the atmosphere in his room to that of a nightclub. But Caray's injuries were serious, and his recovery period was lengthy. He was not released from the hospital until just before Christmas. Even then, he was wearing large casts on both legs.

Gussie Busch assisted Caray's postrelease recovery by arranging to have Harry flown (via private plane) to Busch's beach house in St. Petersburg, Florida. A January article by Jimmy Mann portrayed Caray in fine spirits and even kidding about the accident ("How about that, [the accident happened after] I parked legally for the first time in my life"). While recuperating in Florida, Caray resumed his broadcast work, hosting a daily interview show with such guests as football coaches Joe Paterno and Dan Devine, St. Louis Blues hockey coach Scotty Bowman, and Atlanta Hawks basketball coach Richie Guerin.[6]

Caray's casts were finally removed in February, and he was ready to resume work when the Cardinals began spring training. "They said I would be in the hospital for seven and a half months. But I wound up walking out after three and a half months," he told a reporter in early

1970. "Dave Bristol, who was then managing Cincinnati, told me, 'I'd like to have you talk to my players . . . the ones who take off when they get a hangnail.'"[7]

The night before the start of the regular season, Caray was roasted by a group of about 600 people at a banquet of the Knights of the Cauliflower Ear in St. Louis. "What nice things can I say about Harry that you haven't heard from the man himself?" kidded Caray's broadcast partner, Jack Buck. Regarding Caray's accident, Buck joked, "What can I say to make you believe that I didn't do it?" Another guest, Pittsburgh Pirates broadcaster Bob Prince, said he was astounded that Caray, who was "dumb enough to cross Kingshighway," would pick on someone "without a driver's license and insurance." Gussie Busch, who introduced Caray to the crowd, presented him with a set of cuff links to mark the start of Harry's 25th season with the Cardinals. When it was Caray's turn to speak, he modestly said he wasn't even the "best announcer in the family" and bowed to his son Skip. "If it ended right now," he told the audience, "I'd be tickled to death."[8]

The welcome-back celebrations continued for Caray at the Cardinals' season opener against the Pittsburgh Pirates at Busch Stadium the next day. Caray, who was slated to introduce the Cardinals' players before a packed house of 38,163, hobbled onto the field using crutches—even though he no longer needed to use them. As he passed the first-base line, he theatrically threw away one of the crutches. Then, with the crowd urging him on, he tossed away the other crutch as well, to tumultuous applause. "Well, it's all show biz," Caray admitted later. "I hadn't needed those canes in weeks."[9]

☆ ☆ ☆

Coming off back-to-back National League pennants, the Cardinals were widely expected to return to the postseason in 1969, which was an expansion year and the first season of divisional play in Major League Baseball. The club had lost former Yankees star Roger Maris, a valuable member of the 1967–1968 pennant winners, to retirement; however, Bing Devine, who had returned to the Cardinals as general manager in 1968, had obtained a replacement for Maris in right field by trading for longtime Cincinnati Reds star Vada Pinson. Most of the team's other regular hitters and pitchers were returning (although one of the team's key players, Orlando Cepeda, was traded to the Atlanta Braves in March for another longtime star, Joe Torre). In spring training, the Cardinals posted a 16–9 record, with Pinson batting .449 and driving in 14 runs in only 49 at-bats. "We look so good," said Devine, "that it scares me."[10]

But the Cardinals lost their first three games and didn't get over the .500 mark until mid-July. By then they were well behind the Chicago Cubs and New York Mets, who were leading the National League Eastern Division. The team began playing better ball in August, with Caray singing, "The Cardinals are coming, tra la, tra la" to his listeners after St. Louis victories; however, the Redbirds never advanced higher than third place in the standings or got closer than seven and a half games of first place. When the first-place Cubs faded down the stretch, it was the Mets—not the Cardinals—who took advantage of the slump. The Redbirds finished the season in fourth place in the six-team division with an 87–75 record.

By then Caray had a bigger concern: His job with the Cardinals was rumored to be in jeopardy.

During the 1969 season, Caray wrote in his autobiography, he began hearing rumors that the Cardinals were thinking about not renewing his contract when it ran out at the end of the season. There was talk that Caray, still married to his second wife, Marian, was having an affair with a member of the Busch family; Harry's alleged lover was soon revealed to be Susan Hornibrook Busch, the spouse of Gussie Busch's son August III. At first Caray's response to the rumors was to say, with some amusement, that he'd never raped anyone in his life. "Hell, I wanted them to believe it," he said in a 1975 interview. "The way I looked at it, I'd rather have people believe that at age 50 I could steal the 23-year-old wife of a 30-year-old billionaire whose name was August Busch III."[11] (Ms. Busch actually turned 31 in 1969, and Caray was 55.)

At first, Caray brushed off the thought that the rumors of an affair with Ms. Busch might jeopardize his job with the Cardinals. But then, in August, two newspapers in Pittsburgh reported that KMOX had offered a multiyear contract to Bob Prince, the Pittsburgh Pirates' colorful radio voice and a man whose bombastic style had sometimes been compared to Caray's. Prince told the *Pittsburgh Post-Gazette*, which first reported the story, that KMOX had offered him a five-year contract "for excellent money" but that the "offer did not have anything to do with play-by-play of Cardinals games."[12] Frankly, this stretches credulity. Given that Prince was primarily known as a baseball announcer and KMOX already had Caray and Jack Buck under contract working football and basketball broadcasts along with baseball, it would seem strange that the station would make such a substantial offer to Prince to broadcast sports only *other than* baseball—while keeping all three broadcasters on the payroll.

In a related story the same day, the *Pittsburgh Press*, the *Post-Gazette's* sister newspaper, wrote, "Prince confirmed last night that he has received a lucrative offer to move to St. Louis, where speculation is rampant that Caray may soon be unemployed due to a personal conflict with beer and baseball baron Gussie Busch, who owns the Cards and a large piece of Missouri." The *Pittsburgh Press* story repeated Prince's claim that the offer was for sports other than baseball; however, he told the paper he would be interested in broadcasting Cardinals baseball if "Caray was out of the picture."[13]

The Prince-to-St. Louis story created a firestorm in St. Louis, with the same *Pittsburgh Press* story reporting that, "St. Louis newspapermen burned up the telephone wires to Crosley Field last night during the Pirates–Reds game, peppering Prince with queries concerning his possible move West." KMOX and Anheuser-Busch immediately denied the story. Al Fleischman, the Anheuser-Busch public relations director, told the *St. Louis Post-Dispatch*, "There have been no discussions between Prince and Anheuser-Busch, certainly not about a five-year contract." KMOX general manager Bob Hyland admitted that the station had talked to Prince, but he added, "There has never been any specific contract discussion." But Fleischman's final remark to the *Post-Dispatch* might have been his most meaningful. "Caray's contract is up in November," he said, "but there have been no discussions about his contract, and there never are at this stage."[14]

In the meantime, the rumors continued that Caray's contract would not be renewed. Caray was concerned enough to discuss the situation with Gussie Busch, who was about to leave for a trip to Europe. According to Caray, Busch told him he'd heard Harry's stock answer to the rumors about an affair and that if any relationships he was involved in were consensual, he had nothing to worry about. Caray also reassured Gussie there was no truth to reports that had gotten back to Busch that Harry was about to go into business with Eddie Vogel, a former Anheuser-Busch executive who was now working for Schlitz, one of Anheuser-Busch's chief rivals. The report said Caray was being offered a chance to become a partner in a major Schlitz beer distributorship in Florida. Caray assured Busch the reports were false and wrote that Gussie told him he would hold the matter in abeyance until he returned from Europe.

But in late September, Caray was on the air when a *St. Louis Post-Dispatch* reporter handed him a written request for information on a report that he had been fired. Caray gave his answer into the microphone. "I'd be the last to know that," he told his listeners. "I still have a contract that runs through December 31. I really don't know a thing about it, but if the *Post-Dispatch* has that information, then I'd say it's true. Thanks for letting me know I've been fired." Later he quipped on-air, "The Cardinals are about to be eliminated, and apparently so am I. When I took this job 25 years ago, they said it would be temporary."[15]

On October 9, the official word finally came down: Anheuser-Busch advertising director Donald Hamel informed Caray that his contract would not be renewed in 1970, and that his job as the Cardinals' number-one broadcaster would be going to Jack Buck. Caray said later that he'd been given the news by telephone while in a bar. According to Gussie Busch, the decision was made "based on a recommendation from the company's marketing division." Caray's response: "I'm bruised, I'm hurt, and I feel badly about it."[16]

Caray, who was interviewed that night in a St. Louis restaurant holding a can of Schlitz beer—a move he said he later regretted—expressed disappointment in Gussie Busch. "I think the world of Mr. Busch," he told reporters. "I'd cut off my arms for him. But you'd think that after 25 years, they would at least call me and talk to me face to face about this." He disputed the stated reason for the dismissal, saying that during the years since he began advertising Anheuser-Busch products, beer sales had risen from 200,000 to 3,000,000 barrels annually. In response, the brewery stated that the decision had been made "in conjunction with the entire advertising, promotional, and merchandising plans for next year." George W. Couch Jr. of the company's advertising department said, "We felt Caray would not fit into our 1970 program. I think the announcement speaks for itself." Caray still wasn't buying it. "I want to know why I was fired," he said. "I've heard a lot of rumors involving personal things."[17]

The "rumors involving personal things" concerned Caray's alleged affair with Susan Busch. If some people had the wrong impression about the nature of Caray's relationship with Ms. Busch, their behavior on at least one occasion may have been a contributing factor. William Knoedelseder, author of the 2012 book *Bitter Brew: The Rise and Fall of Anheuser-Busch and America's King of Beers*, wrote,

> The pair could not have been less discreet when they were seen dining together at St. Louis's only four-star restaurant, Tony's, just a few blocks from Busch Stadium, visibly under the influence and so physically affectionate that owner Vince Bommarito had to instruct his whispering waitstaff to stop staring at them.

Knoedelseder, who was working at the restaurant at the time and witnessed the incident, told an interviewer, "The conclusion you would jump to is that there was something going on there."[18]

The rumors gained more momentum in August 1969, when Ms. Busch, who had been separated from her husband since February, sued August III for divorce, on the ground of "general indignities." The divorce was granted in November. Caray probably did not help matters by never quite denying the rumors of his involvement with Ms. Busch, at least for some time. "Hell, I was so flattered that I preferred to have people believe the rumor than tell the truth," he said in 1975. "So what if I got fired—I knew I'd get a job elsewhere."[19]

The truth, Caray later insisted, was much more innocent. "Mrs. August Busch III is, to my knowledge, the finest of ladies, and she also happens to be a true friend of mine," Caray said in an interview in December 1969, shortly after Ms. Busch's divorce was finalized. He added,

> She visited me daily while I was in the hospital, partly in the line of duty as a volunteer nurse and the rest out of unhappiness and loneliness. The young lady, now divorced, was a constant companion for a long time of my wife's and a dear friend of mine. I hope she is still a good friend of mine, and I have now and have always had nothing but friendly affection and respect for her. If this is having an affair, then our society is becoming sick.[20]

"She was a volunteer in the hospital three days a week, like a lot of society gals are," Caray told Richard Dozer in 1972. Caray continued,

And because of her troubles with her husband and because he was away so much, she'd prefer to go to the hospital. My family would be there . . . my children. It was just the idea that she could play cards with a friend or have somebody to talk to. So people began making something out of her frequent visits.[21]

In a 1995 profile of Susan Busch written by Jerry Berger of the *St. Louis Post-Dispatch*, Ms. Busch discussed her relationship with Caray. Asked if she and Caray had been an "item," Ms. Busch replied, "We were a friendship item, but not a romance by any means." Told that a family member had tracked phone calls between Caray and Ms. Busch, she replied, "I could have made a phone call to Harry, easily, because Harry and August and I and Marian [Caray's second wife] used to get together and play cards. But as far as a romance item, no." She said she sometimes joined Caray for dinner, something she did with a lot of friends. She concluded, "And people would see us and I guess decided to go for the romance."[22]

Along with the rumored affair between Caray and Susan Busch, there was unrest about Harry's work for other reasons among people at Anheuser-Busch. As usual, Caray's chief critic was Anheuser-Busch public relations director Al Fleischman, a man who Caray distrusted so much that he told Myron Cope, "I never walk with my back to him."[23] Fleischman even questioned Caray's abilities as a beer salesman, writing to Dick Meyer of Anheuser-Busch that the record failed to show that "baseball broadcasts have thus far been productive in increased beer sales." He asked whether the "intensely partisan and emotional atmosphere created by the present broadcasts" was the most effective way to market the company's beer. Fred Saigh, the former Cardinals owner (and Caray critic), who was now a major Anheuser-Busch stockholder, voiced similar sentiments in a letter to Anheuser-Busch executive vice president John L. Wilson. "Instead of getting better [Caray] is depending on his past good reputation to carry him," Saigh wrote. "He is as stale as last week's opened Budweiser bottle. He is losing money for you and will lose more."[24]

Throughout the years, Gussie Busch had maintained his faith in Caray despite the criticisms of Fleischman and others. But early in the 1969 season, Busch found himself openly siding with Harry's critics. That year, MLB added four expansion teams, one of which was the Montreal Expos, who represented the first non-American city to field a

MLB team. When the Cardinals visited Montreal in mid-April for the Expos' home opener, Caray spent much of the broadcast criticizing the Expos' stadium, Jarry Park; he berated the condition of the field and the quality of the new team's staff. A listener wrote to Busch, "The conduct of Harry Caray in broadcasting Montreal's Opening Day baseball game made me, and I'm sure many others, ashamed of the Cardinals organization, Anheuser-Busch, and even our own country."

After receiving other letters of a similar vein, Busch responded directly in signed letters to the fans. "I am sure Harry's efforts were to report the scene as he saw it," Busch wrote. "But you were very right in that the choice of words and the constant repetition of the situation and the problems up there seemed to detract from what was the most important thing of all . . . namely, the play-by-play description of the game."[25]

According to Jack Buck, Caray may have sealed his own fate. In his autobiography, Buck wrote that Busch had told Caray when the two had met prior to Gussie's trip to Europe that he would deal with Harry's situation when he returned. In the meantime, Busch said, Caray was to keep quiet until Gussie returned to St. Louis. But when Busch, who was on his way to the airport, heard Caray's on-air rant about the *St. Louis Post-Dispatch* story concerning Harry's potential dismissal, he decided it was the last straw.

Whatever the reasons behind the Cardinals' decision not to renew Caray's contract, the news generated enormous criticism. The day the news was announced, a group calling itself the Harry Caray Fan Club scheduled a protest rally for the following morning at Busch Stadium. In Jefferson City, Missouri, a group began circulating a petition asking Anheuser-Busch to reconsider its decision. "Out here in the boondocks," the petition said, "Harry Caray *is* the Cardinals to many of us. He makes the names in the lineup dance with reality, and the quivering faith or haunting doubt that goes into the outcome of every game, every play, gives new reality and lasting emotion to all of us who love the Cardinals."[26] The KMOX switchboards were flooded with protest calls.

Letters to the editors of *Sporting News* and local-area newspapers during the next few weeks were full of outrage regarding Caray's dismissal. Typical was a letter to *Sporting News* from Tom Gettel of Carthridge, Missouri. "I must express my disgust over the dismissal of Harry Caray as voice of the Cardinals," Gettel wrote. "One is hard pressed to find the culprit in this mess. It appears that those responsible had to find a scapegoat and Harry was it. As for Gussie Busch, Anheuser-Busch's marketing division, and the Cardinals—or whoever is to blame—I say, 'A plague on all your houses.'"[27]

Another fan, Robert L. Nussbaumer, of Columbia, Missouri, wrote the following to the *St. Louis Post-Dispatch*:

> To one who was born in St. Louis in 1941, and grew up there in the 1950s and 1960s, the "voice of the Cardinals" has always been Harry Caray. One would always know that he was back home in Missouri and that things hadn't really changed that much when he heard the voice of Harry Caray.
>
> No other baseball announcer could convey the thrill and excitement of the sport. Yea, all other baseball announcers turn pale and colorless next to Harry's "it might be out of here, it could be, but it's curving, curving . . . foul ball!"
>
> I know that I speak for the generations of Cardinal fans from the '40s through the '60s when I say that an era of Cardinal baseball listening has come to an end, and that listening to a Cardinal game in the future will never be the same. Thank you, Harry, for making Cardinal baseball come alive.[28]

But Harry was gone, and the protests failed to change minds at Anheuser-Busch. No one expected Caray to be out of work for long, and he wasn't. In January 1970, Caray announced his new destination: He was headed west to broadcast baseball for Charlie Finley and the Oakland Athletics.

10

SIBERIA

The Oakland Athletics would consider themselves extremely fortunate if we should be successful in having Harry join us.—Charles O. Finley, president of the A's

We think Harry is the greatest announcer in baseball.—*St. Louis Post-Dispatch*, November 1969[1]

Charles O. Finley—the O was for Oscar, but after acquiring the Athletics franchise, Finley often suggested it stood for "Owner"—was born just outside Birmingham, Alabama, in 1918. Both his father and grandfather were steelworkers, and Charlie himself worked in the mills for five years after the family moved to Gary, Indiana, in the 1930s. During that time, Finley began selling insurance as a second job, and he was so successful that after battling a serious case of tuberculosis that hospitalized him for two and a half years, he started his own company. Within a few years, he had become a multimillionaire.

Finley loved baseball, and once he had attained wealth, he made several unsuccessful attempts to buy a major-league team (Philadelphia Athletics, Detroit Tigers, Chicago White Sox, and expansion Los Angeles Angels). In December 1960, he finally succeeded, obtaining a controlling share of the Athletics, who had moved to Kansas City in 1955, from the estate of Arnold Johnson. Finley quickly purchased the remaining shares of the team from its minority owners.

In their six years in Kansas City prior to being purchased by Finley, the A's had never finished higher than sixth place, and their home attendance had declined from almost 1.4 million in 1955, their first season, to 774,944 in 1960. Finley vowed to change that. One of his first moves was to sign one of Gussie Busch's former general managers, Frank Lane, to a multiyear contract. Finley didn't get along with Lane any better than Busch had, and he fired him before the 1961 season was over. Ultimately, Finley became his own general manager, with the front-office staff consisting mostly of family members. It took him a few years, but Finley eventually became quite adept at identifying and sign-ing talented players. He was also extremely creative; Finley ideas later adopted by other teams, or Major League Baseball, included wearing multicolored uniforms, playing postseason games and the MLB All-Star Game at night, and using the designated hitter. He wanted shorter games and campaigned for the use of a pitch clock, an idea being seriously discussed more than 50 years later.

Throughout his tenure in Kansas City, Finley battled constantly with local officials conerning stadium issues, and he had frequent quarrels with the commissioner of baseball, other American League owners, the local media, and even his own players. When his numerous promotional attempts—for example, cow-milking contests, fireworks shows, install-ing a sheep pasture and a zoo beyond the Municipal Stadium fences, and hiring legendary black baseball star Satchel Paige to pitch a game—failed to improve attendance, Finley began campaigning to move the A's out of Kansas City. The other American League owners always voted down his requests. Finley's response was to stop trying to get people in Kansas City interested in his team. In a biography of Finley for the Society for American Baseball Research, Mark Armour wrote, "Finley ignored booster clubs. He gave no support to local groups that organized ticket-buying programs. He made only cursory attempts at selling radio and TV rights. He decided that the city did not care about him, so, by God, he was not going to care about the city."[2]

Finally, with the expiration of Finley's lease on Kansas City's Munic-ipal Stadium, the American League allowed him to move the team to Oakland for the 1968 season. Finley expected a warm welcome in Northern California; however, the Bay Area already had one major-league team, the San Francisco Giants, and though the Athletics were an improving team full of young stars, including future Hall of Famers Rollie Fingers, Catfish Hunter, and Reggie Jackson, the club drew only 837,466 fans in its first year in Oakland—despite posting a winning record (82–80) for the first time since 1952. That was only about 111,000 more fans than the A's had drawn in their final season in Kansas City, when the team had finished in last place, with a 62–99 record. In 1969, the A's continued to improve, posting an 88–74 record, while finishing in second place in the American League West—but the team's attendance fell to 778,232.

Finley knew he needed to find ways to promote his young team, and one of his answers was to hire Harry Caray.

✣ ✣ ✣

Caray did not come cheaply; Finley offered him a salary of $75,000 a year for five years, which was a 50 percent raise from what he had been earning with the Cardinals, plus the freedom to earn additional money doing fringe work. That was a lot more than Finley was paying any A's player; the highest reported salary for an Oakland player in 1970 was $60,000 for Felipe Alou, a 35-year-old veteran playing his 13th major-league season. Still, Caray was hesitant to accept the offer. He was reluctant to leave family in the Midwest—in part, he wrote later, because his marriage to his second wife Marian was having difficulties. Additionally, he did not want to commit to a multiyear contract, and he was concerned about how Monte Moore, who had been the Athletics' main play-by-play voice since 1962, would react to being pushed into a secondary role. Finley assured him that Moore would still get plenty of air time with no reduction in salary, and Caray agreed to a one-year deal that included use of a Cadillac and a penthouse apartment.

Both Finley and Caray expressed enthusiasm about the opportunity to work together. "Baseball needs color," said Finley, adding,

> and I don't just mean green shirts and white shoes. Any time people in baseball can put color into the game, we should do it. I'm doing it with Harry Caray, whom I consider to be the finest baseball announcer in the country. Now we've got an unbeatable combo—Harry Caray and Monte Moore, baseball's best announcing team.

For his part, Caray promised he would be unafraid to criticize the A's on the air when he felt the situation warranted it. "I've criticized the Cards and got into hot situations with the management, and I'll tell the truth about the club here, too," he told the press. "The biggest thing I must have as an announcer is believability. If people don't believe me, what can I sell?" When a photographer asked Caray and Finley to pose together for a shot, Harry quipped, "Better get a lot of pictures now. Charlie might not be speaking to me in July."[3]

Caray quickly got himself situated into Oakland's night life. The same day Finley was introducing Harry to the local sports media, *Oakland Tribune* gossip columnist Perry Phillips was writing about dining with Caray and Finley at Trader Vic's, where, as Phillips put it,

> The Trader's famous Mai Tai's helped get the conversation in high gear a little bit sooner than usual. Between bites of crepe crab Bengal, Caray gave me a rundown on his favorite nightclub acts, with Shecky Greene getting his top vote. A guy who likes Shecky that much has to be a live wire.[4]

Asked in mid-February what it was like to be the Athletics' number-two broadcaster after eight years as number one, Monte Moore replied,

> Number two to whom? Ever since I wanted to be a sports announcer I've considered Harry Caray the nation's number-one broadcaster, and that's still true. I'm just happy to be a part of what I hope is the number-one team of announcers broadcasting the games of the American League's number-one team.

Moore, a devout Christian, admitted he was "momentarily shaken" when Finley told him about Caray's hiring but that, "All my life I've trusted the Lord to know what he's doing and work out the details of my life."[5]

"When I took the job a lot of people told me that my ego would not be compatible with Charlie Finley's," Caray told the *Los Angeles Times* as spring training was coming to an end. "But I found that I really do like the man. He's promotion-minded, and that's my cup of tea"; however, Caray hadn't forgotten his Midwestern roots—or his messy exit from St. Louis. "I haven't seen Gussie Busch since it happened, but if I did, I don't think he could look me in the eye," Caray said. "Someday I may just write a book about it, and it will have all the elements of something that will sell—sex and intrigue." Caray claimed the Busch family had tried to blacklist him in St. Louis, threatening to withdraw advertising from entities that gave him a job. "They failed," he said, stating he was about to launch a daily five-minute radio show that would air on 65 stations in seven Midwest states, and that he would also be writing a weekly newspaper column called "Holy Cow."[6]

When the 1970 season began, the A's got off to a slow start, posting an 8–12 record in April. They soon recovered and finished the season in second place in the American League's Western Division, with an 89–73 record—the most wins for an Athletics team since the 1932 Philadelphia A's went 94–60. But despite the promotional efforts of Finley and Caray, attendance continued to stay at about the same lackluster level as in 1969. After drawing a respectable 26,270 fans for the home opener against the Milwaukee Brewers on April 13, the A's drew fewer than 3,000 fans for each of the team's next three home games.

Caray soldiered on, and his work drew mostly good reviews from the nation's sporting press. "Watching and listening to Caray is a throwback to the excited football announcer of the Jack Oakie and Ronald Reagan football movies," wrote Jack Craig of the *Boston Globe* when the Athletics visited the Boston Red Sox in late April. "Every pitch is a prospective turning point." Caray admitted to Craig that he was concerned at first about his ability to become enthused broadcasting games for a new team in a new league. "I found out baseball is great no matter who is reporting it," Caray said. "I really didn't know that for sure until I left the Cards."[7]

"The TV station that beams the A's games into your living room comes on with 'Charlie O's Movie' after each contest, but what an anticlimax that is," wrote Lowell Hickey of the *Fremont (California) Argus*, who watched Caray broadcast a game on a hot night in Chicago. "No 1918 film contains as many choice lines as Old Harry comes up with in a couple of hours behind the mic. Harry should get an Academy Award, or at least an Emmy, for his performance in Chicago the night before last." Hickey described Caray, telling his listeners, "I've got my shirt off, my tie off, and I'm doing the game in my shorts."[8]

"The people in Oakland are beginning to talk baseball—thanks to Harry Caray," wrote Jerome Holtzman in *Sporting News* in mid-July. "He's getting them interested."[9] Another *Sporting News* columnist, Bob Addie, wrote that Caray is a "smash hit in the Oakland area, where he is now bringing excitement to the otherwise drab Athletics with the colorful boss—Charlie Finley. Harry is a big deal at ballgames, where he leans out the booth to banter with the fans, and they love it." Caray told Addie, "When I first came out here, few people talked baseball, but they're changing. The fans have to identify with the players. It takes time, but it's coming to Oakland."[10]

"It's my kind of town—good eating, good drinking, good fun, good company, good music," Caray told *Sporting News* writer Jim Scott, who wrote that the "Bay Area is just as taken with Caray." Boots Erb, co-owner of Oakland's Bow & Bell restaurant, along with former major-league star Jackie Jensen, told Scott, "Harry gives a new dimension to the game. Why, he even makes baseball sound as exciting as football. Trouble is, he may be just too good. It seems a lot of citizens would rather listen to Harry than go to the games."[11]

Asked by Scott about Finley, Caray said, "Charlie hasn't said a word to me. He knows how I announce a game. And I never change. He has an exciting club, so I naturally get excited, too." Caray did hear from Finley on at least one occasion: Finley, who for many years had used a mule nicknamed "Charlie O." as the team's mascot, suggested to Caray that he change his trademark call from "Holy Cow!" to "Holy Mule!" While Caray continued to express his respect and admiration for Finley, this was one suggestion he was unwilling to accommodate.

But not all the reports about Caray's year in Oakland were positive. In May, Jerome Holtzman's *Sporting News* column led off with a report of an interview of Caray by Bob Elson, the longtime radio voice of the Chicago White Sox. Asked by Elson how he liked things in Oakland, Caray replied, "It's like being in Siberia." That was "true enough," wrote Holtzman, "but courageous, too, because Caray must have known Finley was back in Chicago—and listening."[12] Caray disputed the report in an interview several weeks later, saying it was actually Elson who said, "This is like Siberia," and that Caray disagreed. Nonetheless, he admitted that "it was cold at the early night games. I didn't mind. I find the weather here is invigorating. It's a working man's climate. . . . However, I was assured by Monte Moore that it would warm up. And it did."[13] Whatever was said in the interview with Elson, the word "Siberia" became linked with Caray in summarizing his feelings about Oakland.

In his April 1971 *Boston Globe* story about Caray, Jack Craig mentioned the "Siberia" comment and wrote that Caray's "season there had not always buoyed the city's pride."

> [Caray's] frankness was sometimes difficult to absorb for a relatively new franchise inclined to hard sell. I remember standing behind him at his Fenway Park mic last season as he contended that a ball which had eluded second baseman Dick Green actually was an error, even if the scorer had declared it a hit.
>
> Later he wondered if Reggie Jackson, struggling during the '70 season, was a flash-in-the-pan rather than a superstar.
>
> These were the thoughts fans were liable to express, but Caray was saying them on the air. [14]

While one could argue this was simply Caray being Caray, Craig's point was that Oakland simply wasn't used to this kind of broadcasting.

Caray certainly was not about to change. In July, Lowell Hickey quoted Harry alluding on the air to the fact that Jackson had the same number of home runs (10) as shortstop Bert Campaneris, a player not known as a power hitter. "What would you have done if someone had told you during spring training that, come the end of June, Campy Campaneris and Reggie Jackson would have the same number of home runs?" Caray asked. "Why, you'd have picked up the phone and called the insane asylum and made a reservation." [15]

Three days after the publication of Hickey's story, Don Merry of the *Long Beach (California) Independent* quoted Caray referring to the Athletics, who had lost to the California Angels, 5–1, the previous day, as a "team without character. How could they play so uninspired in the last game of a series?" [16] At the time, the A's were in third place in the American League West but 10 games over .500 (45–35) and only six and a half games out of the division lead.

Caray was not afraid to confront a struggling A's player. In late August, Caray's guest on his pregame radio show was Oakland outfielder Rick Monday. During the interview, Caray remarked that while he hadn't noticed Monday stranding an inordinate number of runners, statistics showed he wasn't driving in many runs, either. "When he brought that up, it sort of ticked me off," Monday said. The next night, Monday drove in the winning run in an A's victory. [17]

In late August, Ed Levitt of the *Oakland Tribune* reported that during Caray's pregame show, Detroit Tigers pitcher Denny McLain had criticized Charlie Finley's handling of Reggie Jackson.

"Ballplayers," said Denny, "aren't little mechanical toys. They're human. They have feelings."

It was, of course, quite a dig at the A's boss.

After the interview, Caray was told by a newsman, "That little session will cost you your job."

Caray countered, "You can't call me a house man anymore."[18]

According to a 1975 *Chicago Tribune* article by Gary Deeb, an "angry Finley was on the phone" after Caray returned to the broadcast booth following his interview with McLain, "spitting fire about Caray having the gall to give McLain air time on Charlie's own broadcast. . . . When the conversation was over, Harry's ears were still burning."[19]

Although Caray had obviously ruffled a few feathers, Ron Bergman wrote in early September that reports indicated Caray could return to the A's broadcast booth in 1971 "if things can be worked out." According to Caray, Finley offered him a five-year deal to work for the A's year-round, plus an interest-free loan to build a house in the Bay Area. Caray wrote that while he'd enjoyed his time in Oakland and had maintained a good relationship with Finley, he wanted to return to the Midwest, and turned down the offer. On October 13, the A's announced that Caray would not be back, and that former Chicago White Sox broadcasters Bob Elson and Red Rush would be joining Monte Moore in the broadcast booth in 1971.

But some reports stated that Finley fired Caray. A column by Bill Soliday in the *Fremont (California) Argus* several days after the announcement that Caray would not return called it a firing and took Finley to task for it. "Caray was not your ordinary house man. That is to say, he wasn't a Finley man," wrote Soliday. "Caray believed in broadcasting freedom of the press. He held back from personally criticizing Finley, whom he did not particularly care for, but he let others do the criticizing for him."[20]

In Curt Smith's *Voices of the Game*, Caray's departure from Oakland was reported as a firing. Former Athletics broadcaster Jim Woods told Smith that he had asked Finley why he'd fired Caray, and Finley responded, "Hell, that line of bull-shit Harry put out might have worked in St. Louis, but nobody was buying it here." Woods also mentioned friction between Caray and Monte Moore, with Caray supposedly telling Moore, "Listen, when I start doing my stuff, I don't want to hear a thing out of you. Just keep your mouth shut." [21] In 1978, Caray told Ron Fimrite that he and Finley "got on famously" but that he'd had problems with Moore. "I could feel the knife in my back every time I walked into the booth," Caray said about Moore. "We couldn't go on like that."[22] Among other things, Caray said Moore had alerted Finley (who was in Chicago at the time) about the Denny McLain interview, which Finley found objectionable. According to Gary Deeb, "Moore, a personal stooge for Finley since 1960, had dialed Charlie on the long-distance horn as soon as Caray started chatting with McLain. The 'Spy in the Sky' had struck again."[23]

"The first thing Harry told me in spring training that year was, 'I'm gonna be number one,'" Moore said in 1987. "I said, 'Harry, you've got to earn number one.' He never did earn it. He did a whole lot of talking. And he couldn't wait to get out of the booth and start drinking."[24]

In a *Sporting News* story about Caray in late October 1970, Pete Rahn wrote, "There have been insinuations from some quarters that Caray didn't cut the mustard for the A's. When he joined the Oakland team, Caray said his goal was to promote a 1 million attendance." If so, it was a goal the A's came nowhere near achieving. Despite their second-place finish and 89–73 record, the team drew 778,355 fans to its home games—only 123 more fans than had watched the A's at home in 1969. Oakland's season-ending three-game series against the Brewers drew a total of just 8,307 fans.

"Granted that's not much of an increase," Caray told Rahn about the slight improvement in attendance, "but the other side of the story is that the Giants—right across the bay—dropped 140,000 people at the gate. In other words, I figure if I hadn't been there, the A's might have lost in attendance. Anyway, Finley and I parted on the friendliest of terms. We got along beautifully."[25]

During the 1970 World Series between the Baltimore Orioles and Cincinnati Reds, there were press reports that Caray's next stop would be Cincinnati, as the Reds were looking for a new play-by-play man. Caray's response was that he had not spoken to Reds management but that the Reds "would be some great ball club to talk about the next couple of years."[26] Ultimately, the Caray-to-Cincy rumors failed to pan out; instead, the Reds filled their opening with a young broadcaster named Al Michaels.

In the meantime, the October 31, 1970, issue of *Sporting News* featured an advertisement announcing Caray's latest venture: the Harry Caray School of Broadcasting. "This is a complete home-study course, covering all phases of broadcasting," stated the ad. "You study at your own pace, with every step under the supervision of experts in the broadcast performance field." In a statement that might have prompted some Caray listeners to suggest that Harry—who was known for sometimes struggling with the pronunciation of players' names—sign up for his own course, the ad stated the course started "with the basics of diction, pronunciation, and vocabulary."[27]

Caray himself would not have to wait long for the next opportunity to exhibit his broadcasting skills. He was not going to be broadcasting games for the National League's defending champions, the 102-win Cincinnati Reds. He was going to be working for the team with the worst record in the major leagues in 1970 (106 losses)—and a team that didn't even have a radio contract for 1971.

Caray was heading to Chicago to work for the lowly White Sox.

11

NEW MAN IN TOWN

Baseball's most unusual deal of the season was completed yesterday by the Chicago White Sox, who suddenly have emerged as wheelers and dealers. Before what probably was the largest crowd White Sox officials have seen in five years, the club announced the acquiring of Harry Caray, the sportscaster who last season raved about the Oakland Athletics, for a salary of $80,000 per.—*David Condon, Chicago Tribune*, January 1971[1]

April 9, 1971, Good Friday, was a pleasant spring day in Chicago, with temperatures reaching the low 60s. Though the forecast called for brisk northwesterly winds, it was unusually warm weather for early April in Chicago. That morning's *Chicago Tribune* proclaimed, "Spring is here," and noted the presence of women in summer attire on Chicago's downtown streets.[2]

At Comiskey Park on Chicago's South Side, there was another harbinger of spring: A group of men in their own summer attire, the Chicago White Sox, was preparing for the home opener against the Minnesota Twins. In tandem with the arrival of spring weather, the White Sox were offering what *Tribune* writer Richard Dozer called the "baptism of a new era in Chicago baseball."[3]

White Sox fans were undoubtedly ready for a new era. After almost winning the American League pennant in a tight four-team race in 1967—they ultimately finished fourth, only three games behind the pennant-winning Red Sox—the White Sox had fallen on hard times, both on the field and at the box office. Table 11.1 shows the club's decline in wins, finish in the standings, and attendance from 1967 to 1970.

Despite the club's strong performance on the field in 1967, the White Sox failed to draw 1 million fans for the second-straight season—the first time Sox home attendance had been below the million mark in back-to-back seasons since 1949–1950. Club management was so concerned that in 1968 and 1969, the White Sox scheduled one "home" game versus each of their American League opponents (nine total games in 1968, 11 games in 1969) to be played in County Stadium in Milwaukee—a city attempting to acquire a major-league team to replace the Braves, who had moved to Atlanta prior to the 1966 season.

The games in Milwaukee proved a godsend for the Sox: In both 1968 and 1969, more than 33 percent of the White Sox home attendance came from those handful of games in Milwaukee. Not surprisingly, the *Sporting News Official Baseball Guide, 1970* reported that there had been negotiations between White Sox ownership and a Milwaukee group eager to move the Sox to that city; however, such a sale needed approval from the other American League owners, and the proposal lacked the required votes. The point became moot when the Seattle Pilots moved to Milwaukee and became the Milwaukee Brewers prior to the 1970 season.

The White Sox hit bottom in 1970, losing 106 games—the most in franchise history—while finishing last in the American League West (despite the presence in the division of two second-year expansion teams, the Brewers and Kansas City Royals). Without the lifeline from those games in Milwaukee, the White Sox drew less than 500,000 fans for the first time since the wartime season of 1942. Edgar Munzel's review of the club's 1970 season in the *Sporting News Official Baseball Guide for 1971* summarized the situation: "For the White Sox, 1970 was sheer disaster. It was a 'lost' season in every sense of the word. There

Table 11.1.   Chicago White Sox, 1967–1970

Year	Won	Lost	Finish	Attendance
1967	89	73	fourth of 10	985,634
1968	67	95	eighth of 10	803,775
1969	68	94	fifth of 6	589,546
1970	56	106	sixth of 6	495,355

were record losses on the field, as well as at the gate, with the result that, in the end, it led to a dramatic shakeup of the entire top echelon of the organization by Owner John Allyn."[4]

* * *

The shakeup began in early September 1970, when Ed Short, who had worked for the White Sox in various roles for the past 20 years, was replaced as vice president and director of player personnel by Roland Hemond, former farm director of the California Angels. Executive vice president Leo Breen was replaced by Stu Holcomb, who had been the Sox public relations director. "The next day, September 3," Munzel wrote, "Allyn completed the shakeup by the firing of Don Gutteridge as manager and the hiring of Charles (Chuck) Tanner, who had piloted Hawaii to a division title in the Pacific Coast League."

The White Sox shook up their roster as well; Dozer's preview of the 1971 home opener noted that 17 of the 25 players on the club's roster had been with different teams when the Sox opened their home season in 1970. The emphasis was on youth: Dozer described the club as "young, exciting, and marked for improvement," with an average age of 25. The players were decked out in newly designed uniforms for 1971, with red the primary color for the first time in franchise history. Writing two decades later, baseball uniform historian Marc Okkonen enthusiastically described the change as "new and dazzling! . . . The S-O-X emblem, the caps, the undersweaters, the stirrup socks, and yes, even the *shoes* and pinstripes were a vivid scarlet."[5]

There was one more significant change for the White Sox in 1971—in the team's radio booth. Chicago legend Bob Elson had been the Sox' primary radio voice since 1946, and he had been describing White Sox (and sometimes Chicago Cubs) games as far back as 1931. In the late 1960s, White Sox games had been broadcast on WMAQ, one of the city's major radio outlets, but with the team struggling, the relationship began to sour. By midseason of the disastrous 1970 campaign, it became apparent that WMAQ had no interest in continuing to broadcast White Sox games in 1971—and neither did any other major Chicago radio station. When the season ended, the Sox had neither a radio outlet nor their primary radio broadcasters. In a stunning move, Elson and his radio partner, Red Rush, announced they had agreed to broadcast games for Charlie Finley's Oakland Athletics in 1971.

It took several months of negotiations, but in January 1971, the White Sox introduced Elson's successor. It was none other than Harry Caray.

※ ※ ※

Apart from the fact that both men were legendary broadcasters, the bombastic Caray could not have been more different from the straight-laced Elson when it came to describing a game. Wrote sports broadcasting historian Stuart Shea,

> Caray was profane, sloppy, often annoying, and completely in tune with the game. His common-man act was at least part salesmanship, but his language and bearing were refreshing to long-suffering fans numbed by stony-faced spokesmen narrating a black-and-white picture of a dull gray team that contrasted with a world that had long since embraced color.[6]

Caray could not have been a better fit for a team desperate to remake its image and energize its fan base. In summary, the White Sox had added new team management, new uniforms, a mostly new roster—and now a new broadcaster, one totally different from the man he was replacing.

Landing Caray had required some creativity on the part of the White Sox. Stu Holcomb, who led the club's search for a broadcaster to replace Elson, told Caray he couldn't match the base salary he'd been paid in Oakland, so he guaranteed the broadcaster $50,000, with a bonus of $10,000 for every 100,000 home fans the 1971 team drew over the 600,000 mark. Caray agreed to the deal. He was gambling, in essence, on his ability to draw fans to Comiskey Park.

Even with Caray in the fold, the White Sox were unable to make a deal with a major Chicago radio station to broadcast the team's games. Finally, in early March, the team unveiled a five-station Chicago-area network, none of them in the city proper, and only one on AM radio. The four FM stations were WEAW in Evanston, WJOL in Joliet, WVTV in Dundee, and WLNR in Lansing. The lone AM station was WTAQ in La Grange. There was a bit of irony in the fact that WJOL in

Joliet was part of the mix: Caray had begun his broadcasting career with the station back in 1940, when its call letters were WCLS.

The financial details of the radio network were more than a little humbling for the White Sox. According to Stuart Shea, "Each station paid the team $25 per game, sold its own ads, and kept all the revenue. This meant that five stations airing all 162 games earned the White Sox a little more than $25,000 in radio rights fees!"[7] That, of course, was half of what the team would be paying Caray in base salary alone.

To say the least, this was quite a comedown for Harry Caray. During most of his tenure with the Cardinals, Caray had broadcast games on KMOX, the 50,000-watt powerhouse whose signal could be heard at night in most of the United States—not to mention numerous foreign countries. WTAQ, on the other hand, dropped its signal at night to just 500 watts.

Chicago Tribune writer Bob Verdi, who would later collaborate with Caray on Harry's autobiography—*Holy Cow!*—recalled the challenges of trying to listen to White Sox games on the underpowered network.

> In those days I lived about 25 miles north of Chicago, and if I was driving downtown from my home to the office, I would literally have to change stations two or three times to find the White Sox. I could maybe pick up WTAQ, but then the signal would fade out and I would have to find one of those other little stations that carried the game . . . which was a crime because this was Harry Caray broadcasting the games.
>
> I recall that Zenith was one of the sponsors on Harry's pregame show on WTAQ. Harry had interviewed a guest on the show, and afterward he thanked the person and then said, "And for being our guest you'll get this wonderful Zenith radio. I'm not sure you'll be able to pick up one of our games on it, though." Typical Harry.[8]

There was also the matter of Caray's radio partner. In St. Louis, Caray had worked alongside (among others) Milo Hamilton, Jack Buck, and Joe Garagiola, all of whom would go on to win the National Baseball Hall of Fame's Ford C. Frick Award (as would Caray). In Chicago, Caray's first partner was WTAQ sales and sports director Ralph Faucher, whose primary experience had been broadcasting high school football and basketball games. Faucher himself had put together the radio network, then approached the White Sox about broadcasting the games.

"We were a last resort," he told Ed Sherman in 2000. "They had no-where else to go."[9]

If the challenge of calling games on a patched-together network for a team coming off a 106-loss season bothered Caray, he certainly didn't show it. His introduction to much of the Chicago media came at the annual Chicago baseball writers' Diamond Dinner on January 10, where he was a featured guest. Reflecting on his 25 years as the voice of the Cardinals, Caray brashly stated, "There were just two names in St. Louis—Stan Musial and me." He expressed enthusiasm for working in Chicago, saying, "I'm gonna be part of this community," and "This is my kind of town." Caray had positive things to say about his lone season in Oakland, "but moving from St. Louis was out of the question. Working in Chicago is a different ball of wax. I'm coming to talk with the people I've spent my life with."

Then, in a statement that would prove to be worth remembering, Caray said, "It's a good thing I'm not doing Cub games, though. With their afternoon games and the four o'clock (a.m.) closing hour here, I'd never make it."[10]

* * *

Caray's first work for the White Sox came in 1971 spring training games, and it was a happy spring for the Sox: The club went 18–10 in Grapefruit League action, the best spring record for any American League club that year. The team opened the regular season with a doubleheader (a rarity for a season opener) on April 7 in Oakland, and the White Sox took both games to continue their momentum.

When the home opener arrived two days later on Good Friday, White Sox fans came out in force: The paid attendance of 43,253 (44,250 total) was the "largest Opening Day crowd in White Sox history," according to Dozer's *Tribune* game story (the record would be broken in 1978). An author's review of daily White Sox attendance figures on baseball-reference.com revealed that this was also the largest paid attendance for *any* White Sox home game since August 1963. According to Dozer, "Nobody in the Sox ticket office thought the crowd would exceed 30,000, a figure that would have been excellent by any standards."[11]

The crowd was treated to an exciting game, and Caray described the action to those listening on radio. Writing more than two decades later, Bob Vanderberg described the scene.

> From the start, (Caray) made obvious that he was going to be the opposite of his predecessor, the legendary but unexcitable Bob Elson. At the 1971 home opener against defending AL West champ Minnesota, Caray, already pumped by the Sox's doubleheader sweep the day before [editor: actually two days before] at Oakland and by the presence of 44,250 fans in the ghost town that had been Comiskey Park, shouted in joy as the Sox rallied to win 3–2 in the ninth on Rich McKinney's pinch single. "Perranoski from the belt . . . the pitch. . . . *Here* it is. . . . Base hit!! Left field!! Sox Win! Sox Win! Holy Cow! The White Sox win!"[12]

Reality set in the next day as the White Sox lost to the Twins, 5–3, in front of only 12,499 fans. That was the first of seven-straight losses. The 1971 White Sox never had a winning record on the season after April 11, when their record was 3–2, and the home opener marked the only time all season that the team played before a home crowd of 30,000 or better. Even the usually optimistic Caray was concerned about his ability to reach the club's fan base, given the makeshift radio network. "For a while, I wasn't sure there was anyone out there listening," he wrote in his autobiography. "Here I was doing my damnedest to convince the people of Chicago that you really can't beat fun at the old ballpark, and I had the distinct impression I was talking to myself."[13]

Yet, somehow the word got out. In late April, when the White Sox visited Boston to play the Red Sox, *Boston Globe* sports television writer Jack Craig wrote a story about Caray that began, "The most exciting announcer in baseball is in town this weekend with the most unexciting team. The improbable combination is Harry Caray and the White Sox." After mentioning Caray's "very small radio network" and the fact that most of the White Sox games were also available on television in Chicago, Craig wrote, "But don't a lot of Chicago fans turn the sound down on TV and listen to Harry on radio? 'You can say that, but I can't,' (Caray) said in an uncharacteristic default."[14]

In another *Boston Globe* story two months later, Craig summarized Caray's style: "His 'Holy Cow' trademark usually is reserved for home runs hit by his club but seemingly so is his most severe criticism. This dual manner may reflect not only Caray's independence resulting from a very large bank account, but also his gregarious nature, his natural style."[15]

※ ※ ※

Early in the 1971 season, Caray brought back a tradition he had first used in St. Louis: broadcasting games on a regular basis from Comiskey Park's center-field bleachers. Larry Everhart of the *(Chicago Suburban) Daily Herald* spent an afternoon in the bleachers with Caray, watching him describe the game while interacting with the fans in the stands. Everhart came away with two conclusions: "It is obvious that Caray's special charisma is a major factor in the Sox' greatly increased attendance this season," and, "For once, even though the Sox had lost the game, I left the park feeling I'd had as much fun as if they'd won." Everhart also wrote, "Nobody has better fan relations than Caray," and he described several features of Caray's work that would soon become familiar to Chicago fans. These included his constant interaction with the fans ("Caray is the only broadcaster I know who will acknowledge any fan addressing him at any time during the game"); the constant chants of "Hey, Harry!" from nearby fans throughout the game; Caray's frequent flirtations with female fans he found attractive; and Caray "chug-a-lugging a beer and waving a white towel in exciting moments."[16]

By mid-August, the White Sox had already surpassed their 1970 home attendance by almost 100,000 fans, and an Associated Press story credited Caray with helping boost the attendance, despite the fact that "Caray has to shout his 'holy cow' from such fringes as La Grange and Joliet."[17] The White Sox finished the year with a home attendance of 833,891—68 percent better than the 1970 total of 495,535. While a greatly improved team was unquestionably a big factor (the White Sox won 79 games in 1971, 23 more than in 1970), much of the credit for the renewed interest in the team was given to Caray—who received a $20,000 bonus based on the attendance clause in his contract.

When the White Sox and Caray settled on a new contract for 1972, the bonus for increased attendance did not begin until the team's home attendance reached the 1 million mark. That was no small challenge, as the Sox had not drawn 1 million fans since 1965. But with the addition of slugger Dick Allen, who would win the American League's Most Valuable Player Award in 1972, the White Sox made a strong challenge for the league's Western Division title; the team finished the year in second place, with a home attendance of 1,177,318—the club's highest attendance since 1964, and a 41 percent increase from 1971. As in 1971, a greatly improved team was a major factor in the rise in attendance. At the same time, Caray's enormous popularity was credited in numerous news stories as one of the big keys to the club's attendance surge.

Although Caray was broadcasting in 1972, on the same network of small suburban stations, with WTAQ and its 500-watt signal at night as the flagship, Stuart Shea noted that the "station still got comparatively huge ratings with Caray behind the mic."[18] The *Chicago Tribune* reported that, "WTAQ beat the local radio giants on the night of May 26, when ratings gave the White Sox 15 percent of the Chicago audience during a late-late game with Oakland. Four 50,000-watt stations lined up behind."[19]

Caray was again broadcasting every Wednesday afternoon home game from the center-field bleachers. *Chicago Tribune* writer Robert Markus, who watched Caray in action from the bleachers during a game in May, wrote, "He is as much a celebrity around White Sox Park as most of the ballplayers. If you don't think he puts people in the park just spend a Wednesday afternoon in the bleachers."[20] Dave Condon, another *Tribune* writer who spent an afternoon in the bleachers with Caray, wrote, "There is nothing like fun at the old ballgame. Not with Harry Caray in the bleachers, assembling his rooters and coaching them like the director of the old Paulist choir."[21]

In August 1972, Caray was the subject of a multipage profile in the Sunday *Chicago Tribune Magazine*. Wrote author Richard Dozer,

> The man called "the gabbiest gadabout in baseball" has dealt with billionaires; told executives how to run their business; managers how to manage. He knows with some intimacy the stars of stage and sport. But he's just as likely to be found casually drinking beer with anybody who happens to be on the bar stool next to him.[22]

As the 1972 season neared the end, Caray's popularity had grown to the point that White Sox ticket manager Tom Maloney reported, "It used to be that the fans wanted to sit along the first- and third-base lines. Now the first tickets to go are the ones in the upper deck, near Harry's broadcast position."[23]

Perhaps the biggest sign of Caray's impact on the White Sox during those first two years in Chicago came in October 1972, when the team made two announcements:

1. Beginning in 1973, White Sox radio broadcasts would be heard on Chicago's powerful NBC outlet, WMAQ. The station estimated that Caray's radio calls would now be able to be heard "in a big slice of the Midwest."
2. White Sox television broadcasts—an estimated 135 games—were moving from WFLD (Chicago channel 32) to WSNS (channel 44). More importantly, plans called for Caray to become the team's main television voice, working "five or six innings" of each telecast on TV and the remainder of the game on radio. While Caray had done a limited amount of television work during his tenures in both St. Louis and Oakland, the bulk of his work would now come from the television booth—and it would continue that way for the remainder of his broadcasting career.

Caray's big gamble in going to the White Sox had paid off. He was back on top of the sports broadcasting world.

12

SOUTH SIDE BLUES

Q. What channel are you going to be broadcasting on now?
A. Channel 44. Can you get it out here? Good. I can't get it where I
stay.—Harry Caray at Q&A with fans, January 1973[1]

After their strong second-place in 1972, the White Sox were expected
to contend for the American League Western Division title in 1973. In
the April 14 preseason edition of *Sporting News*, the Sox were picked to
finish second in the division behind the defending World Series champion Oakland Athletics; Sox staff writer Edgar Munzel wrote in his
capsule preview, "If pitching comes through and (Bill) Melton comes
back, (Sox) could win division title." Publisher C. C. Johnson Spink
wrote, "The Athletics and the White Sox should run a beautiful race in
the A.L. West," adding, "If Dick Allen can have the same kind of year
he had in 1972, when he was the A.L.'s MVP, the White Sox could
overtake the Athletics." The paper also stated that Las Vegas oddsmak-
ers had the Sox at 11–5 to reach the World Series, second in the
American League only to the A's.[2]

Things started beautifully for the White Sox in 1973. The team went
10–5 in April to take the division lead, and at the end of May they held a
three-game lead with a 27–15 record. Used frequently on two days' rest
by manager Chuck Tanner and pitching coach Johnny Sain, knuckleballer Wilbur Wood had 13 of the 27 wins and was on pace to win more
than 30 games. Although slowed a bit by a thumb injury, Allen was
leading the league with a .652 slugging percentage and ranked second
in the American League with 11 home runs.

But the win pace slowed in June, and on June 28, Allen suffered a hairline fracture of his left leg in a collision while trying to field a wild throw. He was expected to miss one to four weeks but wound up getting only five more at-bats the rest of the season. Another key player, center fielder Ken Henderson, missed the last two months of the season with a knee injury. Meanwhile, the heavy workload was taking its toll on Wood, who went 11–17, with a 4.47 earned run average from June 1 to the end of the season. On July 20, Wood started—and lost—both games of a doubleheader against the New York Yankees. That was emblematic of the struggles of the White Sox after the first two months; the club was 20 games under .500 (50–70) after May 31, and finished the year fifth in the six-team division with a 77–85 record.

Despite the club's disappointing finish, it was a mostly satisfying year for Harry Caray. Primarily a TV broadcaster for the first time in his career, Caray could be seen on TV for six innings of each of the Sox' 130-plus telecasts (he switched to radio for innings four through six). He was a hit in the new role; at the end of the season, the team announced that Sox TV ratings on their new flagship station, UHF channel 44 WSNS, had improved by 70 percent from 1972. Caray could also point to the fact that despite the fifth-place finish, the club's home attendance of 1,302,527 was the highest for the White Sox in 13 years, and fourth highest in franchise history. On May 20, the team drew an all-time franchise record 55,555 fans for a doubleheader against the Minnesota Twins.

Caray had new broadcast partners in 1973. On radio, he was paired with Gene Osborn, who had formerly worked for the Pittsburgh Pirates and Detroit Tigers; on TV his partner was ex-Cincinnati Reds broadcaster Bob Waller. Caray did not click with Osborn, who lasted only one year as Harry's partner, but his work with the 31-year-old Waller drew positive reviews. Like Caray, Waller was not afraid to be honest; in a *Daily Herald* profile, Paul Logan wrote, "You'll not hear Bob making excuses for the home team like some Chicago mic men, a fact that's making him more and more appealing to each new fan who turns him on." In a line that might have drawn a different interpretation a year or so later, Logan also wrote, "Coupled with the effervescent Harry Caray, the vocal duo must have been a match made in the same celestial spot as the one that brought together Dick Allen and the White Sox."[3]

As the White Sox began to struggle, Caray became increasingly un-afraid to voice his criticism of struggling Sox players, as well as team management. In 1971–1972, when the Sox were improving on the field and Caray's popularity in Chicago was soaring, he was mainly upbeat, while never abandoning his trademark bluntness. One example: During a game in which Sox shortstop "Bee Bee" Richard committed a couple of errors, Caray cracked, "Richard just picked up a hot-dog wrapper at shortstop. It's the first thing he has picked up all night."[4]

Harry did have one frequent target in 1971–1972: reserve catcher Tom Egan. A modestly talented player with a lifetime batting average of .200, Egan never played more than 85 games in a major-league season, so he was never a key component on any Major League Baseball team. Nonetheless Caray, by most accounts, was unsparing in pointing out Egan's shortcomings. "Harry called Tom Egan the worst catcher he had ever seen, and one of the worst hitters," said Egan's teammate (and fellow catcher), Ed Herrmann. "I think it hurt him mentally and might have hastened the end of his career. His wife told him what Harry said. He'd say to me, 'He got me again last night,' with some expletives you couldn't print."[5] Egan became a frequent target of the Comiskey Park boo-birds, and it got worse after he exploded in May 1972, saying, "The fans are all front-runners, and you can put that in the paper. . . . I guess they'll really be after me now, but to hell with them."[6] He apologized the next day, but it didn't seem to help.

In 1973, Caray's criticism of Sox players and management became more pointed. On June 28, the club released outfielder Rick Reichardt, who was batting a respectable .275 but had hit only three home runs. Prior to being released, Reichardt had told general manager Stu Hol-comb that he was suffering "mental anguish" because of criticism from Caray. "Sure, I've said that he can't throw," said Caray in response, "but everybody can see that. But I haven't been on him in the sense that I ride him all the time. For instance, I blew my stack, gave it all I had the day he won for us with a homer."[7]

Caray was also critical of aging knuckleballer Eddie Fisher, saying on the air (according to *Chicago Tribune* radio-TV critic Gary Deeb), "Fisher never was any good, and at the age of 38 [actually 37] he's not gonna get any better. Get him outta there!"[8] "There's nothing we can do about Harry," said Holcomb. "He blasts me, too, and [manager Chuck] Tanner, and everybody else. That's his style."[9] A few weeks later, on July 27, Holcomb resigned as White Sox general manager, citing his difficulties getting along with Chuck Tanner as the primary reason for his departure. Holcomb mentioned the hiring of Caray as one of the positive moves of his White Sox tenure.

During one of the last home broadcasts of the 1973 season, Caray walked through the Comiskey Park stands and interviewed fans. "He strolled through a near-empty and dark Comiskey talking to anyone who was willing to come on the air," wrote Dan Helpingstine. "This was before the explosion of talk radio, and Caray gave these fans a platform to air their gripes. As he stood in the lower deck conducting man on-the-spot interviews, Caray appeared to be truly listening. This was no stunt."[10]

❋ ❋ ❋

On January 17, 1974, the *St. Louis Post-Dispatch* reported that Harry Caray's marriage to his second wife, Marian, had ended in divorce after 24 years. Mrs. Caray had filed suit in 1972, to end the marriage, charging that Caray "associated with other women in a manner inconsistent with his marital vows." Caray gave Marian custody of their two daughters; the family home in Ladue, Missouri; land valued at more than $100,000; and a cash settlement of $52,500. He also agreed to pay child support and attorneys' fees. The couple divided assets estimated at $570,000.[11]

In an interview a year later with John Smith of *Florida Today*, Caray complained, "I never got my name in the [St. Louis] papers, even though I won all the broadcasting awards. The only time I was mentioned was if I got fired, divorced, or nearly died in an auto accident."[12]

❋ ❋ ❋

Despite their fifth-place finish the previous year, the White Sox were expected to field a strong team in 1974. Dick Allen, who had suffered a broken leg and played in only 72 games in 1973, had returned for the second year of a three-year, $750,000 contract, which, at the time, was the most lucrative in baseball. Outfielders Ken Henderson, Pat Kelly, and Carlos May were also returning from injuries. Left-handed pitcher Jim Kaat, who had joined the White Sox late in the 1973 season after 15 years with the Minnesota Twins franchise, would be around for the entire season. The Sox roster included several promising young players, including shortstop Bucky Dent, second baseman Jorge Orta, catcher-outfielder Brian Downing, and pitchers Rich Gossage and Terry Forster, all of whom would go on to have long and successful major-league careers. The Sox had even acquired longtime Chicago Cubs infielder Ron Santo in a trade. In the *Sporting News* April 6 baseball preview issue, the Sox were picked to finish second in the Western Division, behind the two-time defending World Series champion Oakland Athletics.

Instead, the White Sox managed only a .500 record (80–80) and a fourth-place finish in a season full of contention and controversy. The troubles began on Opening Day, when the Sox lost, 8–2, to the California Angels in front of 30,041 fans, "several of whom probably belong in a place they should have had to escape from to be present," according to George Langford of the *Chicago Tribune*. Langford continued,

> The scoreboard for the number of streakers, strippers, fights, and bottles thrown was incalculable. The outbreaks of fisticuffs counted more than a dozen. One person had to be removed from the left-field upper deck on a stretcher.
>
> At least a half a dozen (and probably more) fans, including one female, removed their clothes. . . . One male, wearing only a White Sox helmet, jumped over the box seat wall in deep left and raced out to the field in the top of the seventh inning and did a dance. . . . Wine bottles and beer cans were thrown from the upper deck at the players. One bottle narrowly missed hitting White Sox reliever Terry Forster in the head. Another struck and cut Sox batboy Rick Sakamoto on the hand. In order to protect the players who were working in the bullpen, pitcher Skip Pitlock had to stand guard beside them during the final three innings.
>
> "It was the worst I've ever seen," said former White Sox catcher Tom Egan, who was now with the Angels. "They must be spicing up the booze," remarked Tom McCraw, another ex-White Sox now with the Angels. "After that I don't see how anybody would want to come out to a game."[13]

Caray was behind the mic for this game, of course, and I was able to listen to some sound clips of his radio call courtesy of White Sox fan and historian Mark Liptak. Frankly, Caray crossed the boundaries of good taste in these clips, particularly in commenting rather crudely on the measurements of a female fan who took off her top ("Boy, you could describe her as 'Holy Cow!'") and enthusiastically describing the mayhem as it began to escalate. As could be said about the behavior of many people in the crowd that day, this game was not one of Caray's prouder moments.

The White Sox lost their first five games of the 1974 season, and although they recovered enough to lead the division for a time during the month of May, their last day in first place was May 19. The team's disappointing performance had a big effect on Dick Allen, the club's biggest star and highest-paid player. "Things were never right for the White Sox in '74 from the start," Allen wrote in his 1989 autobiography, *Crash.* "I felt confused, disoriented, but mostly depressed. My baseball career was slipping through my fingers, and it was getting harder to see where I was going to get a ring for my efforts."[14] Allen was so upset that on September 14, with more than two weeks left in the season, he abruptly announced that he was retiring from baseball—even though he was leading the American League in home runs at the time. Allen later changed his mind about retirement, but he never played another game for the White Sox, who traded him to the Atlanta Braves in December.

Allen's difficulties—which included a well-publicized battle for team leadership with former Cub Ron Santo—were only one of many problems encountered by the 1974 White Sox. At one point the Sox even needed help from the Chicago Fire Department. On June 7, at Comiskey Park, a popcorn machine in a storage room behind the first-base stands burst into flames during the eighth inning of the White Sox–Boston Red Sox game. The field was quickly engulfed by smoke, and the game was delayed for more than an hour—with some fans going onto the field to escape the blaze—while 75 firemen using 22 pieces of equipment attempted to douse the flames and contain the smoke. Fourteen people were treated for smoke inhalation at nearby Mercy Hospital.

Falling attendance at Comiskey Park was another problem—particularly late in the year. During the Sox' final two homestands, the club drew more than 10,000 fans only once—a crowd of 11,874 for a double-header against the California Angels on September 13. Only 1,969 hearty souls showed up for the season finale against the Kansas City

Royals on October 2. For the season, the club's home attendance of 1,149,596 was more than 150,000 fans lower than in 1973.

As the team's troubles escalated in 1974, so did the volume of Caray's criticism. One player who came under fire from Harry was pitcher Jim Kaat, a respected veteran who would retire in 1983, with 283 major-league wins. "In 1974, when I was really struggling, Harry was kind of calling for my scalp," Kaat said in a 2018 interview. "'What are they running this guy out there for?'" he'd say. "'When your fastball and curve are the same speed, it's time to call it a career.' He was really all over me." Kaat recovered and eventually finished the season with 21 wins, but "the problem was that Harry would never actually acknowledge that I had turned things around. He wanted to give me an award at the end of the season for White Sox pitcher of the year. And I said, 'Harry, take that thing and stick it where the sun doesn't shine.'"

Nonetheless, Kaat found it impossible to stay angry with Caray. By the next spring, he said, Caray had forgotten about the unpleasantness and asked Kaat to have a drink with him. Later on, when Caray learned that Kaat's teenage son had broadcasting ambitions, he invited the youngster to come on the air and announce a bit of a game. "Harry was pretty unfiltered, but he was one of those iconic persons that fans loved and players had some issues with," Kaat added. "He was brutally honest and unflappable. He didn't care if the players liked him or not. He felt he was just doing his job." [15]

Dick Allen had been a White Sox hero in 1972, when he won the American League Most Valuable Player Award in his first season with the team. The White Sox rewarded him with a three-year contract at $250,000 a year, and manager Chuck Tanner loosened the reins on Allen, allowing him to show up later than other players. The Sox even found a spot on their roster for Allen's older brother Hank. But in 1973, Dick suffered a broken leg, limiting his play to 72 games, and he was an unhappy player by his own admission in 1974. The culmination was his September announcement that he was retiring. "Allen's dissatisfaction was mirrored in his play," wrote Richard Lindberg. Continued Lindberg,

> Frequently he would forget how many men were out (on one occasion he flipped the ball to the umpire and returned to the dugout while a runner advanced from second to third). He skipped batting practice—with Chuck Tanner's blessing. He had himself taken out of

the lineup in the late innings so that he could avoid the postgame interviews.[16]

Chicago Tribune radio-TV critic Gary Deeb wrote, "Under Tanner, Allen was baseball's number-one poodle, coming and going as he pleased and playing when he felt like it."[17]

Caray did not let this sort of behavior go unnoticed. "Harry was tough on Dick Allen," Jim Kaat related. "He'd say, 'Dick Allen's in the on-deck circle. Nice to see he made it on time today.'" On one occasion in 1974, Allen missed the start of a game, and the White Sox said he was sick. Caray, however, discovered Allen wasn't sick at all; he simply hadn't shown up on time. He told his viewers the excuse was phony and blistered Allen on the air.

Caray completely unloaded on Allen in January 1975, about a month after the White Sox traded the slugger to the Atlanta Braves. He even referred to Allen—who had told the Chicago media when he joined the White Sox that he preferred to be called Dick—as Richie. Said Caray,

> Allen has a lot of charm, you know. But his is a waste of talent. He just doesn't have any feeling for baseball. He thinks he owes nothing to the game. Just because God gave him a great talent, he feels he owes nothing to baseball.
>
> Hell, I came up with another great talent in Stan Musial. He'd spend hours after a game signing autographs. A little black kid comes up to Allen and Allen pushes him away—that's not what I call being a superstar.
>
> Every time I try to compare Richie Allen to Stan Musial, I want to vomit.[18]

* * *

During Allen's three seasons with the White Sox, Caray frequently voiced his disagreement with manager Chuck Tanner's loosening of team rules for him, feeling it created a clubhouse rift and set a bad example for the team's younger players. The Caray–Tanner feud became a major news story in Chicago; Tanner complained that Caray was telling him how to run the team, and Caray responded, "He [Tanner] is not going to force my resignation like he did Stu Holcomb's."[19] In June

1974, at the request of the White Sox, the two met in front of members of the Chicago media for 40 minutes and attempted to make peace; Caray told Tanner, "I'm your greatest fan, you couldn't find a better press agent than me."[20] But the friction continued. When Allen announced his retirement in September 1974, Tanner suggested that being abused by "some sportswriters and an announcer" might have been a factor. Two months later, Caray told David Condon, "He [Tanner] did a horrible job last year."[21] In January 1975, Tanner said of Caray, "He's a front-running, second-guessing liar. He's a liar 90 percent of the time."[22]

The two ultimately became friends, but not until after Tanner had left the White Sox. "Harry Caray was a fan. I was the manager," Tanner said in 1998. "I was young and energetic. He was enthusiastic. . . . He wasn't really ripping me. He was ripping the game and the team. . . . We never really had a feud." Tanner claimed Caray became a big fan of his managerial work with the Pittsburgh Pirates, who he led to a World Series championship in 1979.[23]

Along with battling with Tanner, Caray also had critical words in 1974 for White Sox general manager Roland Hemond, who had been named *Sporting News* Major League Executive of the Year in 1972. "The only reason [Stu Holcomb] hired Hemond was because Tanner said Hemond was a helluva good baseball man," Caray told David Condon after the 1974 season. "Hemond told [White Sox team president] John Allyn it'd be a great vote of confidence to extend Tanner's contract. Who knows what will be happening in 1978? The Russians might be playing here . . . but Hemond isn't just taking care of Tanner, he's taking care of Hemond, too."[24]

✿ ✿ ✿

In his blunt criticism of Chuck Tanner, Dick Allen, Roland Hemond, and others during the 1973–1974 seasons, Caray had an ally in the broadcast booth: his Channel 44 television partner, Bob Waller. As was the case with Caray, Waller caught some heat for expressing his opinions. "If the front office doesn't like what I report, that's tough," Waller told Gary Deeb in September 1974. "I have to present things in an entertaining way, but I still have to present the truth. I can't gloss over. I'm not a cheerleader or a Pollyanna. People deserve better than that.

They're not stupid." Deeb, a fan of both Caray and Waller, wrote, "Both men never had been shy about lowering the boom on Manager Chuck Tanner, General Manager Roland Hemond, and some of the key Sox players. And when the team stunk up the league this season, neither Harry nor Bob pulled the head-in-the-sand, pie-in-the-sky routine." When Tanner praised the White Sox for their effort and hustle throughout the year on the next to last day of the 1974 season, Waller issued a 10-minute rebuttal on the air the next day, stating, "If anybody still believes that this team hustled and put out 100 percent all the time, then the Sox problems just can't be solved."[25]

Caray was popular enough to get away with that sort of bluntness. Ultimately, Bob Waller was not. On November 5, the White Sox announced that Caray would have a new TV partner in 1975. Caray was not pleased, saying, "I'm a little bitter about it. I think a deal was made . . . for a sacrificial lamb. When they couldn't get me fired, I think they told Tanner they'd fire the partner I liked so well."[26] (Years later, Caray told Curt Smith, "One year I had an assistant named Bob Waller—no great shakes there.")[27] Waller's next stop was Caray's previous broadcast home: Charlie Finley's Oakland Athletics. In Oakland, where Waller spent three seasons, he not only worked alongside Caray's old rival, Monte Moore, but also, in 1976, was reunited with Chuck Tanner, who managed the A's that year.

While he couldn't save Waller's job, Caray was able to prevail in a dispute with the management of the Sox' flagship radio station, WMAQ. In August 1974, Caray heard that the station would not be renewing its contract to broadcast White Sox games in 1975. A short time later, Harry aired an interview with a part-time WMAQ producer, Jim Malia, in which both Caray and Malia criticized the station's decision. The station responded by firing Malia and putting Caray's radio broadcasts on a seven-second delay so that it could edit his comments if the station found it necessary. Caray, in turn, announced he would stay off radio completely rather than work for a "lame-duck" station. He also offered to pick up Malia's lost wages. After two weeks off the air, Caray resumed his radio stint at the request of the White Sox. As for WMAQ, the station replaced the general manager who had talked about dropping Sox broadcasts and announced it was renewing its deal with the team for 1975. WMAQ would continue to be the Sox flagship station through the 1979 season.

"Harry Caray, the controversial, freewheeling spirit who this season locked horns with one manager, one radio station, and a chunk of the White Sox front office, will be back for another year of White Sox play-by-play on Channel 44 and WMAQ radio," wrote Gary Deeb in October 1974. "The 57-year-old [actually 60], $100,000-a-year broadcaster reached agreement Tuesday afternoon with Sox vice president Leo Breen on the West Coast."[28]

In 1974, Caray had taken on everyone from White Sox team management to his own radio station—and come out stronger than ever. But that was just a warm-up for 1975, which proved to be one of the most tumultuous years of Harry's long career.

13

A TUMULTUOUS YEAR

Once upon a time, in a land not too far away, there lived a man named Melton the Giant. He was a strong and handsome giant who was so very good at playing a game called baseball that he was paid more than $100,000 a year for doing so.

But Melton the Giant had a tragic flaw. Every time anyone said anything mean to him, he would just sit down and cry. He would weep giant puddles of tears until it became a problem in the place where he worked.

"Why are you weeping such copious tears?" a scrivener asked Melton the Giant on one such occasion.

Melton the Giant dried his eyes.

"It's all because of Harry the Mouth," Melton the Giant said. "He's so mean to me. Every time I make a mistake he talks about it on radio and television. And when I come up to bat the people who come to see me play boo me."—Tom Fitzpatrick, *Chicago Sun-Times*, July 1975[1]

Although Dick Allen was no longer on the roster, the White Sox were expected to field a solid team in 1975. In the *Sporting News* annual baseball preview issue, editor and publisher C. C. Johnson Spink picked the Sox to finish third in the six-team American League West, writing, "The White Sox were a .500 club with Dick Allen last year. They should do better without him if closer-knit team spirit means anything."[2] White Sox fans seemed skeptical, however; the crowd of 20,202 that gathered for the team's first home game against the Texas Rangers on April 15 was the smallest for a Sox home opener since 1970. Even worse, the opener was marred for the second-straight year by an unruly crowd. The *Chicago Tribune* reported that "fights in the stands were rampant" and that Chicago police made 17 arrests during the game.[3]

Each of the Sox' next six home games after the home opener was played in front of fewer than 5,000 fans, including a meager crowd of 1,295 on April 17, the lowest since May 1971. The club's play on the field did nothing to encourage the fans to come to Comiskey Park; the Sox went 7–13 in April and never had a winning record at any point in the season. They finished the year fifth in the division with a 75–86 record. Home attendance was only 750,802, a drop of almost 400,000 from 1974 and second worst in the American League.

While the Sox were struggling on the field, team president John Allyn was struggling to pay his bills. On April 1, the Sox felt it necessary to trade Ed Herrmann, the team's number-one catcher, to the Yankees for four minor leaguers rather than pay Herrmann's $32,000 salary. In August, *Sporting News* reported that the Sox were six to eight weeks behind on paying their bills, including money owed to other American League teams for their share of Sox gate receipts. By the fall of 1975, Allyn's Artnell Corporation had less than $10,000 in the bank. Allyn personally owed the Internal Revenue Service more than $400,000.

Not surprisingly, there were reports in the Chicago and national media throughout the season that Allyn was attempting to sell the White Sox. The solution favored by the other American League owners involved Allyn selling the Sox to a syndicate that would relocate the team to Seattle; Charlie Finley's Oakland Athletics would then move to Chicago and take over both Comiskey Park and the White Sox name. For the other American League owners, this would solve several problems. First, they would still have a team in Chicago, a city they did not want to abandon. Second, a move to Seattle would settle a $32.5 million lawsuit the city had filed against the league for allowing the Seattle Pilots, a 1969 expansion team, to move to Milwaukee after only one year in Seattle. Finally, it would satisfy Finley's desire to move the A's out of Oakland, where the club had never had more than middling attendance, even with championship teams, and into Chicago, where Finley lived and maintained his business headquarters.

There was only one problem with this scenario: John Allyn didn't like it. He preferred trying to find local ownership that would buy the

White Sox and keep them in Chicago; however, the season passed with no serious local bidders stepping up.

* * *

For Harry Caray, the 1975 season contained one event that was undeniably positive. On May 19, Caray married the former Dolores (Dutchie) Goldmann, a 46-year-old mother of five who lived in Ballwin, Missouri. The couple married in a civil ceremony in Chicago's Ambassador East Hotel, where Caray maintained his residence during the baseball season. "No, no, we don't have time for a honeymoon," Mrs. Caray told reporters. "Besides that, I'm going home [to Missouri] tomorrow."[4]

The marriage—the third for Harry and the second for Dutchie—proved to be a happy one. Mrs. Caray, a St. Louis native, had first met Harry in 1970. "A friend of mine and I went to lunch in this little place in LaDue, a suburb of St. Louis," Dutchie later recalled. "Harry was there, and according to the bartender, he said, 'Wow, who in the heck is that over there?'" For several years Dutchie resisted the idea of marriage, "but Harry was persistent. I will say that for him." The couple remained married for the last 23 years of Harry's life. "And as Harry would say," she recalled, "'We never had an argument.'"[5]

* * *

While Caray was embarking on a happy marriage with Dutchie, his relationship with his broadcasting partners was anything but blissful. Caray's primary radio partner in 1974–1975 was Bill Mercer, a broadcasting veteran who had previously worked with the Texas Rangers. (Mercer also worked some games on TV in 1975.) In a 2010 interview, Mercer told Mark Liptak that he and Caray had gotten off to a good start in spring training in 1974, but that things started going wrong once the regular season started. "I don't know exactly how, but it wasn't working," said Mercer. "I don't like to be a homer, but I also don't like to criticize everything that goes wrong in a game. Harry would just beat it to death." He related a particular incident involving Sox pitcher Stan Bahnsen.

Early in 1974, Stan Bahnsen was having trouble in the first inning of games. I actually asked him about it, and he told me that it didn't seem to matter how long he warmed up; it just didn't click right at the start. Some pitchers just have trouble that way. Sure enough, I'm on the radio and Stan gets in trouble in the first and gives up two runs . . . he settled down and it's still 2–0 in the fourth inning when Harry comes in to do the middle innings on the radio. One of the first things he says on the air is, "That Bahnsen doesn't know how to pitch." So I said that I had talked to Bahnsen, and he said it wasn't a question of warming up enough, it just wasn't working. I said that some pitchers are like that. So Harry shoots back *on air*, "You never say anything bad, do you?" After that it didn't matter what I said, he'd put it down on air.[6]

In 1975, on Sox TV broadcasts, Caray was paired with J. C. Martin, a former White Sox player with no previous broadcasting experience. Martin had been selected by White Sox management to replace Bob Waller. The hiring of a neophyte broadcaster did not please Caray, who told Mercer, "You've got hundreds of guys trying to get into the business and instead of starting out down in the low minors like you and me, they're trying to learn here." Caray also perceived Martin to be a management shill. According to broadcasting historian Stuart Shea, "Martin was handpicked by the front office to say nice things about the team, and Caray treated him with barely disguised contempt in their year together."[7] Mercer, who had befriended Martin and was working to mentor him, called it a "miserable year. . . . J. C. would tell me, 'Harry won't listen to me during the game. He just ignores me.' Harry came out and told me, 'I'm not talking to that son of a bitch. He's got nothing to say.'"[8]

Martin related his experience with Caray in a 2002 interview with Mark Liptak.

> I didn't really fit in with Harry. He didn't want to work with me. We didn't hit it off at all. I wasn't used to working with a guy that had that kind of authority, and Harry used that against me. I was only there for one year. Now Bill Mercer was a great guy, he helped me out a lot. If I had Bill when I started out, I think I'd have been a lot better and things would have worked out. Harry just left me out to dry. I'll give you an example. We were in Milwaukee doing a game, and the Brewers had a pregame activity, which saw the Milwaukee

wives playing a game before the regularly scheduled one. That game caused the regular game to start late. Harry opened the telecast and then just left the booth. He left me there by myself for it must have been 15 to 20 minutes.[9]

Chicago Tribune TV-radio critic Gary Deeb, a strong Caray support-er, was merciless in his criticism of both Mercer and Martin. Along with calling Mercer's game descriptions "about as tasty as intravenous feed-ing," Deeb wrote that in 1975, Mercer had become a "shameless elec-tronic flack, pumping up the egos of everybody from Atilla the Hun to Benito Mussolini." In the same column, Deeb mocked the Southern accent of Martin, a native of Virginia, writing, "Last year he was shag-ging flies in the Cub bullpen. This year he's a real live baseball an-nouncer, giving Hee Haw and Gomer Pyle a bad name."[10]

Discussing his White Sox broadcast partners with Curt Smith, Caray said, "Another year they put a former catcher, J. C. Martin, on the air with me, along with some guy named Bill Mercer. Their job was to protect Tanner. I would rap him, and they'd say something good about him. Tanner, Mercer, and Martin had a real cozy little group. Anything to shut me up."[11] Both Mercer and Martin would be replaced in the White Sox broadcast booth after the 1975 season. "The truth is that very few people could work with Harry Caray in Chicago because he rarely let them," wrote Stuart Shea. "If Harry perceived a new partner as a shill or interloper—sometimes both—he refused to collaborate."[12]

✿ ✿ ✿

Along with not enjoying the work of his fellow White Sox broadcasters in 1975, Caray was not enamored of the team's play on the field. His most vehement criticism was directed toward two veteran players: third baseman Bill Melton and outfielder Ken Henderson. Both Henderson and Melton had enjoyed success during their earlier years with the White Sox, but both had experienced declines in production that were at least in part due to injuries. Henderson, who played for the White Sox from 1973 to 1975, had been fully healthy only in 1974, a year in which he played in all 162 games and ranked among the American League leaders in a number of categories. In 1973, he had played in only 72 games due to torn knee ligaments. In 1975, Henderson's pro-duction was hampered by a broken finger suffered early in the year; he admitted after the season that he should have sat out some games but kept playing at the request of manager Chuck Tanner. All Caray could see, however, was that Henderson wasn't playing as well as he had in 1974.

In 1970, Bill Melton had set a White Sox team record (later broken) with 33 home runs; in 1971, Caray's first season broadcasting White Sox games, he hit 33 homers again, becoming the first player in franchise history to lead the American League in home runs. But in November 1971, Melton fell off a ladder and suffered a ruptured disk in his back. He played six more years after suffering the injury but never again hit more than 21 home runs in a season. "I learned from the doctors that when you're in pain you protect your muscles by changing your swing, and that's what I did," Melton said in 2012. "I was never the same hitter."[13]

The effects of Melton's back problems on his home run production probably weren't apparent to Caray, especially since Melton was still basically a full-time player from 1973 to 1975 (he played in only 57 games in 1972). But Caray went beyond criticizing Melton's production; he accused the third baseman of loafing. In a game between the White Sox and the Milwaukee Brewers in July 1975, Melton advanced only from first to second base on a single to the outfield by Bucky Dent; Dent, who had rounded first in apparent expectation that Melton would advance to third, was tagged out to end the inning. On the air, Caray was harshly critical of Melton for what he perceived was lack of hustle. Melton, who heard about what Caray had said, confronted Harry in the team hotel the next day. According to some reports, the two almost came to blows.

The next two weeks featured a war of words between Melton and Caray. "Some of the guys are so worried about what Caray is going to say on the air," Melton complained to a reporter, "we can't relax and play our game." A few days later, Caray fired back, telling Gary Deeb, "Well, when a guy makes $100,000 a year and is supposed to be the team's leading home run and RBI man, and he's having a lousy year, it's pretty tough not to be critical . . . especially when he loafs on the job." Later the same day, Caray backed off a bit, telling a reporter, "I never said Bill Melton wasn't trying. I just said he was playing horsebleep."[14]

Melton, who received words of support from Sox manager Chuck Tanner and general manager Roland Hemond, fired back at Caray to *Chicago Tribune* writer Bob Verdi.

> "He harped on it and harped on it, and all I was doing was playing heads-up baseball," said Melton. "I'm tired of going every place and hearing that Caray is jumping all over me on every broadcast. Then he comes over to me three nights ago real sarcastic and said, 'What's wrong, is little sweetheart Billy upset over something?' I could have popped him one.
>
> "The people of Chicago are down on me now, but I just want them to know that I'm trying. I'm busting my butt. I'm not trying to strike out, I'm not trying to pop up, I'm not trying to be traded. But if I was, the reason I'd be happiest to leave is because of that man upstairs."

In the same article, Caray told Verdi, "There are only two guys [on the White Sox] who are having a horsebleep year, Melton and Ken Henderson. And they're the ones who are supposed to be batting in big runs, and they're the ones who are making the big money."[15]

In December of 1975, the White Sox dealt Henderson to the Atlanta Braves. A few weeks later, they traded Melton to the California Angels. "I had to get out of Chicago," Melton said after the trade. "People turned against me because of that person upstairs. If I had to go back, I'd probably have quit baseball. It was either him or me." Melton also suggested that Gary Deeb, the TV critic whose July interview with Caray also featured some harsh criticism of Melton by Deeb, "should be watching *Sesame Street* and writing his opinion on that."[16]

Caray and Melton weren't done feuding. When Melton and the Angels made their first visit to Chicago in 1976, Caray told reporters he was going to invite Melton to be a guest on his pregame show: "I'm going to the dugout and tell him this is the first time I've ever invited a .205 hitter to appear on my pregame show." Later he added, "Melton has the heart of a canary."[17] Melton would have the last laugh that night, recording three hits to lead the Angels to victory. He insisted his feud with Caray gave him no extra incentive, but he also said, "We're not friends."

Melton would ultimately mellow toward Caray. He reflected on Harry in 1998, shortly after the broadcaster's death.

I was back here [in Chicago] with a friend of mine from California—
I want to say 1986. And we were in a place on Oak Street. And I ran
into Harry at the piano bar. And we both sang "Take Me Out to the
Ball Game."

The hard thing about disliking Harry was he could say something
to you, and it'd be like a knife, a digging thing, but he would laugh.
And you would laugh too, 'cause he was right. That's what he had.

He'd come out on the field before a game and say the damndest
things about you, and you'd end up laughing with him.[18]

In July 1975, John Allyn publicly dismissed the friction between
Caray and Sox manager Chuck Tanner. "There's no good broadcaster
who's ever going to get along with a good manager," Allyn said, "because their jobs are completely different. But I can't see replacing Harry. If he's not the best baseball announcer in the country, he's close to
it."[19]

If that's how he felt about Caray at the time, Allyn soon changed his
mind. "Harry Caray became bigger than the organization," Allyn's son,
John Jr., told Richard Lindberg. He continued,

My dad thought Harry was doing his job to promote Harry. And that
seemed more important to him than objectively announcing ballgames. He showed the Sox in an ambivalent light. He picked on his
favorite targets, and his goals were not in synch with the organization, and at that point something had to be done.[20]

On September 30—two days after the White Sox finished the 1975
season with a 6–4 victory against the Minnesota Twins—Bob Verdi of
the *Tribune* filed a story commenting on the state of the team. After
writing that the club's first offseason move should be to trade Bill Melton, he discussed the "aura of negativism" surrounding the White Sox,
with the players blaming Caray and the media as the cause. On the
team's final road trip of the year, Verdi wrote that Sox pitcher "Wilbur
Wood berated Caray on a bus leaving Chicago and [manager Chuck]
Tanner upbraided him on the plane returning." He also wrote that Ken
Henderson "said Sunday that if the bad vibes pervading the White Sox
don't improve, he would welcome a change of address." Nonetheless,
Verdi felt that to "dismiss Caray would be a monumental public relations gaffe. For every player who shuns him, there are thousands of
listeners who crave him. For every player who claims he killed the club,

there are thousands of listeners who feel that he didn't arrange the team's death, only described it."[21]

John Allyn had already made up his mind. On October 1, the day after Verdi's piece appeared in the *Tribune*, Allyn told Johnny Morris of WBBM-TV, "If I own the club next year, Harry won't be with us." This was a big qualifier, as it was public knowledge that Allyn was attempting to sell the team.

After hearing the news, Caray fired back to John Hillyer of the *Chicago Daily News*.

> I don't want to leave Chicago unless I have to. But Allyn's going to have to sell the club, from what I've heard.
>
> Nobody on the club has said anything to me about not being back next year. Then Allyn goes on TV and said what he said. It's kind of a horsebleep way to handle things.
>
> Hell, the ballplayers like me. Only three of them popped off about me—Woody (Wilbur Wood) and the two popoffs, Melton and Henderson. You never hear a Bucky Dent, a Brian Downing, a Rich Gossage doing it.
>
> I felt that when Melton held that press conference after I criticized his baserunning, it was orchestrated by Tanner. He probably figured he'd been trying for five years to get rid of me, maybe he could be doing it that way.
>
> How about his record for three years? Two fifth-place finishes and a fourth-place finish, for chrissake.
>
> But Allyn's got to be a stupid man. He takes a manager's contract in 1974 and extends it through 1978. Why would he do that? I heard the Seattle people took one look at Tanner's contract and backed off.[22]

Caray told reporters that White Sox TV ad sales had cleared $300,000 in 1975, helping the team reduce its losses. He received support from Charlie Warner, general manager of WMAQ, the team's flagship radio station. "My position is that we're interested in exactly the same deal we had this past season with the Sox," said Warner. "With the kind of mediocre team they have, Harry Caray is a major part of the thing, and the announcers have to be approved by us. There's almost no way we would approve a contract without Harry."[23]

For now, however, Caray was a man without a job, and his "stupid man" comment about the White Sox owner would never be forgotten.

What Caray needed now was a new owner who would buy the team from Allyn—and one who wanted Harry back in the broadcast booth.

Such a man was right around the corner, but he was a most unlikely candidate: Bill Veeck, who had once accused Harry Caray of trying to drive him out of St. Louis.

14

HARRY, JIMMY, AND BILL

It was Thomas Wolfe, the novelist, who long ago decided, "You Can't Go Home Again." Maybe so. But Bill Veeck, a 61-year-old baseball vagabond, is returning to Chicago as a part-owner and chief operating officer of the Chicago White Sox.

If it sounds like you've heard all this before, it's because you have. Veeck formed a similar group more than 15 years ago and operated the White Sox for almost three full seasons, including the Camelot year of 1959—the year of the last Chicago pennant.—Jerome Holtzman, *Sporting News*, October 1975[1]

Bill Veeck liked to say, "I am the only human being ever raised in a ballpark." That wasn't literally true, but it was close enough. Born in Chicago in 1914, Veeck was the son of William L. Veeck Sr., a sportswriter who used the pen name Bill Bailey. Veeck Sr. often criticized the Chicago Cubs in his columns, and after a few years Cubs owner William Wrigley dared Veeck to take control of the team and prove he could do better. Veeck Sr. accepted the challenge and showed himself to be good at the job; he put together teams that won National League pennants in 1929, 1932, and 1935. He died in 1933. By then, young Bill was working for the team, and while he never held a management position, he helped plant the ivy on the Wrigley Field walls and assisted in assembling the park's iconic scoreboard.

In 1941, Veeck began his own career as a baseball executive by assembling a group of investors to purchase the minor league Milwaukee Brewers. In Milwaukee, Veeck first showed his skills as a promoter;

he gave away prizes, brought in animal acts, and scheduled morning games for the benefit of people working the overnight shift at war plants. As Warren Corbett wrote, "He believed a trip to the ballpark should be fun."[2] He also built a successful team that won three consecutive American Association pennants.

Veeck left the Brewers in 1943 to serve in the U.S. Marines during World War II, and suffered a leg wound that later necessitated the amputation of his right leg. When the war ended, he sold the Brewers and put together a group to purchase the Cleveland Indians, a club that hadn't won an American League pennant since 1920. In Cleveland, Veeck staged the same sorts of promotions that had worked in Milwaukee; signed the American League's first black player, Larry Doby, as well as Negro League legend Satchel Paige; and developed a team that won the World Series in 1948. The club was successful not only on the field, but also at the box office, drawing a major-league record 2.6 million fans in 1948. That total would not be surpassed until 1962, when the Los Angeles Dodgers would draw 2.7 million.

Needing cash, Veeck sold the Indians after the 1949 season, but in 1951, he was back in baseball, heading a group that purchased the St. Louis Browns. In St. Louis, he briefly clashed with Harry Caray, accusing Harry of trying to convince Browns minority stockholders not to sell their shares to Veeck's investment group—a charge Caray denied (see chapter 4). After two years of battling the Cardinals, Veeck gave up trying to compete when Gussie Busch purchased the Redbirds in 1953. He worked out a deal to move the Browns to Baltimore, but in a clear effort to force Veeck out of baseball, the American League refused to approve the move; he had alienated his fellow owners not only with such stunts as using 3-foot-7 dwarf Eddie Gaedel in a game as a gag pinch-hitter, but also by proposing that visiting clubs share in the home team's television revenue (they considered the idea to be "socialistic"). Facing bankruptcy in St. Louis, Veeck was forced to sell the Browns to a Baltimore syndicate that had the approval of the league.

He was back in 1959, this time heading a group that purchased a majority share of the White Sox. In his first season, the Sox won their first American League pennant in 40 years. Veeck's White Sox tenure was once again filled with stunts and promotions, along with such soon-copied innovations as installing baseball's first exploding scoreboard and putting players' names on the backs of their uniforms. As in Cleveland, Veeck's team was a hit at the box office; after setting a franchise home attendance record in the pennant-winning season of 1959, the Sox drew 1,644,460 fans to their home games in 1960, a club record that wasn't broken until 1977, during Veeck's second Sox ownership tenure. But Veeck's health was not good—along with having to deal with problems involving his amputated leg, he was a heavy smoker and drinker. In 1961, he sold the White Sox to members of his investment group, headed by John Allyn's brother Arthur (Art Allyn, in turn, would cede control of the team to John in 1969).

Now, in late 1975, Veeck was angling to reacquire the White Sox from John Allyn. He put together a group of 40 investors who pledged to keep the team in Chicago, and Allyn, who would retain a 20 percent share of the club, was amenable to the terms; however, Veeck still had a number of enemies among the other American League owners. Most recently, he had upset MLB executives by testifying in support of Curt Flood's unsuccessful challenge to baseball's reserve clause. The league voted him down, saying the purchase plan included too much borrowed money. When Veeck restructured the deal, they were ready to vote him down again until Detroit Tigers owner John Fetzer—no friend of Veeck's—pointed out that Veeck had met the conditions outlined by the league to win approval of the sale. The owners voted again, and Veeck's purchase was approved, 10–2. He was back in baseball, and back in control of the White Sox.

In an interview, longtime Chicago-area sportswriter Rick Telander spoke about his experiences with Bill Veeck.

> Bill was such an engaging personality. He was a character beyond fiction. With that wooden leg—he had an ashtray in that thing, and he used to dump his cigarette ashes into it—he seemed like someone out of a Jack London story. He was a brilliant man, and really well-read. He could talk about absolutely anything. For instance, my wife is a psychologist, and Bill could talk about psychology. To think, this was a guy who owned a major-league team.
>
> I remember when I asked him for his phone number. He said, sure, but it's in the phone book (this was back when everybody had phone books). I couldn't believe it; I said, "Don't people call you all the time?" He said, "Yeah, they call . . . they say, 'Bill—is this Bill Veeck?' And I say 'Yes, what can I do for you?' They're astounded. We'll talk for a little bit, and finally they'll hang up." I said, "Don't

you get calls in the middle of the night?" He said, "Yeah, sometimes." After that I kept my own number in the phone book. I figured if Bill can do it, so can I. He was an astounding person, a man of the people . . . he was like Harry Caray in a lot of ways.[3]

Interestingly, Harry Caray also kept his number listed in the phone book during his Chicago years. But as Veeck took control of the White Sox in late 1975, Caray did not have a contract to broadcast games. Would these two men of the people, Veeck and Caray, get together?

It wasn't guaranteed, as Veeck, who was busy making trades and hiring a new manager (Paul Richards) to replace Chuck Tanner, had yet to make Harry an offer. In the meantime, Caray was weighing other opportunities. In St. Louis, Jack Buck had left the Cardinals at the end of the 1975 season to host a NBC-TV studio show called *Grandstand*. The gig did not work out, and Buck would return to the Redbirds in time for the 1976 season, but in the interim Gussie Busch offered Caray an opportunity to come back to the Cardinals. Caray turned it down. In December, Caray went to New York and auditioned for a job doing play-by-play for ABC's *Monday Night Baseball* network telecasts; auditioning with Caray for the role of analyst was Ken (Hawk) Harrelson, the future White Sox television voice who was then early in his broadcasting career; however, Caray's preference was to return to the White Sox. "Not many guys would say this, but I'd take the White Sox job over the network any day," he told David Condon. "I don't know if I'll get the Sox job or not, but either way, Bill Veeck is the best thing that could have happened to Chicago baseball."[4]

In early January, Caray turned down another opportunity, this one from Charlie Finley, to return to the Oakland Athletics. By that point, Caray and Veeck were well along in their discussions, and Harry felt confident he would be returning to the White Sox. "If I wasn't confident, I might have panicked," Caray said a few days later. "I could have taken Charlie Finley's offer. But I told myself that Veeck had reasons for delaying any announcement and that I'd just have to sit things out. I was determined to stay in Chicago no matter what."[5]

On January 13, Veeck made it official: Caray was returning to WSNS-TV and WMAQ radio at a salary of more than $100,000. Veeck made it clear that the stations—not the White Sox—would be paying Harry's salary. "It's one way to eliminate a source of possible aggravation," Veeck said. "Even though the ball club has the right of refusal on an announcer, if he's paid by the station, I won't have players coming up to me complaining."

He continued,

> We don't want a house dog as our announcer. I think Caray is too great an asset to leave the city, particularly since the White Sox needed assets. He's not always kindly, but he's never dull. If we're bad, I expect him to say we are. He has a style, and I have no qualms about it. Some days I won't like what he says, but some days I won't like what I see on the field, either. Sometimes the truth hurts.

Veeck called Caray the "best play-by-play man in the country," adding that Harry "beat our brains out in St. Louis when I had the Browns, and he was with the Cardinals. I have the tapes to prove it."[6]

Still to be determined was the identity of Caray's broadcast partner (or partners, as it was certain that both J. C. Martin and Bill Mercer would not be back). Veeck said publicly that he was interested in hiring an African American broadcaster to work with Caray, and former St. Louis Cardinals great Bob Gibson was said to be under consideration. Caray himself spoke in favor of the return of Bob Waller, who had been fired by the Sox after the 1974 season following his vehement criticism of the team and then-Sox manager Chuck Tanner. In late January, Gary Deeb reported that a different candidate was being considered: WMAQ and WSNS were talking to Skip Caray, Harry's 36-year-old son, about joining the broadcast crew. At the time, the younger Caray was working in Atlanta as the radio voice of the National Basketball Association Atlanta Hawks and was under consideration for a broadcast position with the Atlanta Braves. It wasn't to be, as Skip turned down an offer to come to Chicago; instead, he took the play-by-play job with the Braves, for whom he became a franchise icon. (Interestingly enough, the man Skip replaced in Atlanta was Harry's lifelong rival, Milo Hamilton.) "Dad and I have worked together before," Skip said in announcing that he was turning down the Chicago offer. "It would have been interesting to find out how that combination would have worked in Chicago. Unfortunately, we'll never know."[7]

After discussions with Lanny Frattare (who wound up going to the Pittsburgh Pirates) and Pete Van Wieren (who would join Skip Caray with the Braves), the White Sox gave their vacant broadcast job to Lorn Brown, a South Side native who, at the time, was working Chicago Bulls

NBA games. Brown and Caray did not work side-by-side in 1976—each did solo stints on either radio or TV—but Brown, who worked for the Sox through 1979, and then returned in the 1980s, said he developed a good relationship with Harry. While Brown told an interviewer that Bill Veeck gave him the freedom to report the game as he saw it, he related that Caray told him that if something controversial came up during a game, to leave it alone and let Harry handle it. That method seemed to produce harmony between the broadcasters. Caray was never hesitant to rip a fellow broadcaster who he considered to be either a management shill or someone who tried to take the limelight off Harry, but if he ever voiced a negative opinion about Lorn Brown, I could find no record of it.

※ ※ ※

The club Brown and Caray would be describing in 1976 was complexly different from the Sox club that had finished the 1975 season in fifth place in the American League West. After taking control of the team in December 1975, Veeck and Sox general manager Roland Hemond put an "Open for Business" sign in the hotel lobby at the baseball winter meetings and started making trades. But Veeck's ability to strengthen the team was hampered by a landmark decision on December 23, from arbitrator Peter Seitz, abolishing baseball's reserve clause. The decision ushered in the era of free agency for veteran players whose contracts had expired. Veeck, who lacked the working capital to compete for high-salaried players, was immediately put in a precarious position. "The Seitz decision ushered in a gold-rush era for the players," wrote Richard Lindberg, "but at the same time it put the small-market teams and financially strapped ownerships like Bill Veeck's group in Chicago on less than equal footing with George Steinbrenner's Yankees and Gene Autry's California Angels."[8] Timing was everything; had Seitz issued his ruling two weeks earlier, Veeck likely would have chosen not to buy the White Sox. "As soon as he got back into the game," wrote Warren Corbett, "he was on his way out."[9]

Nonetheless, Veeck did his best to field a competitive and entertaining team in 1976. On Opening Day, Veeck, 67-year-old manager Paul Richards, and Sox executive Rudie Schaffer celebrated America's Bicentennial by dressing in Revolutionary War uniforms and marching to home plate with a fife, drum, and American flag; Bill's peg leg added a nice touch of authenticity. The stunts continued throughout the season, and although the Sox wound up finishing last in the division with 97 losses, home attendance improved by 20 percent.

One of Veeck's most popular innovations involved Harry Caray. White Sox organist Nancy Faust had always played "Take Me Out to the Ball Game" during the seventh-inning stretch at Comiskey Park. Caray would sing along from the broadcast booth; however, no one except the fans sitting near the booth could hear him. One day during the 1976 season, Veeck decided to add Harry's voice to the stadium sound system as Faust played the song. Suddenly, Caray's singing could be heard throughout the ballpark. When Caray protested to Veeck that he was no singer, Bill replied, "Yeah, that's the reason . . . if you could sing, nobody would sing with you. This way everyone will sing." A beloved tradition was born, one that would be associated with Caray for the rest of his life.

Veeck, who had always seen the fan-participation potential in playing "Take Me Out to the Ball Game" during the seventh-inning stretch, said he'd tried getting the fans involved with playing the song at his previous stops in Milwaukee, Cleveland, St. Louis, and his first ownership stint in Chicago, "but it never worked. Finally, I got the right guy. It does a lot for the game and gets the fans involved even if the Sox are losing."[10]

Despite the team's last-place finish, 1976 was a year in which Caray found harmony, even with White Sox players. In February, future Hall of Famer Rich "Goose" Gossage said that unlike the departed Bill Melton, he'd never had problems with Caray. "I've always liked Harry," Gossage said. "Most of the players think he's a good announcer."[11] Another young Sox pitcher, Bart Johnson, claimed Caray's biting criticism of his work was actually beneficial. One night after a game, Caray and Johnson were part of a group of White Sox personnel having drinks. Right in front of Johnson, Caray did an exaggerated imitation of Johnson throwing a pitch and then fixing his hair. "Bart, you just don't have enough guts," he told Johnson. "You pay more attention to your hair than to the hitters." Then he pounded his chest above his heart and told Johnson, "You just don't have it here."

St. Louis native Harry Caray was the lead broadcaster of his hometown Cardinals for 25 years (1945–69). Immensely popular with the team's fan base, Caray was credited with helping make the Cardinals a favorite team of fans across the U.S. and even in foreign countries. His dismissal in 1969 generated a wave of protest from the club's followers. *National Baseball Hall of Fame and Museum, Cooperstown, N.Y.*

After managing the Cardinals to the National League pennant in 1930 and the World Series championship in 1931, Gabby Street became a radio broadcaster for the Cardinals and Browns. He worked with Caray from 1945 until his death in 1951. Of Street, Caray wrote, "no broadcast partner I've ever had meant as much to me." *National Baseball Hall of Fame and Museum, Cooperstown, N.Y.*

A broadcast partner of Harry Caray with the Cardinals in 1954 and the Chicago Cubs from 1982–84, Milo Hamilton had a tempestuous relationship with Caray, whom he blamed for the loss of both jobs. Winner of the Baseball Hall of Fame's Ford C. Frick Award in 1992, Hamilton never reconciled with Caray. *National Baseball Hall of Fame and Museum, Cooperstown, N.Y.*

After working as Caray's Cardinals broadcast partner from 1954–69, Jack Buck served as the team's No. 1 broadcaster from 1970 until his death in 2002. He won the Hall of Fame's Ford C. Frick Award in 1987. Buck's *New York Times* obituary called him "Voice of the Cardinals"—a title that had once belonged to Caray. *National Baseball Hall of Fame and Museum, Cooperstown, N.Y.*

A St. Louis native and boyhood friend of Hall of Famer Yogi Berra (pictured here), Joe Garagiola became one of Caray's broadcast partners after retiring as a player in 1955. Garagiola saw his relationship with Caray cool as his own fame grew, and the two seldom spoke after Joe left the Cardinals following the 1962 season. Garagiola won the Hall of Fame's Ford C. Frick Award in 1991. *National Baseball Hall of Fame and Museum, Cooperstown, N.Y.*

A star third baseman for the Cardinals from 1955–65 and winner of the National League's Most Valuable Player Award in 1964, Ken Boyer had a contentious relationship with Caray, who was often critical of Boyer's performance in clutch situations. According to some observers, the friction began when Boyer refused an interview request from Caray. *National Baseball Hall of Fame and Museum, Cooperstown, N.Y.*

After leaving the Cardinals and spending the 1970 season broadcasting for the Oakland Athletics, Caray returned to the Midwest with the Chicago White Sox—a struggling team with a tiny broadcast network—in 1971. An immediate hit with Sox fans, Caray was given major credit for helping revive interest in Chicago's South Side franchise. *Courtesy of the author*

1971 American League home run champion **Bill Melton** became a frequent **Caray** target as he (and the White Sox) began to struggle. "People turned against me because of that man upstairs [Caray]," said Melton after being traded to the California Angels. "If I had to go back [to Chicago], I'd probably have quit baseball." *National Baseball Hall of Fame and Museum, Cooperstown, NY*

As president of the St. Louis Browns in the early 1950s, Bill Veeck often clashed with Caray, the Cardinals' lead broadcaster. When Veeck took control of the White Sox in 1976, the two began working together. One of Veeck's most enduring innovations was to feature Caray leading the stadium crowd in singing "Take Me Out to the Ball Game" during the seventh-inning stretch. *Courtesy of the author*

Caray's ability to connect with his teams' fan base was legendary wherever he worked. "If he saw a person and they recognized him, he would immediately engage with them," recalled broadcaster Pat Hughes. "That stays with people." *Courtesy of the author*

During Bill Veeck's White Sox years, Caray's most popular broadcast partner was colorful and unpredictable former major league outfielder Jimmy Piersall. "When Harry and Jimmy were on the air," said writer Bob Verdi, "I don't care what the score was or what the standings were; it was must-listen radio because you never knew what you were going to hear." *Courtesy of the author*

In 1982, Caray stunned the baseball world by leaving the White Sox to broadcast games for the crosstown Cubs. With Cubs broadcasts available to the entire country via the WGN-TV cable "superstation," Caray and the Cubs reached new heights of popularity. Caray remained with the Cubs until his death in 1998. *National Baseball Hall of Fame and Museum, Cooperstown, N.Y.*

During Caray's White Sox years, Steve Stone was one of the team's best pitchers. After retiring as a player, Stone became one of Caray's favorite broadcast partners, holding the job from 1983 until Caray's death. *Courtesy of the author.*

Johnson stayed relatively calm but fired back, "I may be a (bleep) pitcher, but you're a (bleep) announcer." But after defeating the Texas Rangers the next night, he admitted Caray's criticism had been helpful. "I
think maybe Harry's the best psychologist in the world," he told reporters. "He really woke me up and I'm grateful. In fact, I told him, 'Harry,
maybe we ought to room together.'" Johnson admitted he was thinking
of Caray's words during the game and was grateful for the incident.
"Harry and I are super," he said. "He's a fan and interested in the club,
and if he thinks that way, a lot of the fans must be thinking the same
way." He concluded, "Harry Caray is a definite asset to the White
Sox."[12]

   The Sox front office seconded Johnson's assessment. "Let's face it,"
one of the club's stockholders said after the season. "Caray has a magic
appeal. He personally brought in more season ticket revenue last season
than he was paid in salary."[13]

✽ ✽ ✽

When the 1976 season ended, wrote Corbett, "Veeck told general manager Roland Hemond, 'Don't bother drawing up a budget. We don't
have any money. We'll think of something.' But he still worked and
played for 20 hours a day, drinking two dozen beers and smoking up to
four packs of Salem Longs, stubbing out the butts in an ashtray built
into his prosthetic leg. Hemond said, 'I tell people I worked for Bill
Veeck five years, but it was really 10 because I never slept.'"[14]

   The plan Veeck and Hemond came up with was dubbed "rent-a-
player." It consisted of trading for players who were a year short of free
agency—talented players who Veeck was unlikely to sign but figured to
give the Sox a good effort. The scheme resulted in the acquisition of
power-hitting outfielders Richie Zisk and Oscar Gamble. The Sox also
signed two moderately priced free agents, pitcher Steve Stone and third
baseman Eric Soderholm, who proved to have value. It was strictly a
short-term strategy, but Veeck couldn't afford to think on a long-term
basis.

   There were two new additions to the Sox broadcast crew as well.
One of them, Mary Shane, had come to Caray's attention when she was
working for a Milwaukee radio station in 1976. Caray invited Shane to
do play-by-play for a few innings, and the Sox liked her work well

enough to sign her to work about 30 games on radio in 1977. Shane, one of the first women to call play-by-play for a major-league game, was regarded as a Veeck stunt by some observers and also encountered the sort of pushback often experienced by women trying to win a position in a male-dominated world. Her inexperience on the air showed at times, and Veeck elected not to bring her back in 1978. Many people thought Shane should have been given more of a chance to establish herself in baseball broadcasting—but within a few years, Mary had established herself in another male-dominated position in sports. As a sportswriter with the *Worcester (Massachusetts) Telegram*, she became one of the first female beat reporters covering a NBA team. Mary Shane was only 42 when she died of heart failure in 1987.

The other addition to the Sox broadcasting crew was a well-known baseball figure. Jimmy Piersall had spent 17 years in the major leagues and then served as a public relations specialist, part-time coach, and occasional broadcaster with the Oakland Athletics and Texas Rangers. In 1952, his rookie season, Piersall had suffered a nervous breakdown, which resulted in hospitalization and shock treatment; his recovery was chronicled in a best-selling autobiography, *Fear Strikes Out*, as well as two movies based on the book. His career as a player was filled with on-field incidents with players, fans, and umpires; his behavior was frequently described in such terms as "temperamental," "spirited," "high-strung," and "brutally honest." Those terms could also be applied to Piersall's broadcasting work.

In 1976, while working for the Texas Rangers, Piersall had served as a guest analyst for Caray during several White Sox broadcasts. His chemistry with Caray was evident from the start, and in 1977, Piersall was added to the broadcast crew of Caray, Lorn Brown, and (occasionally) Mary Shane. Usually, he was paired with Caray, and the tandem was an immediate hit. "Harry had been telling it like it was since he joined the Sox in 1971," wrote Mark Liptak, "and now that Piersall was on board, no one and nothing was off limits. Both men asked no quarter and gave none in return. Everything was tackled . . . players, fans, even owners. The fans loved it."[15] Chicago sportswriter Bob Verdi told me, "When Harry and Jimmy were on the air, I don't care what the score was or what the standings were, it was must-listen radio because you never knew what you were going to hear."[16]

Caray and Piersall had a lot to talk about in 1977. With Zisk and Gamble leading the way, the "rent-a-player" team Veeck and Hemond had put together slugged 192 home runs—at the time a club record—and led the American League West well into August before fading and finishing in third place. Dubbed the "South Side Hit Men," the team was a hit at the box office as well; for the year, the Sox drew 1,657,135 fans to their home games, breaking the team record set by Veeck's 1960 Sox team (the record would be broken by the 1983 division-winning club).

The Caray–Piersall pairing was a big success with Sox fans. In August, *Chicago Tribune* TV-radio critic Gary Deeb reported that Sox broadcasts on UHF channel 44 were averaging 500,000 viewers per broadcast, easily their highest total in the five years the station had broadcast the team's games. On radio, White Sox games on WMAQ were averaging about 100,000 listeners a game, almost twice the station's normal evening audience, and Deeb wrote that advertisers were lining up to buy commercial time.

In June, Piersall was the subject of a lengthy feature in the Sunday *Chicago Tribune Magazine*. Author Clifford Terry was candid about Piersall's history of mental-health problems, writing that during Piersall's career, other players gave him nicknames like "Gooney Bird" and "Nutsy." He wrote that Piersall was deeply active in mental-health work and that, "He recognizes that he is still a tightly strung, moody person, and takes regular doses of lithium carbonate, an antidepressant." Terry noted that Piersall "doesn't treat every player as a potential Hall of Famer" and quoted some of Piersall's irreverent broadcasting, which was, if anything, even more blunt than Caray's. ("If this guy Jim Mason hits you, you shouldn't be pitching. You know how he sticks around the majors so long? He's a good-looking guy.")[17]

As a lifelong White Sox fan who lived in the Chicago area, I can personally attest to the magic of the 1977 Southside Hit Men—and the brilliance of the Caray–Piersall tandem. Although I was working a job that required me to start at 6 a.m., I attended almost 40 White Sox games that year, easily a personal record. Fans brought banners; insisted that Sox players come out of the dugout for curtain calls after home runs (at the time, a much-criticized innovation); and sarcastically sang "Na, Na, Na, Na, Hey Hey . . . Goodbye!" when an opposing pitcher was removed from the game. Piersall and especially Caray were as popular as any of the players, and the whole park would erupt during the seventh-inning stretch when Harry led the crowd for "Take Me Out to the Ball Game."

I have a personal collection of about 300 color slides that I took during that memorable season, including many shots of Caray and Piersall. When I wasn't at the park, I could watch or listen to the broadcasts, and no one could capture the excitement like Harry Caray. The following is a transcript of Caray describing a Chet Lemon home run in front of a capacity crowd on July 31. Caray not only captured the excitement of the action with his voice, but also stayed silent for almost 30 seconds and let the crowd help tell the story.

> Let's see if Lemon will be taking or trying to hit one out of here. Two balls, no strikes, the pitch. . . . There it goes! Way back! It might be . . . it could be . . . into the upper deck! Holy cow! Listen to the crowd! (Silent for 28 seconds as crowd erupts) Holy cow, did he give that ball a ride . . . high into the upper deck, and all the banners are being unfurled!

On the South Side of Chicago, there had never been another year quite like it.

15

DEMOLITION

Howard Cosell branded Harry Caray a "grade-school cheerleader" after listening to a portion of Caray's televised description of the White Sox's Opening Day victory over Boston Friday.

"I was amazed when I heard Harry Caray leading the fans in singing 'Take Me Out to the Ball Game,'" Cosell said. "The FCC is investigating the [ABC] network for just this sort of thing."

Asked if it is not true that nearly all television sports announcers are cheerleaders to some extent, Cosell replied:

"That's true. We all are. But some are more housemen than others. I once had high hopes for Brent Musburger. I thought he would be the next Howard Cosell. But Brent has disappointed me. He has become a high-school cheerleader. He's not as bad as Harry Caray, though. Caray's broadcasts are on the grade-school level."—Cooper Rollow, *Chicago Tribune*, April 1978[1]

When the 1977 season ended, the White Sox, as expected, were unable to resign "rent-a-players" Richie Zisk and Oscar Gamble; Zisk signed a multiyear contract with the Texas Rangers, and Gamble agreed to a multiyear pact with the San Diego Padres. "But," wrote Gary Deeb, "the REAL power hitter in the Sox lineup is staying right here, and the crowds at Comiskey Park still can look forward to their seventh-inning chorus of 'Take Me Out to the Ball Game.'" Harry Caray, Deeb reported, had agreed to a new contract to broadcast White Sox games in 1978; he would be receiving a substantial raise to a reported $135,000 a year. "Let's face it—until last season, the Sox were a depressed product," Caray said. "They were in deep financial trouble. I went along without any raise primarily because of Bill Veeck. I was committed to help him turn the club into a success. Now I think I should start making more money." Deeb also wrote that Jimmy Piersall's contract had been renewed "only after Veeck had a long talk with the volatile ex-player. Some fans complained last year that Piersall sometimes used vulgarity on the air."[2]

In 1978, Caray was the subject of long feature articles in two national publications. In August, he was profiled in *People* by Dennis Breo. The article began as follows:

> It's game time in that solar oven called Comiskey Park, and the 10th starter on the Chicago White Sox, the one the fans come to see, tune their radios to, and turn on their TVs for, is suited up and ready to go. Not wearing spikes but baby-blue sneakers, scruffy shorts, no shirt, carrying neither glove nor bat but a frosty pop-top instead, belly not trim but jiggling comfortably, the man grins at the cheers that greet him.
>
> "Harrreee! Harrreee!"
>
> ❉ ❉ ❉
>
> Who is this clown? Ask almost anybody on the South Side of Chicago: This is Harry Caray. The fans know him on sight, or from the instant he opens what has been called the only mouth with a mind of its own. Loud, contentious, brash, seething with wild joy and vigorous despair, Harry Caray is the play-by-play broadcaster for the White Sox who personifies in his delivery—and in nearly every minute of his waking life—the essence of the species baseball fan.
>
> Make that superfan. Caray goes about his work as if he, single-handed, were keeping the Sox in Major League Baseball and the fans in the park. Maybe he is.

Breo quoted Caray on Caray, with a swipe at his old St. Louis broadcast partner, Joe Garagiola: "Vin Scully [Los Angeles Dodgers] and I are four rungs above the rest, and the worst are in the biggest markets—the New York Yankees broadcast team and NBC's Tony Kubek and Joe Garagiola. They'll put you to sleep." Caray had kind words for his current broadcast partner, saying that working with Jimmy Piersall "is like playing the outfield with Ted Williams. He's the best." As for Howard

Cosell, who earlier in the year had said that Harry broadcasted at the "grade-school level," Caray admitted he would like to have Cosell's national reputation. "But I've done on a regional basis what Cosell's done nationally—except I've told it like it is. Cosell has told it like he thinks [ABC Sports president] Roone Arledge wants it told."[3]

In September, Caray was the subject of another laudatory article, "The Big Wind in Chicago," by Ron Fimrite in *Sports Illustrated*. "Cabdrivers stall traffic to hail him. Barflies press against dusty windows seeking a glimpse of him," wrote Fimrite. The writer accompanied Caray to a couple of night spots, "and in each he was accorded the sort of welcome John Travolta [who had recently starred in the hit movie *Saturday Night Fever*] might receive should he appear in the girls' locker room of a small-town junior high school."[4]

But 1978 was a difficult year for the White Sox, who followed their 90-win season in 1977 with a 90-loss year in 1978. Not everything was smooth for Caray and Piersall, either. "Frankly, I hate to listen to [Caray] when we're losing because he can put the greatest degree of contempt in what he's saying," Bill Veeck told Fimrite. One player who took offense to Caray and Piersall was Sox outfielder Ralph Garr, who said, "Caray and Piersall like to sit around and run off at the mouth all the time and that makes it hard for a man to hit. If I swing hard, I'm swinging 'too hard.' If I swing easy, I'm swinging 'too easy.'"[5] When 1977 Sox hero Richie Zisk came to town with his new team, the Texas Rangers, Caray suggested that Sox fans were justified in booing Zisk when he came up to bat. Zisk's teammate, Jon Matlack, said Caray should have "his lights punched out."[6]

In August, Caray feuded with Milwaukee Brewers team president Bud Selig, who refused to let Caray's voice be heard over the Milwaukee County Stadium audio system when he sang "Take Me Out to the Ball Game" for the benefit of visiting Sox fans. Selig, the future commissioner of baseball, called Caray's on-air commentary "disgusting, disgraceful, and immoral," and said, "Harry Caray has been known through the years to create self-aggrandizing controversies to feed an ego that is already five miles wide. All Harry Caray cares about is Harry Caray." Caray responded by calling Selig a "jerk" and suggesting that Sox fans not travel to Milwaukee for games. "What did Bud Selig ever do—except have money?" he said.[7]

Caray even came in for criticism from Gary Deeb, who had long been a supporter. In an article that noted that WGN-TV, the Chicago Cubs flagship station, had discouraged their broadcasters from announcing the names of fans who had alerted the station that they were attending the game, Deeb criticized Caray for his career-long habit of doing exactly that. "There are times, however, when the plugs and howdies overshadow exciting situations on the field," Deeb wrote. "So far the new attitude at WGN is drawing the admiration of Cubs viewers and listeners. Let's hope it spreads to the Sox."[8]

Speaking in Caray's defense was a man whose presence at Comiskey Park was frequently mentioned by Harry: Jimmy Gallios, owner of Miller's Pub, a bar/restaurant described by David Condon as one of the "nerve centers for White Sox fan groups." Noting that the White Sox drew almost 1.5 million fans to their games in 1978, Gallios told Condon, "Caray is responsible for drawing many of those fans. Harry has the personal touch. Harry can't mention 1,491,100 names. He hasn't even gotten around to every restaurant owner, yet. But what's wrong with Caray mentioning us guys who buy the Sox season tickets?"[9]

Caray would go on mentioning the names of people at the ballpark—from restaurant owners to casual fans who wanted their names mentioned on the air—for as long as he was broadcasting games.

* * *

By the time the 1979 season started, Bill Veeck was struggling to keep the White Sox franchise viable. His operations were bare-bones. "When Veeck ran the White Sox, it was really a small family business," recalled writer David Israel. "Bill was at the top. His son Mike ran marketing. Rudie Schaffer and his son ran concessions and what would now be called merchandizing. The Bossard family, father and son, ran the ground crew. Roland Hemond ran baseball operations with Dave Dombrowski. And there were a couple of people running the ticket operation. That was it. If you went there in the winter to see Bill and sit in the Bards Room [the Comiskey Park dining room], it was completely empty except for the bartender. It was unbelievable."[10]

Veeck's signs of desperation were impossible to ignore. Less than five weeks into the 1978 season, the White Sox traded away their big offseason acquisition, outfielder Bobby Bonds, rather than continue to pay Bonds's $175,000-plus salary. (The Bonds trade had cost the Sox catcher-outfielder Brian Downing, who would be a major-league star for the next 15 years.) In June 1978, Veeck fired popular manager Bob Lemon and replaced him with hitting coach Larry Doby; the hope was that Doby, the major leagues' second African American manager, would help lure fans to Comiskey Park. (Meanwhile, Lemon was quickly hired to manage the New York Yankees and led them to the 1978 World Series championship.) When that failed, Veeck fired Doby and attempted to interest fans by making a player-manager out of Don Kessinger, a popular infielder who had starred for the crosstown Cubs for many years. Kessinger would not survive the 1979 season; he was replaced as manager in August by Tony La Russa, who would ultimately prove to be a sound choice, but only after Veeck had sold the team.

The ultimate fiasco for Veeck and the 1979 White Sox came on July 12, with a promotion that would live in baseball infamy: Disco Demolition Night. The promo was the brainchild of Veeck's 28-year-old son Mike and Chicago disc jockey Steve Dahl, a vocal hater of disco music. Fans who brought a disco record to Comiskey Park would be admitted for 98 cents (Dahl's station was WLUP, FM-98); then, between games of the Sox–Detroit Tigers twi-night doubleheader, Dahl would blow up the disco records on the field using dynamite.

The promotion was out of control from the start. An estimated 70,000 fans showed up, far greater than Comiskey Park's seating capacity. "We were trying to hold the main gate closed, but some fans forced it open. Some ushers got beat up," said a Sox security guard. [11] During the first game, fans were throwing records at Sox and Tigers players like Frisbees. When the promotion started between games, with Dahl riding onto the field in a Jeep and then blowing up a crate of disco records, fans stormed the field; others in the stands threw beer and lit firecrackers. Some people dug up home plate and gouged holes in the outfield grass. Sox players reported that fans were pounding on the clubhouse door trying to get in.

When Veeck had no luck getting the fans to leave the field, he asked Harry Caray to help; Harry sang "Take Me Out to the Ball Game" and pleaded with the fans to return to their seats, to no avail. "Harry was a pro," said Mike Veeck later. "He was the dance band on the *Titanic*, playing through the disaster." [12] Ultimately, the field was cleared with the help of Chicago police (39 people were arrested), but the umpires deemed the field unplayable and cancelled the second game of the doubleheader—a move that infuriated Veeck, who felt the game could be played. He was even angrier a day later, when the American League forfeited the cancelled game to the Tigers.

Howard Cosell, never a fan of Caray's, suggested that Harry was at least partially responsible for the fiasco. "It almost seemed as if that riot was a culmination of an attitude that has for some time been in the making," Cosell said on ABC radio. "There's just too much of the carnival atmosphere, from the very on-air presentation of the White Sox games to the front office itself." Caray's response: "He's a fraud. I've been singing 'Take Me Out to the Ball Game' forever, and when you've got as bad a ballclub as we've had, sometimes that's the only piece of fun the fans at the park can look forward to."[13]

While Cosell was a well-known critic of Caray's broadcasting style, Harry had plenty of defenders—beginning with Bill Veeck. "Sure, there are things I wish he wouldn't say. But I'd be the last to contest them," Veeck said in July 1979, the same month as Disco Demolition Night. "The fans identify with him because he is a fan. They know he's not going to give them a lot of Pablum. He's not a house man."[14] A month earlier, *Chicago Tribune* sports columnist David Israel had called Caray a "civic treasure," writing,

> Since the death of Mayor Richard J. Daley [in December 1976], Harry has emerged as the most recognizable personality in town. . . . Mediocre players, incompetent owners, and thin-skinned managers have complained about Caray and [Jimmy] Piersall over the years. But they ought to thank them. Because Harry and his various partners have kept people coming to the ballpark and interested in the product no matter how shoddy the performance on the field has been.[15]

✿ ✿ ✿

When the 1980 season started, Caray and the White Sox had a new radio outlet: WBBM had replaced WMAQ as the Sox' flagship station. During the 1979 season, WMAQ general manager Burt Sherwood had complained about Caray's on-air mentions of the bars and restaurants he frequented. He had also barred the station from broadcasting Caray's popular "Take Me Out to the Ball Game" sing-along. This annoyed both Caray and Veeck, who opted to take the White Sox to another station. Along with the new station, Caray had new radio partners in 1980. Joe McConnell replaced Lorn Brown, who had taken a job broadcasting Milwaukee Brewers games; when McConnell, who was also the primary radio voice for the Chicago Bears National Football League team, was unavailable, Rich King filled in.

Brown left the White Sox with words of praise for Caray. "Somebody referred to me as [Harry's] sidekick," said Brown, "He said, 'Lorn isn't my sidekick. They kick horses in the side, not people. Lorn is my partner.'" Joe McConnell was less glowing about the two years he worked with Caray. "I remember sitting down with [Bill] Veeck and he told me, 'I know what you're going through working with Harry, don't let it bother you,'" McConnell said in a 2009 interview. "Harry was going to do things his way. I understood that and just did my job."[16]

Rich King's experience with Caray was more like Brown's. "Harry was very kind to me, very gracious, and I really enjoyed my two years with him," King said in an interview. "He and I got along very well." Perhaps the difference was that, like Brown and unlike McConnell, an experienced broadcaster who would cover games for five major professional sports leagues (MLB, NFL, AFL, NBA, ABA), King was new to broadcasting on a major-league level and happy to let Caray be the star. Comparing his experience and reputation to Caray's, King kiddingly described it as a "giant against a peanut. That was why we got along."[17]

For Harry Caray's main broadcasting partner, Jimmy Piersall, the 1980 season was chaotic, stressful, and—on one occasion—violent. It began in May, when Bill Veeck and his wife, Mary Frances, criticized Piersall on their Sunday morning radio show for Jimmy's negative comments about Sox players. Piersall responded by calling Mary Frances Veeck a "colossal bore" and suggested that her best place was in the kitchen.[18] The Veecks were not pleased, but Veeck assured writers that he was not about to fire Piersall. A month, later, however, Piersall *was* fired from his job as a volunteer White Sox outfield coach by Tony La Russa. The Sox manager said he felt that Piersall's critical remarks on the air about Sox players' performance did not mesh with working for the team as a coach.

Then, on July 2, Piersall attacked suburban sportswriter Bob Gallas in the White Sox locker room about 90 minutes before a game. Piersall was apparently incensed that Gallas was questioning Sox players about the team's decision to remove him as part-time coach. "I couldn't believe it; he was yelling at me and then he just started strangling me," said Gallas. "I thought he would stop, and he didn't. The look in his eyes—it was scary."[19] Sox personnel intervened and Gallas, whose neck was covered with bruises, was taken to the hospital and then released. (In his 1984 book *The Truth Hurts*, written with Richard Whittingham, Piersall wrote that the incident with Gallas was a "little scuffle" that took "all of about three to five seconds," and that it was Sox trainer Herm Schneider, not Piersall, who put his hands on Gallas's neck in attempting to separate Gallas and Piersall.)[20]

About a half-hour after the incident with Gallas, Piersall was involved in a physical confrontation with Veeck's son Mike, who apparently initiated the action. Afterward, Piersall was hospitalized for several days and given a leave of absence by the White Sox. He returned to the broadcast booth on July 13, after receiving strong support from Sox fans, White Sox executives, the team's radio and television crews, and Harry Caray. Meanwhile, Gallas reported receiving hate mail, and he was booed by fans when he returned to Comiskey Park.

"I love Jimmy, but you can't get hyper about every hate letter you receive, and you can't take every good letter and carry it around with you in your back pocket," Caray told Bob Verdi the day after the incident. He added,

> Jimmy is a great broadcaster, but for the first time ever, I'm beginning to have second thoughts about whether we all haven't done Jimmy a disservice. Maybe, emotionally, he would be better off away from the game. I don't know. I just don't know. But I do know that you don't fire a man because he is not well.

Bill Veeck was widely praised by Caray and others for supporting Piersall and treating the Gallas incident as an emotional breakdown that could be treated medically. "Bill has been unbelievably good to me," Piersall said the day after the attack.[21] But in a 2005 interview with Mark Liptak, Piersall said, "He [Veeck] was a fraud. He never had any money to run the team with. Harry didn't like him either."[22]

* * *

Dealing with Jimmy Piersall was far from the biggest problem faced by Bill Veeck in 1980. "It was apparent that 1980 was going to be the end of the baseball road for Veeck, 66 years old, short of money, and with not enough talented players," wrote Gerald Eskanazi. "His illnesses seemed to be coming with increasing frequencies, his falls more serious."[23] At a high school reunion following the 1979 season, Veeck slipped on a wet floor and broke the kneecap on his left (nonamputated) leg. Although the 1980 White Sox got off to a promising start under Tony La Russa, the club ultimately faded to fifth place with a 70–90 record. For the third-straight year, the Sox had a drop in attendance, to 1.2 million.

Veeck let it be known that he was entertaining offers to purchase the White Sox. In 1979, he had talked to Marvin Davis, a Denver oil billionaire who wanted to buy the team and move it to Denver. The man who had saved the White Sox for Chicago in 1975 was interested; however, the Sox board of directors refused to consider selling to any group interested in moving the team. In 1980, Davis was back, and so was a group headed by Edward DeBartolo, a Cleveland-based real estate magnate whose family owned racetracks and two sports franchises (the San Francisco 49ers and Pittsburgh Penguins). DeBartolo was said to be interested in moving the team to New Orleans. "I think Bill is fed up with Chicago's failure to support the team, and with the way baseball is operated today," said a member of the Sox board of directors in explaining Veeck's amenability to selling the team to a group interested in moving it.[24]

A group headed by Sox directors Nick Kladis and Fred Brzozowski was also interested in buying the team and keeping it in Chicago—and in August, Harry Caray announced that he wanted to be part of the group. Caray stated on his WBBM radio show,

> I want you to know that of this moment I am offering my money and my interest to the group of men who already have proven their dedication to the Chicago White Sox—the guys who raised the money in those desperate hours when the owners threw Bill Veeck a curve . . . the people who helped Bill Veeck keep the White Sox in Chicago in the first place.[25]

Having Harry Caray as a part-owner of the White Sox was a fascinating concept, but even with the addition of Caray, the Kladis–Brzozowski group did not have the capital to compete with DeBartolo or Davis.

According to Marvin Davis, he and Veeck reached a handshake deal at one point in 1980: Davis would buy the team for $15 to 16 million (the offer from the Chicago group was several million dollars lower); Davis would move the club to Denver; and Veeck would come along as an assistant to Davis. But once again, Veeck lacked the support to move the team, both from the Sox board of directors and the other American League owners. So Veeck went back to DeBartolo, who agreed to keep the White Sox in Chicago. In October, they announced a deal, with the sale price an estimated $20 million.

The White Sox board of directors was amenable to the DeBartolo offer, but MLB commissioner Bowie Kuhn spoke out against the sale, as did American League president Lee MacPhail. When the league voted on the sale, only eight of the 14 owners favored it, two fewer than needed. The stated objections were that DeBartolo would be an absentee owner, that he might attempt at a later point to move the team to New Orleans, and that he owned three racetracks. When Veeck tried again at the league meetings in December—with DeBartolo threatening a lawsuit if the sale was turned down—the vote was 11 to 3 against him. This time there were whispers that because of his wealth and Italian American ethnicity, DeBartolo must have had ties to the Mafia. "It was nasty—as nasty as it gets," said Ray Grebey, head of MLB's Player Relations Committee. Yankees owner George Steinbrenner, who Veeck had labeled a "liar" and a "convicted felon," said that the real problem was Veeck. "I think I can safely say that the last vote, which went so strongly in numbers against Mr. DeBartolo, was, in fact, a vote against Bill Veeck," Steinbrenner said in December. "I think if Bill Veeck was applying for membership today in the American League, he would find it hard to get one vote."[26]

Within a short time, however, Veeck found another group of bidders with ties to Chicago. Jerry Reinsdorf, a Brooklyn native and Northwestern law school graduate who owned a real estate business in the Chicago suburb of Skokie, had been interested in the White Sox for some time. Once the DeBartolo bid was officially dead, Reinsdorf stepped forward again, this time allying himself with Eddie Einhorn, a Northwestern law school classmate who had made millions in sports television syndication. As a student, Einhorn had once sold hot dogs and soft drinks at Comiskey Park. The addition of Einhorn, who brought broadcasting expertise along with additional capital to the new ownership group, proved to be a key factor in winning approval from both the White Sox board of directors and the American League. The Reinsdorf–Einhorn group was able to match DeBartolo's $20 million bid for the team, agreed to keep the team in Chicago, and also agreed to keep in place the Sox management team headed by general manager Roland Hemond and field manager Tony La Russa. When the sale bid was submitted to the American League owners in January, it passed unanimously.

But as Reinsdorf and Einhorn took control, a key issue yet to be settled was whether Harry Caray would be returning to the broadcast booth. Shortly after the league approved the sale, Bob Markus wrote of Caray's uneasiness.

Caray is as popular in Chicago as any player and more recognizable than most. The choicest seats in Comiskey Park are considered to be those just under his announcing booth, where Caray can be seen and heard toasting the fans with whichever beer he is currently plugging. Caray also leads the crowd in singing "Take Me Out to the Ball Game."

No wonder, then, that White Sox fans were growing concerned that Caray had not yet been rehired for next season. As Christmas came and went, Caray was getting concerned, too.

"I keep hearing, 'They want you, they want you,'" said Caray, but nobody's contacted me."[27]

"It is Jerry's and my desire to retain Caray and Piersall," said Einhorn at the end of January, "but the stations, not the ball club, have the final say on that."[28] Those stations were yet to be determined, and Einhorn and Reinsdorf were exploring their options. One of the options was putting White Sox broadcasts on pay cable television.

The sports broadcasting business was undergoing some major changes, and the new White Sox owners wanted to be in the vanguard.

16

EDDIE AND JERRY AND HARRY AND JIMMY

The new owners of the White Sox might like to know that not every Sox and potential fan is wild about Harry. In fact, I was a Sox fan until about 1970 when Harry Caray arrived from Oakland.

* * *

I like to watch Sox telecasts, and used to turn down the sound and listen to radio. Then Caray kept popping up on radio, so I just turned off all the sound. Jimmy Piersall is kind of grating, too, but at least Piersall knows baseball.

This isn't intended as criticism of Caray any more than it is criticism of rutabaga, which I also don't like. Sox manager Chuck Tanner said Caray was a "front-running, second-guessing liar," but my reaction is merely that he is an overly loud flannelmouth who postures as the "mayor of Rush Street" but runs off to his home in California in the winter.

If you're a real Chicagoan, you love Chicago summer *and* winter.—Jack Mabley (columnist), *Chicago Tribune*, February 1981[1]

When Jerry Reinsdorf and Eddie Einhorn assumed control of the White Sox in January 1981, they were often referred to as "co-owners," but Reinsdorf held the higher rank; he became chairman of the Sox' board of directors, while Einhorn took the title of president (later he became vice chairman). Nonetheless, Einhorn was the ownership group's most frequent public voice in their early days of running the team. Einhorn's background and expertise in sports broadcasting was a major reason for this.

In college (at Penn) and law school (Northwestern), Einhorn had broadcast play-by-play for the schools' baseball and football games. After finishing law school, he launched an independent sports television network called TVS. The network's main sport was college basketball. Concentrating on such independent teams from the Midwest as Notre Dame, Marquette, and DePaul, Einhorn put together a package of games that he marketed to independent television stations. For a few years, he struggled to make money, but in 1968, Einhorn achieved his big breakthrough when TVS became the high bidder for a much-anticipated regular-season game between national powerhouses UCLA and Houston. Traveling the country visiting one station at a time, Einhorn was able to put together a network of 120 stations to broadcast the game, which was played at the Houston Astrodome in front of more than 50,000 people. The television audience for the stations that purchased broadcast rights from TVS was more than 20 million. Other successes followed, and a few years later Einhorn was able to sell TVS to Dun and Bradstreet for $5 million, 100,000 shares of D&B stock, and a five-year contract to continue running TVS. When the contract expired, Einhorn became an executive at CBS Sports, a position from which he resigned when he joined the White Sox ownership group.

Einhorn immediately turned his attention to the White Sox TV broadcasting contracts, which he described as the "worst business deal that I've ever seen in my life."[2] In 1980, UHF station WSNS had paid the Sox only $400,000 for broadcast rights, about $3,000 a game; by contrast, the New York Yankees were getting $5 million for their local broadcast rights. Since the Sox games were broadcast on free TV, Einhorn calculated that the team would be losing money if only 700 fans per game opted to stay home and watch the broadcast rather than come out to Comiskey Park.

Before selling the team to the Reinsdorf–Einhorn group, Bill Veeck had arranged a new TV plan for 1980: The Sox would leave WSNS and return to WGN-TV, their flagship station until the late 1960s, for their road telecasts; Sox home games would be broadcast on cable TV via Cablevision. This wasn't a great deal for the White Sox, either. Returning to WGN for some games was preferable to a smaller UHF outlet, but WGN had a long-term relationship with the crosstown Cubs—and that relationship was about to become even deeper. As for the Cablevision part of the deal, it made little sense; in 1981 Chicago was several years away from being wired for cable TV, and the same was true for most of the city's suburbs. Einhorn was able to pull out of the Cablevision deal and add a few Sox home games to the WGN package for 1981. But he made it clear that he had more ambitious plans for the future. "As Einhorn sees it," wrote Ron Alridge, who had succeeded Gary Deeb as the *Chicago Tribune* TV-radio critic, "television, especially pay television, is much more than loose change and promotion. It's the key to baseball's financial future; it's a goose that'll lay tons of golden eggs; it's a way of expanding paid attendance to enormous proportions."[3]

In the meantime, there was a season to be played, and a broadcaster to be signed. The negotiations between Caray and the new Sox owners were far from pleasant. In 1980, Caray had earned about $200,000: $110,000 from Channel 44; $58,000 from WMAQ Radio; and an estimated $30,000 from the White Sox, who sweetened the pot after WMAQ threatened to walk away from the deal. In mid-February, Reinsdorf reported an impasse, claiming Caray had demanded a raise to $225,000. "Bull," responded Caray, saying that he had actually lowered his price. According to Reinsdorf, WGN didn't want to pay Caray the same amount as Channel 44 had, as it was broadcasting far fewer games; the Sox, who would have to make up some of the difference, were unhappy about potentially having to pay $100,000 or more of Caray's salary. "I can't believe he's paying $100,000 out of his own pocket," countered Caray. "And if he is, he's a horrible businessman. I could sell the radio and TV rights myself and not have to dig into my own pocket." Caray also pointed out some of the salaries the Sox were paying to players, including $250,000 for Jim Essian, a "third-string catcher for the Oakland A's . . . and they can't afford to pay an announcer?"[4] Caray and the Sox finally came to terms in early March; he reportedly got the $225,000 Reinsdorf had mentioned. The Sox resigned Jimmy Piersall as well. But the friction between Caray, Piersall, and the new club management would continue.

✧ ✧ ✧

The Reinsdorf–Einhorn ownership group began the 1981 season with high hopes. They did commit one public relations gaffe. After acquiring control of the team, Reinsdorf announced that the Sox wanted to create a "first-class operation." Although Reinsdorf insisted that he and Einhorn were not being critical of Bill Veeck, the former Sox owner took offense; he pointedly stayed away from Comiskey Park after the ownership transfer and instead was often seen in the bleachers at Wrigley Field, watching the Cubs. "I couldn't be at home in such a class operation as they're operating there," Veeck said sarcastically. "The new owner, Fast Eddie—that's his name, isn't it?—is such a professional he doesn't want me and my kind of people spilling beer on the furniture." Veeck also was still upset that the American League had chosen the Reinsdorf–Einhorn group rather than Edward DeBartolo, saying the "wrong people got the team."[5]

Although alienating Veeck was unfortunate, Reinsdorf and Einhorn were aggressive about strengthening the White Sox on the field. Rather than losing free agents, as had often happened under Veeck, the Sox signed a pair of premium free agents, catcher Carlton Fisk and outfielder Ron LeFlore. They also traded for slugging outfielder-designated hitter Greg Luzinski, a Chicago native whose Polish heritage helped make him a favorite with South Side fans. At the first Sox game on April 14, played in front of 51,560 fans (a club record for a home opener), Fisk hit a grand slam home run in a 9–3 victory. The club had a 31–22 record and was only two and a half games out of the division lead when the season was abruptly halted in mid-June due to a strike by the players. The work stoppage, primarily concerning free agent compensation, wasn't settled until August; when play resumed the major leagues opted to create a split-season format, with the pre- and poststrike division leaders qualifying for the playoffs; however, the Sox played poorly in the second half, finishing the year out of the postseason running with a 54–52 overall record.

While this was going on, Reinsdorf and Einhorn were dealing with issues involving their broadcasters—particularly Piersall. It began in spring training, when, during the broadcast of a White Sox–Pittsburgh Pirates exhibition game, Piersall, Harry Caray, and Joe McConnell criticized Pirates outfielder Dave Parker for being overweight. Piersall went the furthest, saying Parker looked like a "baby whale" (some reports said the term he used was "baby hippo"). Parker took offense at the

reference and confronted Piersall about it, but nothing more trans-
pired.

About a month into the season, Reinsdorf and Einhorn met with
Caray, Piersall, and McConnell to "get a few things on the table." After
denying that he intended to fire Piersall, Einhorn said Piersall "has to
be taught professionalism," and that Piersall agreed to be more professional in the things that he said. "It's easy to play God when you're on
TV with 700,000 people listening," said Einhorn. "The announcers can't
use it as a forum for subjective opinions about the players. Once that
point was made, I think all three announcers accepted our point of
view."[6]

A few weeks later, on May 31, Piersall was involved in a confrontation with umpires Dale Ford and Joe Brinkman during a game between
the White Sox and California Angels. Ford claimed Piersall had used
exaggerated hand gestures to demonstrate his disagreement with the
way Brinkman, the plate umpire, was calling balls and strikes. "He was
leaning over the booth doing it," said Ford, "trying to incite the crowd
against us." According to Brinkman, he and Piersall then exchanged
gestures—but Piersall's response was an obscene one-finger salute.
Piersall insisted he was "using my thumb" and that "I thought we were
having fun," but Brinkman was firm that Piersall "flipped me the bird."

The game was the first of a Sunday doubleheader, and between
games the umpires informed the White Sox that if Piersall continued
with his behavior during the second game, they might stop the contest
and forfeit it to the Angels. "We could have had a riot," said Ford. "It's a
crime that a class organization like this has to put up with Piersall and
the things he says and does." Piersall responded by calling the umpires
"gutless and lazy," and he said that "Brinkman blew calls all day." He
also referred to Ken Kaiser, another American League umpire, as a
"whale." Harry Caray, meanwhile, stood behind his partner. "I never
saw Jimmy use any obscene gesture," said Caray. "And I was right there
in the booth with him. Besides, what are umpires doing looking at the
booth? No wonder they blow so many plays."[7]

While Caray was not directly involved in the confrontation between
Piersall and the two umpires, Chicago-based sportscaster Mike Leiderman felt Caray was not just an innocent bystander in Piersall's misad-
ventures during their years together. "Harry would play Jimmy like a

fiddle," Leiderman said in describing the dynamic between the two broadcasters. He continued,

> He would get Jimmy revved up, and Jimmy would go cuckoo and then he'd say, "I'm sane and I have the papers to prove it," that whole thing. Anytime Harry wanted a rise out of Jimmy, he knew how to press his buttons. Harry wasn't looking to be mean to Jimmy; he was looking to make good television. He knew by getting a rise out of Piersall, the fans would be entertained. Of course, Harry knew when to draw the line; Jimmy did not. [8]

Sportswriter Ron Rapoport, who was working for the *Chicago Sun-Times* during the same period, said in an interview that Caray and Piersall were making so much news that his newspaper used to monitor the Sox broadcasts. "The guys at the desk who were receiving our copy would sit and listen to the game in case they said or did something outrageous," he related. [9]

In late June, shortly after the players' strike had begun, the Sox announced a plan that would greatly limit the amount of time Caray and Piersall would work together. The team said that once play resumed, there would be a new member of their broadcast crew: former St. Louis star Lou Brock, who had played several years for the Cardinals when Caray was broadcasting there. While the addition of Brock was described as part of Reinsdorf and Einhorn's plan to expand their television options in future years, Reinsdorf said that when Brock came on board, he would usually be paired with Caray; Piersall would work primarily with Joe McConnell on radio. Reinsdorf denied that the Caray–Piersall tandem was being permanently broken up; however, he added, "Jimmy will end up doing some games with Harry, but probably just the ones on radio." He insisted that Brock's hiring did not mean he was planning to fire Piersall; Caray, after confirming that Brock was an addition rather than a replacement, welcomed him as a "good friend." But the Caray–Piersall team was effectively being broken up. [10]

Shortly after the strike ended and games resumed, Piersall once again ran into trouble. During the broadcast of a White Sox–Toronto Blue Jays game on September 3, he criticized slow-footed Sox designated hitter Greg Luzinski for not running hard to first base after hitting a ground ball to the infield. According to Sox outfielder Ron LeFlore, Piersall said, "As much money as he's making, he should run the ball out. He ought to be shot." (Piersall admitted to the first comment but denied saying that Luzinski should be shot.) Luzinski wound up winning the game for the White Sox with a double in the bottom of the ninth inning, but he refused to talk to reporters afterward. Sox manager Tony La Russa, who had often clashed with Piersall, defended his player, saying Luzinski had a bad leg and was under orders not to run hard. "Our color commentator took a cheap shot at him," said La Russa. The White Sox took no action against Piersall but told him to work out his issues with Luzinski face to face. [11]

Two days later, on September 5, Piersall and Caray were guests on a TV show hosted by Chicago newspaper columnist Mike Royko. During the show, Royko asked the broadcasters how they handled the reaction from wives of Sox players who Caray and Piersall had criticized on air. Caray, who spoke first, admitted that there could be problems and that the wives often misinterpreted comments made during a broadcast. Then Piersall spoke. "I think each ball club should have a clinic once a week for the wives," he said to Royko. "I don't think they know what baseball is. First of all, they were horny broads who wanted to get married. They want a little money, they want a little security and a big strong-looking ballplayer. I traveled, I played. I got a load of them broads, too." White Sox players were incensed when they heard about Piersall's "horny broads" comments, and on September 9, the White Sox suspended Jimmy "indefinitely"—with pay.

Caray once again defended Piersall, saying he didn't think his partner's comments were serious enough to cost him his job. "Jimmy's said a lot more damaging things than that, and nobody's cared," said Caray. "Why don't the players concentrate on playing baseball? They're more concerned with what their wives have to say than with what they're doing on the field." Eddie Einhorn, who announced Piersall's suspension, said he respected the popularity of Caray and Piersall but added, "You'll never have a winning team with a situation like this. I'm not knocking them, but this is unprecedented—a broadcasting team that upstages the team on the field." [12]

On September 15, the White Sox announced that Piersall's suspension would last the rest of the season. Reinsdorf reiterated that Piersall had not been fired and the White Sox had not yet made a decision about whether to ask Jimmy to return in 1982. For his part, Caray said, "I worked with the Sox before Piersall, and I'm not going to quit or resign in protest if they do fire him." But he insisted that he wasn't going to change his broadcasting style. "Just because I might embarrass them [Einhorn and Reinsdorf] isn't going to stop me from speaking out as I always have," Caray said. "I'm not going to change my character for anyone. There are other jobs around."[13]

As the 1981 season came to an end, there was speculation that one of the "other jobs" that Caray mentioned might be on the North Side of Chicago.

* * *

On June 16, five days after the start of the Major League Baseball players' strike, there was stunning news that had nothing to do with the strike: The Chicago Cubs had been sold to the Tribune Company, which operated the *Chicago Tribune* and WGN-TV and radio, among other entities, for $20.5 million. The Cubs had been part of majority owner William Wrigley's family since 1916. In reporting the sale, the *New York Times* called the Cubs "one of Major League Baseball's least successful franchises on the field in recent years" and said that the club had lost $1.7 million in 1980. The club had not posted a winning record since 1972, and would finish 1981 with the worst record in the National League; however, the Tribune Company saw potential in the purchase. "Although mired with a losing record," wrote the *Times*, "the Cubs play in a prosperous market, and they have a long baseball tradition. Further, the Tribune Company's ownership of cable television subsidiaries, in addition to newspapers and radio and television stations, offers opportunities to highlight the team."[14]

In announcing the sale, the Tribune Company named Chicago business executive Andrew J. McKenna, a man who admitted that he "was never as much of a Cubs' fan as I was a Sox fan,"[15] as the new chairman of the board of the Cubs. McKenna was familiar to people on the South Side. In the summer of 1975, when the Sox appeared to be headed for Seattle, McKenna had traveled to Maryland to visit Bill Veeck, a personal friend, to see if Veeck was interested in assembling a group of investors to purchase the team and keep it in Chicago. McKenna became one of the investors and, after Veeck's group acquired the team, served as temporary White Sox chairman of the board for a period of time. In 1980, when Veeck put the team up for sale, McKenna played a key role in the transfer of the team to the Reinsdorf–Einhorn group after Edward DeBartolo's bid had been rejected by the American League. McKenna and Harry Caray were very well acquainted.

In a *Sporting News* article about the Cubs several weeks after the sale of the team to the Tribune Company, Dave Nightingale discussed the various positions that the new ownership group would be filling. He included the role of lead broadcaster.

> The heavy betting here is that, after 1981, the mayor of Rush Street—Harry Caray—never again will have to work south of the Chicago River.
>
> The redoubtable broadcaster, whose golden tonsils commanded a $225,000 contract from the rival White Sox this season, has been at odds recently with the new Sox owners, Reinsdorf and Einhorn. The two men are on record that they think Caray has the misguided notion he is "bigger than the team" and they sent up more than a couple of balloons that Harry has outlived his Comiskey Park usefulness. [16]

At the time Nightingale wrote his article, Caray going to the Cubs appeared to be a reach, as the Cubs already seemed to have their broadcasting plans in place for 1982. Those plans did not include Harry Caray. In November 1979, WGN had hired Harry's old adversary, Milo Hamilton, to become part of their broadcasting team. The plan was for Hamilton to work alongside legendary Cubs broadcaster Jack Brickhouse in 1980; then Brickhouse would retire and Hamilton would become the Cubs' number-one TV voice. When the 1980 season ended, Brickhouse opted to stick around for another year, but the succession plan was kept in place. On August 5, 1981, a little less than six weeks after the Tribune Company purchased the team—and shortly after the publication of Nightingale's *Sporting News* article—WGN-TV president Sheldon Cooper announced that Brickhouse would definitely be leaving Channel 9's Cubs broadcasts at the end of the season and be replaced as the number-one voice by Hamilton. That seemed to settle the issue; however, Ron Alridge's *Tribune* article announcing the succession plan included a paragraph that seemed unimportant at the time: "Cooper stressed that all announcers will be subject to 'club approval.' But with Tribune Company, WGN's parent corporation, buying the team, approval is all but assured." [17]

In the meantime, Caray was beginning to talk with the White Sox about their television plans for 1982. Although the plans were radical, he expected to be part of them.

17

HARRY HEADS NORTH

So, Harry Caray, "one of two sport announcers who overshadow the event," left the White Sox at the altar when it was time to renew the vows in that tumultuous marriage and signed for two years of broadcasting bigamy with the Cubs and WGN-TV and radio, both wholly owned by Tribune Company.

Well, there goes Tribune Company. It was nice being with you guys (37 years) while it lasted. One wonders how long Harry will be a member of the family before he starts telling Stanton Cook how to publish the *Chicago Tribune*?—David Condon, *Chicago Tribune*, November 1981[1]

Before coming to the White Sox, Eddie Einhorn had made his fortune broadcasting sporting events on television. From the time he took his position with the Sox, Einhorn made no secret that he hated the fact that the vast majority of White Sox games were being broadcast free of charge to the viewer. Commenting in 1983 on how the crosstown Cubs were still televising virtually their entire schedule, home and road, on WGN-TV, Einhorn said, "How can anybody say that works for the Cubs? They've never drawn more than 1.6 million in any year, and they don't have a winning team. The best organizations, the ones that draw the most people at the gate, don't go that way. They have limited TV."[2]

Einhorn had a different plan for the White Sox, a service called SportsVision. He unveiled it in October 1981, during the same time period he and Jerry Reinsdorf were talking to Harry Caray about renewing Harry's broadcast contract for 1982. SportsVision was a subscription television service that sent a scrambled signal to a UHF channel on the user's TV. The user would unscramble the signal with a decoder box connected to the TV. Subscribers would pay $21.95 per month to receive a minimum of 425 sports broadcasts during the year; along with 112 White Sox games, the service included selected Chicago Bulls (NBA), Blackhawks (NHL), and Sting (NASL soccer) games, along with about 100 other events (mostly college basketball). SportsVision used the same type of decoder box as ON-TV, a subscription service that broadcast movies, concerts, and other entertainment; users of both ON-TV and SportsVision would receive a discount for subscribing to both services.

Using pay-TV to broadcast sporting events was not a new concept. As far back as the 1950s, Walter O'Malley, owner of the Brooklyn Dodgers, had discussed putting Dodgers games on pay television. After the Dodgers moved to Los Angeles, O'Malley and the owners of the San Francisco Giants worked out a plan with a company called Subscription Television, Inc. (STI) to make the clubs' games available on a fee-per-game basis. The system was put into place for several months during the 1964 season; however, the subscriber base was low, and hostility toward the plan on the part of movie theater owners (who feared competition) led to a successful referendum to outlaw pay-TV in California. The referendum was eventually ruled unconstitutional, but by then STI had gone bankrupt.

At the time Einhorn announced the launching of SportsVision, there were several other sports pay-TV systems already broadcasting. The most successful was in Philadelphia, where a profitable pay channel called PRISM broadcast selected games of the MLB Phillies, NHL Flyers, and NBA 76ers, along with extensive entertainment programming. New York had both SportsChannel (MLB Yankees and Mets) and Madison Square Garden Cable (MSG), which broadcast the NBA Knicks and NHL Rangers. In those cases, however, the teams using pay-TV also had a substantial number of games available on "free" (at least for the viewer) television. The White Sox would be the first MLB team to put the bulk of their schedule on pay-TV.

For Einhorn and Reinsdorf, it was a question of survival. "It's clear that if we [owners] are to build a winner," Reinsdorf said as SportsVision was being unveiled, "we have to increase revenue to pay higher player salaries. Either we raise ticket prices or we find a new source of revenue."[3] Simultaneous with the unveiling of SportsVision was an announcement that the White Sox had resigned Greg Luzinski to a multi-year contract at $700,000 a year. According to Luzinski's agent, Jack Sands, the timing was intentional; it was a way of showing that the White Sox were serious about spending (and needing) money to field a competitive team.

Einhorn and Reinsdorf's SportsVision plans were quickly panned by local observers. *Tribune* columnist David Condon referred to Einhorn as a "self-designated patent medicine man" and suggested that "Eddie's recent overseas trip was to negotiate with China, the Soviet Union, and other contenders, for exclusive live TV coverage rights of World War III (at $21.95 monthly per home subscriber, slightly higher for saloons)."[4] Condon pointed out the obvious weakness of a pay-TV sports plan in Chicago: The Sox would be charging money to watch their games, while Cubs broadcasts were available for free. Jim Dowdle, head of broadcasting for the Tribune Company, the new owners of the Cubs, was a little more sympathetic, but he thought the Sox were making a big mistake by making only about 30 games available on free TV. "You've got to crawl before you walk," he said.[5]

Meanwhile, there was another major question about the SportsVision plan: Would Harry Caray be part of it? At first, the answer seemed to be no. On October 10, Linda Kay wrote in the *Chicago Tribune*, "Harry Caray and Jimmy Piersall almost certainly are through" with the White Sox, and that the Sox were talking with Don Drysdale about joining their broadcast crew. She added that Caray's agent, Saul Foos, had contacted Cubs chairman Andy McKenna three times but that McKenna had been noncommittal. "I told him our priority was the ball club, not the announcers," said McKenna.[6]

On October 15, however, Ron Alridge reported that Caray would meet with Einhorn and Reinsdorf the next day to see if the Sox wanted him back; if so, negotiations would continue. According to the story, "Caray says he definitely wants to return to the Sox broadcasting booth. He might even be willing to sign for more than the one year to which he traditionally limits his contract. 'I don't want to go through this every year,' he says."[7] Reporting about the October 16 meeting, Kay wrote, "Good vibes were in the air." Caray described the meeting as "very healthy, very wholesome," that, "My number-one priority is to work in Chicago, preferably for the Chicago White Sox," and that Reinsdorf and

Einhorn "seemed as interested as I am."[8] On October 28, Kay reported that Caray and Reinsdorf had met again and quoted Jeffrey Jacobs, the attorney whose firm was handling Caray's negotiations, as saying that another meeting would take place to "discuss dollars and cents." She quoted Reinsdorf as saying that Caray had a "reasonably decent" chance of being rehired.[9] On November 6, Alridge wrote that Caray had struck out on trying to get the Cubs interested and that it was "time for the White Sox to cut out the silliness and sign announcer Harry Caray to a new contract."

> Although neither side will admit it, Caray has a cushy, $225,000-a-year job in a city he likes and understands. Duplicating it won't be easy, as shown by his unsuccessful behind-the-scenes efforts to get his foot in the door of the new Cubs owners.
>
> But if Caray needs the Sox, the Sox need him even more, especially now. Reinsdorf and Einhorn are trying to persuade Sox fans to fork out $22 a month for the privilege of seeing Sox games on pay TV next season. . . . What could the ailing Sox better use than popular, proven Harry Caray? And what could they least afford to lose?
>
> For one thing, Caray is an announcer who can give the risky pay TV package the edge it needs to succeed. You don't have to be a Sox fan, or even a dyed-in-the-wool baseball fan, to enjoy listening to his outbursts of "Holy Cow" or his skillful play-by-play work. If Caray is worth only a thousand or so pay TV subscribers, he'll earn his keep.[10]

But Caray and the White Sox were never able to get together. On November 16 came the stunning news: Harry Caray was moving crosstown to broadcast games for the Cubs.

☼ ☼ ☼

What had happened? In his autobiography, Caray wrote that when he began talking to the White Sox about a renewal, he was dubious that SportsVision could succeed unless the Cubs were part of the package; when he expressed his unwillingness to broadcast for the Sox on Sports-Vision without a multiyear contract, they balked. At that point, he wrote, he contacted Andy McKenna and expressed his interest in working for the Cubs.

Contemporary reports make it clear that Caray had approached the Cubs much earlier in the process—several times, in fact, according to the *Tribune*; however, it took several weeks before the Cubs gave the green light to making Caray an offer. McKenna, wrote Jerome Holtzman in 1998, "had known the applicant [Caray] for many years but was uncertain if Tribune Co. would be interested. He didn't seem to be its kind of guy." The key pro-Caray voice at the Tribune Company, by most accounts, was Jim Dowdle, president and COO of Tribune Broadcasting, which included WGN-TV. His fellow executives, who were well aware of Caray's stormy years with the White Sox, were dubious. "I told them I thought Harry was the epitome of show business," Dowdle recalled. "He did a good job and was very colorful. My job was to try to get as large an audience as we could." None of his colleagues felt the same way, but ultimately the decision among the broadcasting group belonged to Dowdle. "I was the new man at the *Tribune*, less than a year on the job. I knew they were giving me my head."[11]

Caray's hiring also had to be approved by Dallas Green, who had been hired by the Tribune Company as Cubs executive vice president and general manager. Green, who had come to the Cubs after leading the Phillies to their first-ever World Series championship as a field manager in 1980, was a tough, no-nonsense type who Cubs outfielder Bob Dernier compared to John Wayne. Green was concerned about the controversies Caray had generated during his White Sox years and made it clear that Harry needed to keep his criticism within bounds. "I talked to him," Green recalled in 1998. "All I said was I don't mind at all the normal play-by-play, say if the player doesn't have his sunglasses on and should have. That's fine. But I didn't want to get into personalities and the personal side of things. . . . I think he recognized what he had to do."[12]

The Cubs gave Caray a two-year deal. Ron Alridge reported that the Sox also had offered Caray a two-year contract, but one that gave both sides the option to cancel after the first year. That wasn't enough to satisfy Caray, who felt he was taking a major risk moving his talents to a new, fee-based network with a small subscriber base. "The White Sox did make me a good offer, finally," Caray said at the press conference announcing his move to the Cubs. "It came down to do you want to go into 8 million homes free or 50,000 homes on pay TV." In future years, White Sox followers would wonder how different Chicago sports history might have been had Reinsdorf offered Caray the three-to-five-year deal he said he was seeking. But it might not have made a difference once the Cubs began showing serious interest in hiring him. "I kept thinking about Channel 9," Caray said at the press conference. "I kept thinking about my people—the bartenders, the taxi drivers, the post office guys. I'd be without something that made this job worthwhile all these years—the people." [13]

As for the possibility of Caray transferring one of his most popular White Sox traditions to Wrigley Field, he would prove to be an inaccurate prophet. "Caray said he would bring his 'Holy Cow' style of broadcasting to the Cubs," wrote Robert Markus, "but doubted that McKenna and Green would approve of his rasping rendition of 'Take Me Out to the Ball Game' that he traditionally sang during the seventh-inning stretch at Comiskey Park." [14]

❀ ❀ ❀

Not everyone was thrilled that Caray would be joining the Cubs' broadcast crew. Milo Hamilton, in particular, was stunned.

For several months, Hamilton had assumed he would be the Cubs' number-one television broadcaster now that Jack Brickhouse had retired. Hamilton said he had no idea Caray would be getting the job until he arrived at the press conference during which the announcement was made. "I was told as recently as five days ago that I was going to be the announcer," he told Ron Alridge. Asked who had given him the information, he replied, "Well, I didn't ask the janitor." [15] In his autobiography, *Making Airwaves*, Hamilton claimed that Andy McKenna told him he had advised Jim Dowdle against hiring Caray but that Dowdle decided to do so anyway. Hamilton considered leaving the Cubs but ultimately agreed to work with Caray in 1982—at a slightly increased salary.

Hamilton was not alone in feeling unhappy that Caray was joining the Cubs' broadcast crew. On November 22, six days after the move was announced, the *Chicago Tribune* published the results of a survey in which readers were asked for their opinions about the switch. More than 2,500 fans responded, split pretty evenly between Cubs (42 percent) and Sox fans (43 percent), with 15 percent expressing no preference between the teams. The results are summarized in table 17.1.

Among White Sox fans, Caray's popularity was enormous: A total of 89 percent of the respondents who identified themselves as Sox fans said they liked Caray (only 9 percent said they disliked him). Stunningly, 44 percent of the pro-Sox respondents said they would become Cubs fans; only 31 percent said they would stick with the Sox. Meanwhile, 76 percent of Cubs fans said they disliked Caray, and 77 percent were unhappy with the move. But the vast majority of Cubs fans (73 percent) said they were sticking with their team.

Many of the Cubs fans expressed disapproval of the way Caray had taken the job that had presumably belonged to Milo Hamilton. "You think you pulled a coup," wrote one Hamilton supporter. "You made a grave error signing Caray—that flamboyant buffoon. Milo was your best bet and then stupidly you probably lost him." Another fan wrote that hiring Caray was shifting attention from the team to the broadcasting booth. "The thought of a beer-guzzling clown leading the cheers and bringing followers of similar ilk turns my stomach," he wrote. "Dallas Green will inject new lifeblood and new spirit; Harry Caray will tear it apart."[16]

On the South Side, the White Sox replaced Caray and Jimmy Piersall with two former major-league players, Don Drysdale and Ken Harrelson; the colorful Harrelson would prove to be an enduring presence with the Sox and still be broadcasting games for the club in 2018, which he announced would be his final year. Piersall was retained in a reduced

Table 17.1. Fan Survey on Caray Switch to Cubs, November 1981

	Cubs Fans	Sox Fans
Like Caray	20 percent	89 percent
Dislike Caray	76 percent	9 percent
Doesn't matter	4 percent	3 percent
Happy with move	21 percent	36 percent
Unhappy with move	77 percent	54 percent
Doesn't matter	2 percent	10 percent
Will be a Sox fan	4 percent	31 percent
Will be a Cubs fan	73 percent	44 percent
Will be both/none	23 percent	25 percent

role as a pre- and postgame studio commentator. "It's the battle of the baseball announcers," said a headline in the *Chicago Tribune* a few days before the start of the 1982 season.[17]

❀ ❀ ❀

When the season began, the White Sox were red-hot, winning their first eight games; however, the promising start did not send Sox fans flocking to sign up for Eddie Einhorn's SportsVision channel. With subscriptions lagging, the team delayed the start of the channel's paid broadcasts until May 13; until then the Sox showed the broadcasts for free in an effort to lure customers. That didn't seem to help much; in July, Ron Alridge reported that SportsVision had only 17,000 subscribers, far less than the 50,000-subscriber target Einhorn had set for the inaugural season.

Meanwhile, the White Sox were once again dealing with adventures involving Jimmy Piersall. When the club went through a midseason slump, Piersall resumed his on-air criticism of manager Tony La Russa, an old adversary. In late July, La Russa became so upset at Piersall that after a game, he and Sox coaches Jim Leyland and Art Kusyner went to the SportsVision offices to confront Piersall. No punches were thrown, but heated words were exchanged. Famed *Boston Globe* sports columnist Peter Gammons was sympathetic to La Russa, writing, "The fact is that Piersall makes his living on other people's blood. Piersall is to journalism what dumping over a paint can is to art, and his absurd, second-guessing rantings have thrown fuel on the fire." Eddie Einhorn described the soap opera atmosphere surrounding the team as the "Bill Veeck legacy," saying, "This is what we inherited when we bought the club—the whole Harry Caray, Jim Piersall thing."[18]

The White Sox recovered well enough to finish the season in third place, with 87 wins, their most victories since 1977. On the North Side, the Cubs were enduring another difficult season, finishing fifth in the six-team National League East with a 73–89 season. The Cubs had their own soap opera involving broadcasters. For the most part, Caray and Hamilton maintained a professional relationship, but it wasn't easy; Caray described it as an "arms-length relationship" and by saying that he was "bending over backwards to make it work." He told Ron Alridge that he was willing to work with anyone that WGN selected but put in a plug for Jimmy Piersall. "I miss Piersall," he said. "We're a hell of a team."[19]

There were some rough moments between Caray and Hamilton. When the Cubs decided to bring Caray's tradition of singing "Take Me Out to the Ball Game" during the seventh-inning stretch to Wrigley Field, Hamilton, who loathed the ritual, vented his opinion of Caray's singing to a reporter. WGN management quickly called in Hamilton and told him Caray was their number-one broadcaster and that they wouldn't tolerate such sniping. In July, Hamilton became ill and needed to be hospitalized. According to Milo, he was watching a Cubs broadcast from his hospital room when he heard Harry say on the air, "You know, I never missed *any* games. I don't understand how a guy can take time off during the season."[20]

Caray and Hamilton made it through the rest of the season without major incident, but in November, the Cubs announced a new broadcast lineup for 1983. Caray would be paired on television with Steve Stone, a former Cubs and White Sox pitcher who had drawn praise for his broadcasting work on ABC national telecasts. Meanwhile, Hamilton would become the Cubs' primary radio voice, succeeding Vince Lloyd, who would primarily work as a pre- and postgame host. During the middle innings, Hamilton would switch with Caray, moving to television while Harry switched to radio. In contrast with the friction between Caray and Hamilton, the Caray–Stone pairing would prove to be enduring and popular, with each speaking warmly of the other. The duo worked together for the last 15 years of Caray's life.

While the first season of SportsVision could hardly be called a success, Eddie Einhorn could point with pride to the fact that, without Caray, the White Sox had a home attendance more than 300,000 higher than that of the Cubs: 1,567,787 for the White Sox, 1,249,278 for the Cubs. Caray's impact on the Cubs would become apparent soon enough, but in the meantime, the Cubs and White Sox would wage a competitive battle for supremacy in the city of Chicago.

18

SUPERSTAR OF THE SUPERSTATION

Harry Caray, the Chicago Cubs broadcaster, recently received a letter from a glutton for punishment. The letter came from a fellow in the Soviet Union who says he picks up telecasts of Cub games on an illegal satellite dish. Condemned by wanton fate to live in the Soviet Union, he turns to the Cubs to assuage his suffering.—George Will, *Washington Post*, August 1985[1]

Cable television originated in the United States in the late 1940s to alleviate the problem of poor reception in remote areas. Until the 1970s, government regulation prevented cable operators from importing distant signals, so cable offered viewers little original programming of its own and nothing on a national basis. The regulations were gradually loosened, and to take advantage of new opportunities, RCA launched its own communications satellite in 1975. The satellite enabled Home Box Office (HBO), at the time a regional service offering movies and entertainment programming to cable subscribers, to become a national pay-TV network available to any cable operator willing to invest in a satellite dish. HBO's success as a national network encouraged other operators to take advantage of satellite technology.

One of them was Ted Turner, who owned Atlanta UHF station WTCG. Intrigued by the success of HBO, Turner realized he could turn his local station into a national cable network via satellite. With Turner offering the rights to broadcast WTCG basically free of charge, the first cable "superstation," whose call letters Turner soon changed to WTBS (for Turner Broadcasting System), was born. From the beginning, sports were part of the TBS broadcast schedule. Turner's station had the rights to broadcast Atlanta Braves games, and to ensure he could continue to broadcast the games nationally via cable, he bought the team.

Other superstations soon entered the field, one of which was WGN-TV in Chicago, which first uplinked its signal to satellite in October 1978. "Turner's success with the Braves," wrote James R. Walker and Robert V. Bellamy Jr., "was a clear impetus for the Tribune Company to purchase the Cubs from the Wrigley family."[2] WGN was almost as popular as WTBS, with cable operators interested in adding programming. A big reason was the popularity of its sports broadcasts—especially the Chicago Cubs, whose schedule of home day games offered sporting events to viewers at a time of day when there was little competition on the sports calendar. Having a popular announcer didn't hurt, either. By the time Harry Caray joined the Cubs broadcast crew in 1982, the growth of cable had set the stage for him to become a national TV star.

☆ ☆ ☆

In 1983, their second year without Caray, the Chicago White Sox didn't seem to miss Harry at all. The Sox started the season slowly and were under .500 in late June, but then the club caught fire and rolled to the American League Western Division title with 99 victories, winning by a 20-game margin. It was the first division title or pennant for a Chicago baseball franchise since the White Sox had won the American League pennant in 1959. Although the White Sox were eliminated by the Baltimore Orioles in the American League Championship Series, it was a triumphant season on the South Side. The club drew a team-record 2.1 million fans to Comiskey Park, becoming the first Chicago team to draw more than 2 million spectators. For the year, the Sox (home attendance 2,132,821) outdrew the Cubs (1,479,717) by more than 650,000 fans.

The Sox accomplished this without either Caray or Harry's former sidekick, Jimmy Piersall, in their TV booth. Piersall had begun the year as a SportsVision pre- and postgame commentator, but the team fired him in early April after Piersall made several negative comments about the club. "We cannot go through another season of tension and disruption that is counterproductive to everything we are trying to accomplish," Jerry Reinsdorf wrote in a telegram informing Piersall of his dismissal.[3] (Piersall continued to host a postgame call-in show on WMAQ Radio, the Sox flagship station, until the end of the season, when he was fired from that job as well.)

Before the September 17 game, in which the White Sox clinched their division title, Reinsdorf addressed his rocky relationship with Piersall and Caray. He told *Chicago Tribune* writer Linda Kay,

> My biggest mistake was not firing Harry Caray and Jimmy Piersall before the first game of the 1981 season. There was an atmosphere of negativism here that made it hard to win and difficult to attract good ballplayers. That negativism was, in large part, fostered by Harry and Jimmy, who I truly believe didn't want the Sox to win, because if they did, the two of them wouldn't be the biggest attraction—the club would.

Reinsdorf also told Kay that Caray felt that "Jimmy was getting too big" and that on four different occasions told Reinsdorf, "You have to get rid of Jimmy. He's crazy." Regarding Caray and Piersall's broadcasting style, Reinsdorf said, "Harry was never asked to be a house man. He was just asked not to tear down. He didn't like it, and he left. We tried to do the same thing with Piersall. In his first broadcast this year, he breached the promise. So we had to move him out."[4]

Reinsdorf wasn't done. During a postgame interview with Ken Harrelson in the White Sox clubhouse after the division-clinching victory, Reinsdorf said, "Wherever you're at, Harry and Jimmy, eat your hearts out. I hope people realize what scum you are."[5] A day later, Reinsdorf said he regretted using the word "scum," but added, "I don't regret the feeling I had behind the word. I stand by my feeling. The word I used wasn't very gentlemanly. I regret it. But it felt good to say it."[6] Sox manager Tony La Russa supported Reinsdorf, saying he didn't understand why Caray and Piersall "would be upset because Jerry Reinsdorf called them scum. I heard them say many times that their job was to tell it like it is. So why can't they accept someone else's opinion about them?"[7]

While things were rosy for the White Sox on the ball field and at the box office in 1983, SportsVision continued to struggle to add fans to its pay-TV service. The *Chicago Tribune* reported that SportsVision finished the season with approximately 25,000 pay-TV subscribers, 13,000 cable subscribers, and 1,300 subscriptions from bars and restaurants. That was far below Eddie Einhorn's 50,000-subscriber target, and the service was said to be losing $300,000 per month. The unavailability of cable in Chicago was cited as one reason the subscriber base was low; another was the easy availability of pirate decoder boxes. Einhorn said there were four or five pirate boxes in operation for every legitimate box.

In late November, Einhorn worked out a new plan that not only cut his losses, but also left him and the White Sox with a profit. He sold the rights to the games that had been broadcast on SportsVision to the ON TV movie/entertainment subscription service for $4 million a year, got another $4 million-plus for the channel's cable TV rights from Sports Channel, and received a minimum of $1.5 million from UHF channel WFLD to broadcast at least 30 Sox games per year on "free" TV. The deals transformed SportsVision "from a $300,000-per-month-loser into a substantial moneymaker," wrote Skip Myslenski. "I've been vindicated," said Einhorn.[8]

"Think about it," said Chicago-area broadcaster Mike Leiderman, who spent eight months as a SportsVision anchor in 1983. Leiderman added,

> You had WGN giving away everything for free, and you had Sports-Vision, this new thing trying to break into a town that was a Cubs town. 1983 was the best year the Sox could have had; they won 99 games and the division, they were great, and they still couldn't make this thing go. Eddie knew it would take years, but he said they couldn't make it go, so they sold it off.[9]

Leiderman, among others, is dubious that it would have made much difference to the success of SportsVision had Caray signed on with the channel. Author Dan Helpingstine, however, noted that Caray didn't just leave the Sox and reject SportsVision; he went to work for the team's biggest rival. Caray's move to the Cubs, he felt, completely changed the dynamic between Chicago's two major-league teams.

> Not buying into the SportsVision concept for a variety of reasons, Caray left the White Sox. But he didn't just leave. He went to the North Side and took his common-man approach with him. Instead of helping the Sox sell a new TV concept, Caray spent the next 15 years

selling Wrigley Field and everything connected to the Cubs. And for a good portion of that time, he did it on free TV.[10]

While the White Sox were basking in on-field glory in 1983, the Cubs continued to stumble along, losing 91 games—two more than in 1982—and finishing fifth in the six-team National League East. It was the fifth-straight year that the North Siders had ended the season in either fifth or sixth (last) place. At times, the Cubs became the butt of jokes. After a loss to the Dodgers at Wrigley Field on April 29, Cubs manager Lee Elia went into an expletive-loaded rant against the fans who had booed his team, saying (among other things), "About 85 percent of the world is working. The other 15 percent come out here."[11] The rant, which was recorded by a Chicago radio reporter, became an underground classic that can still be heard on the internet.

In May, Caray found himself responding to criticism in a Chicago magazine that he had become a "house man" for the Cubs who was intimidated by general manager Dallas Green. "Dallas Green never once mentioned what I should or should not say on the air," said Caray. "It happens that I admire and respect Dallas Green. Does that make me a house man?"[12] Caray could be critical of Cubs players—Steve Stone mentioned Keith Moreland and Dick Ruthven as Caray targets, and there were some nasty words, in 1986, between Harry and Cubs pitcher George Frazier. Jim Frey, who managed the Cubs from 1984 to 1986, and later served as the team's general manager, described Caray as a "guy who could aggravate a manager. He was just like millions of other fans who could criticize or second-guess."[13]

Yet, many people felt that—especially compared with his White Sox years—Caray had toned down the amount of criticism he directed at his team. "With the Cubs, Harry completely turned," said Ron Rapoport, who was a reporter with the *Chicago Sun-Times* during this period. "The days of ripping the Cardinals (especially Ken Boyer) and the White Sox (Bill Melton) were over. He became a cheerleader; he was very favorable to everything."[14] Cubs executive Mark McGuire, who was with the team throughout Caray's Cubs tenure, agreed that Caray "modified his act," while continuing to be critical of the players and team personnel from time to time.[15] Former Cubs executive Ned Colletti also felt Caray lowered his level of criticism toward players and management during his years with the Cubs, but he added that Caray's past reputation encouraged the players to stay on Harry's good side.

> I think everyone was aware of his relationships with the Sox, and players walked a little softly around him. I can remember some players who would say, "I'm never crossing that guy. I don't ever want him on the wrong side of *my* performance." There was always the potential for issues, but I think by then that Harry had toned down the harsh criticism that he could level. And I think the players knew they needed to be on their toes to keep peace with him.[16]

One person not on Caray's good side was fellow broadcaster Milo Hamilton. Unlike their first season, Caray and Hamilton were no longer working together directly in 1983, but the tension between them continued. "Harry and Milo would cross on the ramp going from radio to TV at Wrigley Field and never acknowledge each other. It was terrible," said Bob Verdi.[17] Dan Schlossberg, one of the coauthors of Hamilton's autobiography, *Making Airwaves*, said in an interview, "Milo would stand and turn his back when Harry was leading the crowd in 'Take Me Out to the Ball Game' during the seventh-inning stretch. He thought it was rather disgraceful, and unprofessional."[18]

While the Caray–Hamilton relationship was tense, Caray's relationship with his new television partner, Steve Stone, was harmonic. As a player, Stone told *Chicago Tribune* writer Skip Myslenski,

> You've been there, and you can offer the insight that experience provides. . . . I have a very dry sense of humor, and I use it, but I'm an analyst, and I don't think you want two Harrys in the booth. I think it's nice Harry wears his Budweiser red jacket and I wear a tie, that Harry sings and screams and tells stories, and I just analyze. The Smith Brothers were good on cough drops, but I don't think they'd be good on the air.[19]

❄ ❄ ❄

If Caray did indeed tone down his criticism while working for the Cubs, he had a good reason to do so in 1984: With a roster that included National League Most Valuable Player Ryne Sandberg, National League Cy Young Award winner Rick Sutcliffe, and a mixture of solid veterans and improving young players, the Cubs caught fire and won the National League East. It was the first postseason appearance for the team since 1945. The Cubs stumbled in the National League Championship Series against the San Diego Padres, losing the best-of-five series after winning the first two games, but it was still a memorable year. When the Cubs clinched the National League East title with a 4–1 victory in Pittsburgh on September 24, Kevin Klose wrote in the *Washington Post* that in the area near Wrigley Field, "Fans carrying radios multiplied the voice of Cubs announcer Harry Caray, sending it echoing through the street."[20]

Caray described the final pitch of the division-clinching win—a called strike three from Cubs pitcher Rick Sutcliffe to the Pirates' Joe Orsulak—to the audience throughout the nation watching on the WGN-TV superstation.

> Listen to this crowd! Might as well join 'em! (Sutcliffe throws final pitch) The Cubs are the champions! The Cubs are the champions! The Cubs win! Look at that mob scene! Orsulak out on strikes. Rick Sutcliffe his 13th in a row . . . 16–1 for the year. He faced only 28 men. He pitched a two-hitter. Let's just watch 'em! The fans are getting out on the field! You'd think there were 50,000 here![21]

For the year, the Cubs reached the 2 million mark in home attendance for the first time in club history, drawing 2,107,655 fans. Somewhat surprisingly, they were outdrawn by the White Sox, who, riding the crest of their 1983 division title, drew 2,136,988. It was the fifth-straight season that the Sox had a higher home attendance than the Cubs. But in terms of popularity in the city of Chicago, 1984 would prove to be something of a "last hurrah" for the White Sox. In the 34-season period from 1985 to 2018, the Cubs would outdraw the White Sox at home in all but two seasons: 1991–1992, when the White Sox enjoyed a brief honeymoon period in their first two seasons in the new Comiskey Park (now known as Guaranteed Rate Field).

If the Cubs in 1984 were on their way to becoming the dominant team in Chicago, they were also experiencing a surge in national popularity thanks to the WGN-TV superstation—and Harry Caray. "The Cubs already had an almost-nationwide fanbase because of WGN Radio," said Chicago broadcaster Al Lerner. Continued Lerner,

I heard countless stories from Cub fans who made the pilgrimage to Wrigley Field because they listened from places like Denver and Nebraska and the Dakotas, which 50,000-watt WGN could reach. When they went to the superstation, the Cubs became a true national team. Harry became their national face, a national superstar. He carried the Cubs on his back. Their merchandizing probably increased 10 or 20 times.[22]

In June 1984, Caray was the subject of a long feature in the *Boston Globe* by Ian Thomsen entitled, "The Master's Voice: Harry Caray's Whiskey Baritone Is the Sound of Chicago Baseball." The article chronicled a day with Caray broadcasting from the Wrigley Field bleachers in front of his adoring fans, a tradition that had worked well with the White Sox. Thomsen wrote of Caray chugging a beer for his fans ("'How can they make it taste so good,' he enthused, 'and sell it so cheap?'"); singing a parody of the Disney "Davy Crockett" theme in tribute to Cubs catcher Jody Davis ("Jody, Jody Davis, catcher that knows no fear"); and waving his trusty butterfly net, which he used for catching foul balls (from the broadcast booth) or home run balls (from the bleachers). Thomsen also wrote that superstation WGN-TV was now reaching 16,483,970 homes.[23] Caray had truly become a national superstar. (Two days after the fawning Caray article, the *Globe* ran a piece by Bob Ryan entitled "Einhorn's Minor Folly," in which he wrote the following of the White Sox vice chairman: "In the eyes of Eddie Einhorn, the White Sox are naught but a vehicle for [cable] television programming.")[24]

The nationwide reach of the WGN superstation—and the strong passions Caray's work aroused—could be seen in the "Voice of the Fan" section of baseball's national newspaper, *Sporting News*, in 1984.

- May 28: A fan from Cedar Rapids, Iowa, nominated Caray for the National Baseball Hall of Fame's Ford C. Frick Award.
- June 18: A fan from Scottsdale, Arizona, ridiculed the idea of Caray for Cooperstown, saying, "To put Harry Caray in the same class as Vin Scully or Red Barber is nonsense."
- August 6: A fan from Darien, Illinois, "cannot understand why fans of the Cubs criticize Harry Caray. He's the best acquisition Dallas Green has made."

- September 10: A fan from Sarasota, Florida, wrote of Caray, "I have never experienced a more obnoxious individual on the airwaves."
- September 17: A fan from Mount Prospect, Illinois, listed some of the "favorite baseball clichés" from the mouths of Caray, Steve Stone, and Milo Hamilton.
- October 15: A female fan from Johnson City, Tennessee, wrote, "Harry Caray singing 'Take Me Out to the Ball Game' does an old lady like me more good than a bottle of Geritol."
- November 26: A fan from Akron, Iowa, expressed disappointment concerning the dismissal of Milo Hamilton, writing, "Harry Caray gives me a big pain."

A fan from Winchester, Kansas—famed baseball writer Bill James—wrote in the *1985 Bill James Baseball Abstract* about rediscovering Caray via the arrival of cable television to the "distant Balkan outland that I call home." The fact that Caray—unlike broadcasters based in New York or California, like Mel Allen and Vin Scully—had not been honored by the Hall of Fame, wrote James, was "almost comically ignorant," "personally offensive," and "beyond any question, an egregious example of the regional bias of the nation's media. But besides that," James continued, "the man is *really* good. His unflagging enthusiasm, his love of the game, and his intense focus and involvement in every detail of the contest make every inning enjoyable, no matter what the score or the pace of the game."[25]

※ ※ ※

In November 1984, the Cubs dismissed Milo Hamilton from their broadcasting crew. "The reason they gave was because of differences, quote, between Milo and Harry, unquote," said Hamilton. "This came as a shock and out of the blue. I was totally happy with my job and there were no indications during the season." Caray denied any responsibility for the move. "If there were any differences, Milo created them," said Caray. "People who know the situation know I leaned over backwards to try and be nice. . . . Milo's a fine announcer, and I'm sorry to see him go. But I don't want to be the fall guy."[26]

Hamilton would have none of that. In his autobiography, he wrote that the dismissal by WGN was the third time Caray had cost him a job.

> Caray resented the fact that I had a decent following among Cub fans. . . . Some would come over and tell me how much they enjoyed my work, and how they would watch the game on TV but turn the volume down on their television and listen to the radio broadcast. Caray would be within earshot, and the "Canary" only had to hear that once or twice and he was ticked.[27]

In a magazine article in September 1985, Hamilton said, "I don't have any respect for him or the way he goes about his business. . . . I don't like his singing—if it's so great, why doesn't anyone else do it? . . . He's a self-promoter. His line is how much he loves the game and the fans, but the bottom line is that he's promoting Harry Caray."[28]

Hamilton landed on his feet. Taking his place with the Cubs was Dewayne Staats, who had spent the previous eight years broadcasting for the Houston Astros. With the help of Cubs general manager Dallas Green, who Milo claimed never wanted him to leave Chicago, Hamilton wound up going to Houston to replace Staats. Hamilton became a fixture with the Astros and continued to broadcast for them until his death in September 2015, at age 88.

✷ ✷ ✷

In January 1985, Ted Turner and WTBS agreed to make annual payments to other major-league clubs in exchange for permission to continue beaming Atlanta Braves games into their broadcast areas. Other teams whose games could be seen nationally via superstations (Texas Rangers, New York Yankees, and New York Mets) followed suit. In May, WGN-TV, the final holdout, signed a similar agreement covering the 1985–1989 seasons.

The 1985 Cubs started the season strongly and led the National League East in mid-June, but the club faded and wound up fourth in the division with a 77–84 record. At one point the team lost 13 straight games. Nonetheless, the club set a new home attendance record with 2,161,534 fans and outdrew the White Sox (1,669,888), who had posted a winning record (85–77), by almost a half-million. When the Cubs had another lackluster season in 1986 (70–90 record, fifth in the division),

Cubs home attendance still totaled 1,859,102 and topped the White Sox (1,424,313) by more than 400,000. From that point onward, except for the strike-shortened seasons of 1994–1995, the Cubs never again failed to draw at least 2 million fans to Wrigley Field. At the same time, White Sox home attendance was heading in the opposite direction. After setting a franchise record with a home attendance of 2.1 million in 1984, the Sox saw their attendance drop in each of the next five seasons, to 1,045,651 in 1989—less than half of what the Cubs were drawing the same year (2,491,942).

By now, Caray had become something akin to a rock star. "When Harry would show up in spring training [in Mesa, Arizona] on March 1," said WGN-TV director of production Bob Vorwald, who has worked on Cubs broadcasts since the 1980s, "he'd go over to old Fitch Park, and when his limo pulled up there'd be about a thousand people around his car, like Springsteen had just showed up. It was like watching the Pied Piper."[29] Rick Sutcliffe, who pitched for the Cubs from 1984 to 1991, and won the National League Cy Young Award in 1984, said, "There's no question that Harry Caray was more popular than any five players that we ever had. When he came on the field, you didn't have to see him. You knew he was in the area somewhere."[30]

In July 1986, Caray was a guest on *Late Night with David Letterman*—a show Harry admitted he had never seen—during a Cubs visit to New York. Fred Mitchell of the *Chicago Tribune* reported that "Caray was hugged and kissed backstage by female producers and stagehands after his 10-minute stint," and that Letterman "seemed genuinely enthralled with meeting Caray." Asked by Letterman if he had ever been "a little, you know, hung over" during a broadcast, Caray replied,

> Listen, David, you've never succeeded in this business until you've had the experience of working with a terrible hangover. Not until then, when you've been able to come through with flying colors under those circumstances, can you consider yourself a professional. And Lord knows I've had more than my share of hangovers. But I've never missed a day, folks. Never missed a night, either.

After the show, Letterman said, "The man is truly amazing. He's a walking billboard . . . for what, I don't really know."[31]

The 1986 season was not without some moments of controversy for Caray. In July, after the Cubs traded relief pitcher George Frazier to the Minnesota Twins, Frazier said Cubs players paid more attention to what Caray was saying on television than to general manager Dallas Green "because Harry is bigger. He has a bigger influence on the fans." Caray shot back, declaring,

> How did he last two years as one of the most inept major-league pitchers we have ever seen in Wrigley Field? If what he says is true . . . then that's disgraceful. These guys are being paid to play baseball. You mean to tell me that guys are sitting in the clubhouse, watching television. I hope that Frazier lied about it. Because otherwise, it's a bad reflection on the ball club.[32]

After his battle of words with Caray, Frazier would go on to pitch in the 1987 World Series for the champion Twins before retiring as a player. Frazier then embarked on a new career: He became a baseball broadcaster, primarily with the Colorado Rockies, before retiring in 2015.

19

STROKE AND RECOVERY

A cabbie honked, a guy trimming a tree yelled from above, a lady came out from behind her grocery store counter to the sidewalk with a handful of tomatoes, and a group of college students screeched to a giddy halt, forgetting for the moment that they were on a walking tour of Chicago's architecture.

Here was an original piece of work, after all, heading for lunch along State Street on a shiny day: Harry Caray in the flesh, though 41 pounds less of it. The voice of summer had returned, after a brief stint on the involuntary disabled list, and come Tuesday at Wrigley Field, Cubs vs. Cincinnati, it will be baseball as usual again. Your regular programming will be resumed after some technical difficulties. Man's back where he belongs, on the air.—Bob Verdi, *Chicago Tribune*, May 1987[1]

In February 1987, Harry Caray was in Palm Springs, California, where he and his wife Dutchie had a winter home. On the afternoon of February 17, Caray was playing gin rummy at the Canyon Country Club when he noticed that he was having trouble picking up his cards with his right hand. He felt no pain, but his companions could see that something was wrong and thought he might be having a stroke. They wanted to take him to the hospital, but Caray said he wanted to go home, and one of his friends drove him there.

"When they brought him through the door, my first reaction was that maybe he had been in an automobile accident," said Dutchie. "I realized something was wrong." One of Caray's friends had called 911, and paramedics arrived and took Caray to Desert Hospital. He had indeed suffered a stroke. "You know Harry, he wants to get out of the hospital right now," said Mrs. Caray, but Harry wound up spending several weeks in the hospital.[2] "I feel terrible," he admitted to Bob Verdi on February 28. "I gotta get out of here." Verdi recalled that Caray's hospital room was jammed with letters and gifts from fans: "It looked like a U.S. Post Office. Boxes and boxes of mail and packages."[3]

Caray returned to his Palm Springs home in March, with his doctor telling him to moderate his lifestyle and lose 40 pounds. Caray, who had never missed an inning of work in his major-league broadcasting career, hoped at first to be able to broadcast Cubs spring training games, but that proved unrealistic, as did being ready for Opening Day in April. "Every spring we played the Angels a game or two in Palm Springs, and I made arrangements to stop by his house the morning of one of our games," recalled former Cubs executive Ned Colletti. "At that point he still had a lot of recovery to go. I didn't know if I'd ever see him in a broadcast booth again."[4]

"The first few days, when I looked at my right arm, my right leg, the inability to talk . . . it was frightening," Caray recalled several months after the stroke. "I just don't know what a stroke is. . . . I never recognized the word, and suddenly, you find out you've been a victim. . . . I had plenty of doubts [about recovering] in the first few weeks when I was really down in the dumps." Ultimately, he lost 41 pounds. "[I'm] staying away from things we know are bad. No bread, no butter, no sweets," said Caray. "Only a couple of drinks a night rather than 50 or 60. . . . Did we ever count 'em?"[5]

As is often the case with stroke victims, Caray's speech was affected, and voice therapy was part of his recovery process. "Want to know what I did in voice therapy class?" he said. "Pa, pa, pa, pa, pa. Ta, ta, ta, ta, ta. La, la, la, la, la. Ka, ka, ka, ka, ka." He also practiced broadcasting games from home.[6] "He was a strong-willed guy, and he was determined to get back into it," recalled Dutchie. "When he was recovering in Palm Springs, the Cubs sent him tapes of their games, and he would go through them and broadcast the games as he was watching them on television. He did very well with that."[7]

The Cubs scheduled Caray's return for the start of a homestand on Tuesday, May 19, against the Cincinnati Reds. In the meantime, they used guest broadcasters to fill in for Harry. The list of 32 substitutes for

Caray included name broadcasters like Brent Musburger, Bob Costas, Dick Enberg, and Jack Buck, and such celebrities as George Wendt, Jim Belushi, Dennis Franz, and—most memorably—Bill Murray ("He skies it. Jody . . . it's all you. Ahhh. My favorite. The popup to the catcher. You've missed this kind of excitement all day.")[8]

On the day of his return, Caray was honored in a pregame ceremony featuring Illinois governor James R. Thompson, who proclaimed it Harry Caray Day. Caray admitted he was nervous and wondered if he would be able to remember the words to "Take Me Out to the Ball Game." He didn't realize that WGN director Arne Harris had spent much of the morning on the phone with the White House. President Ronald Reagan, a former baseball broadcaster who did re-creations of Cubs games in the 1930s, wanted to call Caray during the broadcast to welcome him back.

When the call came through during the early stages of the game, WGN viewers heard the president's familiar voice saying, "Harry, this is Ronald Reagan." Caray, who was shocked to receive the call, said, "Well, Mr. President. What a pleasant surprise." The two chatted for a few minutes, with Reagan reminding Caray that he had broadcast a lot of Cubs games himself in his younger days, and saying, "It wasn't the same without the real voice of the Chicago Cubs." Caray was obviously moved by the call ("I can't get over it," he told the president).[9] Later, when he began to sing "Take Me Out to the Ball Game" during the seventh-inning stretch, the screams of the crowd nearly drowned out his voice.

After his emotional return, Caray resumed his normal broadcast schedule, working six innings on television and three on the radio. He insisted on working road, as well as home, games. At Caray's request, the Tribune Company agreed to provide him with limousine service when he was on the road—an expense that cost the company about $50,000. "The whole idea was that he wouldn't have to wait for the team bus to go to or from the ballpark," recalled Verdi. "He could leave the booth after the game, and the limo would be waiting to take him back to the hotel so that he could get his eight hours of sleep. The problem was Harry didn't go back to the hotel. I don't want to say that the Tribune wasted 50 grand, but the idea of Harry getting his eight hours sleep didn't quite work out the way they planned it."[10]

Another concession to Caray's recovery was for Dutchie to accompany him on road trips, along with veteran WGN-TV executive Jack Rosenberg. That idea didn't work out as planned, either. "For a little while, Dutchie came with him and tried to manage his postgame meals and nightlife activity," said Ned Colletti. "I think she lasted a trip or two before she bailed out and said, 'I hope he's going to be okay because I can't keep the pace.' Right then and there you knew he was feeling better."[11] (When I asked Mrs. Caray how she kept up with Harry's nightlife, she laughed and said, "I just couldn't do it.")[12]

* * *

On the field, the 1987 season was a long one for Chicago's baseball teams: The White Sox finished fifth in the seven-team American League West with a 77–85 record, while the Cubs were dead last in the National League East with a 76–85 mark. But the teams made plenty of news off the field. On the South Side, the White Sox were beginning a battle for public funding to replace Comiskey Park; the Sox threatened to move to suburban Addison, and then leave town completely, before the state of Illinois finally came through with last-minute funding for a stadium plan in July 1988. Meanwhile, the Cubs—since 1946 the only major-league team without lights to play night games—were pushing the city of Chicago for permission to install lights and play 18 night games per year. Like the White Sox, the Cubs' battle included a threat to abandon Wrigley Field and move to the suburbs.

Caray, a traditionalist, was dead set against installing lights at Wrigley Field. "Night baseball will be the absolute ruination [of the Cubs]," said Caray. He continued,

> These people cannot walk here at night. The won't ride the El at night, like they do in the daytime. There's no place to park. You know what has made the Cubs franchise—generation after generation. When you're little, your mother puts you on the El to come to the park. You won't be able to do that at night. I hope they never have night baseball.[13]

Caray was not alone in his sentiments, and there was strong opposition to the Cubs' plan—particularly from property owners in the Wrigleyville area. But ultimately, the Chicago City Council capitulated, voting

29–19 in February 1988, to permit the Cubs to install lights and play their first night game late in the 1988 season.

By the time the 1988 season opened, Caray had become an entrepreneur. In October 1987, Harry Caray's Italian Steakhouse, a 175-seat restaurant with two private dining rooms, opened for business in Chicago's River North area. At the time, a number of Chicago sports celebrities were operating or lending their names to restaurants or bars, including Chicago Bears coach Mike Ditka and Bears players Walter Payton, Jim McMahon, and Gary Fencik. Caray himself had no ownership interest in the restaurant, but he was paid for lending his name and helping to promote the business. He ate and entertained people regularly at the restaurant, helping ensure its success. This was considered a high-risk business, but Harry Caray's, which earned a three-star review from *Chicago Tribune* restaurant critic Paul A. Camp, was still thriving in 2018, with seven different Harry Caray's restaurants operating in the Chicago area.

In March 1988, Vess Beverage, Inc., of St. Louis, announced the marketing of a new beverage called Holy Cow, with Caray's face and facsimile autograph on the packaging. It came in five flavors: cola, orange, lemon-lime, root beer, and cream, plus a diet version. Caray himself had input into the ingredients of the drinks, which contained no sodium or caffeine. The drink was introduced at Caray's restaurant, with a cow brought in from a suburban farm as part of the ceremony ("That cow looks like me a few years ago when I had 41 more pounds," said Harry).[14] Chicago radio-TV personality Al Lerner, who was host for the event, recalled, "They brought out the cow with a halo on top of it, and Harry was supposed to walk down the aisle leading it. He wouldn't do it . . . he was deathly afraid of cows! I had to stand next to the cow instead of Harry, which ruined the publicity pictures. The soda failed miserably."[15]

☼ ☼ ☼

"I feel great," said Caray in the spring of 1988. "I'm down 41 pounds, and I'm keeping it off—kept it off for a whole year. We all know what causes stroke: weight and high blood pressure."[16] For the Cubs, 1988 was another disappointing season on the field: a 77–85 record and a fourth-place finish in the National League East. But the team had added such young stars as Greg Maddux, Mark Grace, Shawon Dunston, and Rafael Palmeiro, and for the first time in several years, there was genuine optimism about the future. The biggest news for the team during the season was the first night game at Wrigley Field, against the Philadelphia Phillies on August 8. The light switch was thrown by 91-year-old Harry Grossman, who had been a Cubs season ticket holder for 83 years. The Chicago Symphony Orchestra played pregame music and then the National Anthem, with the first pitch thrown out by former Cubs greats Ernie Banks and Billy Williams. Fans unable to get tickets could watch the game on a giant television screen set up in the Petrillo Band Shell in Chicago's Grant Park downtown.

Unfortunately, it began to rain torrentially in the fourth inning, and play was stopped and could not be resumed. The official first night game at Wrigley Field took place the following night, August 9, with much less fanfare. Caray, the traditionalist who was dead set against lights at Wrigley, didn't see what all the fuss was about. "I don't know why it's history," he said. "We've had night baseball for a long time." He still insisted that day baseball, not Harry Caray, was the secret to the Cubs' nationwide popularity. The reason the Cubs were so big, he said, "is that they're the only team playing day baseball. At night, everyone's on TV, so not many fans are going to be able to see the Cubs. They're watching their own team."[17]

On a personal level, a source of frustration for Caray in 1988 was his continued failure to receive the National Baseball Hall of Fame's Ford C. Frick Award. The award, presented annually to a broadcaster for "major contributions to baseball" and named after the late broadcaster, National League president, commissioner, and Hall of Famer, has been presented annually since 1978. A separate award for writers, the J. G. Taylor Spink Award, has been presented annually since 1962. To be clear, the winners of these awards are *not* Hall of Famers, nor are there "Writers and Broadcastings Wings" in the Hall of Fame. As Hall of Fame president Jeff Idelson put it, "We continue to remind the winners that they are award recipients and not Hall of Fame members. . . . Our museum does not have wings"; however, Bill Deane, who was senior research associate for the Hall from 1986 to 1994, said, "It is fair to say that winning the Spink or Frick award is as near to Baseball Hall of Fame election that a writer or broadcaster can get."[18]

The first two winners of the Frick Award in 1978 were broadcasting icons Mel Allen and Red Barber, best known for their work with the New York Yankees and Brooklyn Dodgers, respectively. In 1979, the award went to Chicago's Bob Elson, voice of the White Sox for several decades. Then came Russ Hodges, Ernie Harwell, Vin Scully, Jack Brickhouse, Curt Gowdy, and Buck Canel, all basically contemporaries of Caray, as were Bob Prince (1986), Jack Buck (1987), and Lindsay Nelson (1988). By this time, it was more than fair to ask: Why hasn't Caray won the award?

"I was personally embarrassed when I got mine before Harry," said Jack Buck, who had worked with Caray for 14 years before succeeding him as the main voice of the St. Louis Cardinals in July 1970. "Not many people compare to Harry. He was the first in the business to tell it like it is. That might have hurt him. Harry makes friends his own way." Ernie Harwell said, "The real criteria is supposed to be contribution to baseball, and Harry's certainly done that." Jack Brickhouse agreed that Caray was deserving of the award, saying, "I don't know what the qualifications are, but Harry belongs there in spades." Caray himself, mindful of the fact that the Hall had not honored Bob Prince with the Frick Award until after Prince's death, said, "I've told my son Skip if they put me in after I'm gone to nicely turn it down. If my peers don't want me in the Hall of Fame, it's fine with me. Obviously, I must have stepped on somebody's toes."[19]

As was often the case with Caray, his worthiness for the Frick Award, and even his merits as a broadcaster, were the subjects of debate in 1988, with fans and writers expressing their opinions in the local and national sports media:

- May 23: A fan from Cedar Rapids, Iowa, wrote *Sporting News*, nominating Caray for the "broadcasters' wing [*sic*] of the Baseball Hall of Fame."
- June 20: A fan from Seguin, Texas, disagreed, writing *Sporting News* that, "Caray does not belong, and any effort to induct him is a grave reflection upon those who deserve to be there and those who already have been enshrined."
- August 1: *Chicago Tribune* TV-radio sports critic Steve Nidetz, while espousing Caray's qualifications for the Frick Award, wrote that Harry "has obviously stayed too long in the booth, plugged

too many restaurants, mispronounced too many names, missed too many plays. He has become an annoying, unfunny parody of himself who detracts from the games he broadcasts."

- August 11: A fan from Chicago defended Caray in response to Nidetz's column, writing, "Caray, even with the gaffes, still stands head and shoulders above all play-by-play sports announcers, and I go back to the days of Bob Elson." The fan described Caray's play-by-play work as "truly a work of art."
- August 15: A fan from Chicago wrote the *Tribune*, saying, "One reason [Caray hasn't won the Frick Award] may be his constant reading of names of people at the ballpark. While he may be satisfying the egos of a few hundred fans, he is also annoying a million others."
- August 15: A fan from Corpus Christi, Texas, wrote *Sporting News*, saying, "Harry Caray mispronounces names, loses interest in the game when his team is losing, says hello to everybody in the Free World while missing the action on field, plugs his restaurant in Arizona, and clears his throat between words." In the same *Sporting News* issue, a fan from Lawrenceville, Virginia, wrote, "Eventually, Harry Caray of the Cubs and son Skip Caray of the Braves will be the first father–son combination in the broadcasters' wing of the Hall of Fame. And rightfully so."
- September 5: A fan from Glendale, Arizona, wrote *Sporting News*, saying, "A Baseball Hall of Fame without room for one-of-a-kind guys like Bill Veeck, Charley Grimm, and Harry Caray must be an awfully dreary place."
- October 17: A fan from Hoffman Estates, Illinois, responded to the previous letter writer that neither Veeck, Grimm, nor Caray "belongs in Cooperstown. I see Veeck in the Barnum & Bailey Hall of Fame, Grimm in the Inept Managers Hall of Fame, and Caray in the Beer Salesmen's Hall of Fame."[20]

Caray did have at least one friend in a high place. On September 30, President Ronald Reagan, who was in Chicago to campaign for Vice President George H. W. Bush's presidential bid, found time to ride over to Wrigley Field, throw out the first pitch for that day's Cubs–Pittsburgh Pirates game ("high and outside," according to Caray), and then join Harry in the broadcast booth for a little play-by-play.

"You know, I'm going to be out of work in a few months," Reagan said. "I just dropped by for an audition." The onetime baseball broadcaster recounted to Caray the time in the 1930s when, while recreating a Cubs game from a telegraph transmission for an Iowa radio station, he made up an entire segment of the game when the wire stopped functioning. At one point during his play-by-play stint, Reagan said, "It's wide and inside for ball two"; Caray corrected him that the pitch was actually a strike. During a lull in the action, Reagan looked over at Caray and said, "I want to know about your suspenders." Caray responded by reaching over to open the president's coat to check out *Reagan's* suspenders, only to discover that Reagan was wearing a belt. "Fortunately," wrote the *Washington Post*, "no Secret Service men grabbed Caray and wrestled him to the floor."[21]

On November 8, Vice President George Bush was elected to succeed Reagan and become the 41st president of the United States. A little less than three months later, on January 27, 1989, Reagan's friend Harry Caray received his own election news: Ed Stack, president of the National Baseball Hall of Fame, announced that Caray was the 1989 recipient of the Hall's Ford C. Frick Award—a unanimous selection by the 11-man committee. "He sailed right through," said committee member Ernie Harwell.

"I'm very, very thrilled by it all. It's a great day for me," said Caray, who was in Atlantic City, New Jersey, to receive another honor: induction into the National Italian American Sports Hall of Fame. "For an orphan kid from the wrong side of the tracks in St. Louis, this is a great moment. I only wish my father and mother could be here to witness this," he told Bob Verdi, "for they might be proud. I never knew who they were, and still don't, but that's life."[22]

20

THE MAYOR OF RUSH STREET

This is *not* why the people love Harry Caray:

"The way I do a game is the way the average fan would do a game if they could be behind a microphone."

Wrong.

If the average fan got behind the microphone he would never do a game like Harry Caray. What's the fun in that? No, the average fan would do a game like Vin Scully.

Of course, he would fail miserably. Not even an experienced announcer such as Caray, who is 72 [actually 75] and has been in broadcasting for 45 years, can sound like Scully.

"I can't say something lyrical about a popup," Caray said. "I don't know any big words. I just say, 'Popped it up.'"

Nothing to it. Except don't forget the proper tone of disgust if it's your guy who pops it up. Caray never does.—Bill Modoono, *Pittsburgh Press*, September 1989[1]

The year 1989 was a memorable one for the Chicago Cubs. The Cubs, who had endured four-straight losing seasons since winning the National League East in 1984, came together under manager Don Zimmer and won the division title with 93 victories. The Cubs' roster included future Hall of Famers Greg Maddux, Ryne Sandberg, and Andre Dawson; longtime stars Mark Grace, Rick Sutcliffe, and Shawon Dunston; and rookies Jerome Walton and Dwight Smith, who finished one–two in the National League Rookie of the Year voting. The first full season of night baseball at Wrigley Field was a hit with the fans; the Cubs' home attendance was a franchise-record (later broken) 2,491,942. As in 1984, however, the Cubs failed to reach the World Series, falling to the San Francisco Giants in the National League Championship Series, four games to one.

The year was memorable for Harry Caray as well, starting with the January announcement that he was the 1989 winner of the Hall of Fame's Ford C. Frick Award. In March, Caray's autobiography—*Holy Cow!*—written in collaboration with Chicago sportswriter Bob Verdi, was published. Reviews were mixed, with the most common criticism being that the book lacked the take-no-prisoners honesty that was the trademark of Caray's broadcast work. Novelist William Brashler (*The Bingo Long Traveling All-Stars and Motor Kings*), who reviewed the book for the *Chicago Tribune*—Verdi's paper—wrote,

> If Harry's name weren't on the cover, you would have thought this one had been done by Milo Hamilton, the beige former Cub announcer whom Harry loathed and bounced a few years back but who gets nary a mention in this book. "Holy Cow!" is gloss, a nostalgic sacrifice bunt, a barstool yarn that is to memoirs what beef jerky is to sirloin.[2]

Don McLeese of the *Chicago Sun-Times* wrote, "The contradictions in Caray's larger-than-life persona are part of what makes him such a provocative character. But this book barely addresses these contradictions, and Caray himself might not even acknowledge them."[3]

Paul Lomartire, who reviewed the book for the *Palm Beach (Florida) Post*, wrote that the book "will sell, sell, sell," and thought it worth reading. "But Chicago Cubs and Harry Caray fans will be left to wonder what really makes Harry Caray so unique," he concluded. Lomartire felt that the choice of Caray's collaborator made an important difference in the tone of the book. He wrote that *Holy Cow!* originally had been scheduled for publication a year earlier, in collaboration with David Israel, a former sportswriter "who had a meteoric career based on a reputation for being aggressive and vitriolic. The publisher says Israel's schedule prevented the project from being completed. Publishing competitors say Caray and Israel learned to hate each other."[4] I interviewed both Verdi and Israel in the course of researching this book; while Israel declined to talk about his involvement with *Holy Cow!*, he did not have much good to say about Caray. "Harry was popular because he acted goony," Israel told me. "That was the beginning of era of the goon comedy in Hollywood. There was 'Bachelor Party' . . . 'Porky's' . . . Harry. Harry was the 'Porky's' of baseball announcers." Israel, who was born in 1951, said,

> To me, Harry seemed a lot better at his job when I was in my early 20s than he did in the years since then . . . especially since I worked in television for a long time and realized what professionalism is. He was, in retrospect, selling all the wrong things. Yes, you can't beat fun at the old ballpark, but basically he was selling beer 24/7.[5]

Despite the lukewarm reviews, *Holy Cow!* was successful in the marketplace, at least in the Chicago area. In April, the *Chicago Tribune* listed it as the number-10 best seller in Chicago among nonfiction books (number nine was *Leadership Secrets of Atilla the Hun,* by Wess Roberts).

❁ ❁ ❁

On Sunday, July 23, 1989, Johnny Bench, Red Schoendienst, Carl Yastrzemski, and umpire Al Barlick were formally inducted into the Baseball Hall of Fame in Cooperstown, New York. Until 2011, the Ford C. Frick and J. G. Taylor Spink (writers) award honorees were also presented at the induction ceremonies, with the winners of those awards giving acceptance speeches along with the Hall of Famers, although—as previously noted—they were technically not being inducted into the Hall. (As Bill Deane, former research associate for the Hall of Fame, wrote, "This no doubt accounts for most of the misconception in this matter.")[6] But if Caray wasn't formally being inducted into the Hall of Fame on this day, it was hard to tell the difference.

Caray was warmly received by a crowd estimated to be about 8,000 as he accepted the Frick Award. "I've really wondered what I would say today," Caray said after acknowledging the applause. "Many people have said I would be affected by the emotion of the moment. And I am. You can't possibly stand here and not feel the presence of the legendary figures who have been here before. The more I think of all the history which surrounds me, the more inadequate I feel." He paid tribute to the fans, saying, "I think of the fans, and perhaps that's who I represent today. We are all fans, and I know it's the fans who are responsible for my being here. They are the unsung heroes." Jerome Holtzman of the

Chicago Tribune—winner of the Hall of Fame's J. G. Taylor Spink Award in 1989—wrote that when Caray arrived at the ceremony, "[he] was immediately surrounded by what became a constant procession of autograph seekers," and that Harry was "certainly as big an attraction as players Johnny Bench, Carl Yastrzemski, and Red Schoendienst, and umpire Al Barlick, the other Hall of Fame inductees [*sic*]."[7]

⁕ ⁕ ⁕

Three days after the Hall of Fame ceremonies, *Chicago Sun-Times* writer Terry Boers offered "congratulations to Harry Caray on his enshrinement into the Baseball Hall of Fame"—and then turned his focus in a different direction.

> At the risk of sounding too cold, let me add—and this comes with all due respect—that the time has come for Caray to grab his gold watch and call it a career.
>
> Why?
>
> Because he has turned just about every Cubs game into a comedy of bloopers that's lowlighted by repeated mispronunciation of visiting players' names, misidentification of Cub players (How many times early this season did he refer to Andre Dawson as Andre Rodgers?), and his incessant slobbering over the Cubs.

Boers wondered "what happened to that terrible swift sword Caray used to wield so wonderfully during his days with the White Sox, when he was paired with Jimmy Piersall, who, love him or hate him, always says what's on his mind." He added,

> I always had thought Caray's total loss of that hard edge was simply a case of mellowing with age, but I got the real answer the other day when I saw where Caray and Jim Dowdle, the president of Tribune Broadcasting Co., have an understanding. In essence, their little deal seems to be that Caray can say what he thinks—as long as it doesn't too badly offend any of the precious Cubbies.[8]

Boers certainly was not alone in commenting that, after moving crosstown to work for the Cubs, Caray had dropped the "hard edge" that had often characterized his years broadcasting for the White Sox (see chapter 18). As for mispronouncing names and making gaffes on the air, that was always an issue with Caray to some degree. The problem became worse after his 1987 stroke and would increase as he got older. For the most part, however, Caray's fans seemed to accept the mistakes because he brought so much else to a broadcast.

In late 1989, for example, after *Sporting News* published a letter critical of Harry's award from the Hall of Fame, the paper reported that subsequent letters on the subject were running about three-to-one in defense of Caray. "Harry was lucky to get the names right, especially after the stroke," said Mike Leiderman. "But it was part of the charm. As a play-by-play guy, he just made the game so interesting and fascinating and fun."[9] For Caray to retire in 1989, with the WGN-TV superstation at its peak of popularity, the Cubs setting attendance records, and a division-winning team on the field, would have been pretty unthinkable.

* * *

With the 1989 season coming to a close and the Cubs hoping to finally win their first World Series since 1908 (something that would not happen until 2016), William Gildea of the *Washington Post* wrote of the excitement at Wrigley Field and its environs, where a "three-story-high painting of Harry Caray adorns a brick house on Addison Street." He continued,

> The Cubs are a much-loved team. While they have broken hearts over the decades and had a losing record 10 of the last 11 years, they nevertheless have added fans by the millions, because of cable television. Signs adorn Wrigley's neighborhood bars ("Good luck in the stretch drive"); the team lifts a city's psyche. But more, Caray's voice carries across America the story of love in the afternoon.[10]

There were two more highlights for Caray before 1989 came to a close. At a National Basketball Association game between the Atlanta Hawks and Orlando Magic on November 29, Caray joined his son Skip, the voice of the Atlanta Hawks, and his 24-year-old grandson Chip, who was in his first year of broadcasting games for the Magic. In New York, a month later, Harry was inducted into the American Sportscasters Hall of Fame—the third time he had been honored by a Hall of Fame during the year. During his brief acceptance speech, Caray said, "Remember, I'm only one of three generations [of one family] doing major-league sports—and I'm very proud of that."

Then came the highlight of the evening. "It was a sound you had to see to believe," Steve Nidetz wrote. "There, on the dais of the American Sportscasters Association Hall of Fame Dinner, were former Metropolitan Opera star Robert Merrill and Cubs broadcaster Harry Caray, belting out a duet of "Take Me Out to the Ball Game."

> "Whenever I go the ballpark and sing, 'Take Me Out to the Ball-game,' people shout, 'Hey, you're no Harry Caray,'" said Merrill. "My ambition has always been to sing [it] with Harry."
> And they did.
> And when they finished, it was Caray who got the last word.
> "Hey," said Caray to the baritone who has thrilled opera-lovers for years, "you can sing!"[11]

Caray began the 1990 season with some new broadcast partners. Dewayne Staats, who had broadcast on WGN television and radio since 1985, left to take a job broadcasting New York Yankees games for MSG. Staats, who grew up in the St. Louis area listening to Harry and Jack Buck on KMOX, spoke warmly of his experience with Caray.

> I had a great working relationship with Harry. When I went to Chicago, I recall the first spring in Arizona, Harry and I drove out together to Sun City to play the Brewers, and on the trip back, Harry said to me, "Listen, I'm not going to be your mentor . . . you've been around the big leagues long enough. But if you ever want to know anything about anybody, just ask me." I thought that was pretty gracious of him to make that offer and treat a young broadcaster coming in that way. From that first spring it was really a treat for me. There was never any conflict with him. He was just great to be around.[12]

Also moving on was former major-league infielder Dave Nelson, who had worked as an analyst for WGN radio in 1988–1989. Nelson, who according to *Chicago Tribune* TV-radio sports critic Steve Nidetz "never seemed as comfortable on the air as he was off," felt he had good chemistry working with Staats but said, "It was intimidating with Harry at first, because this guy's the legend and he's the man. I wouldn't say a lot [when working with Caray]. I found listening to tapes that I was very repetitive."[13]

Replacing Staats on his combination radio/television stint was Thom Brennaman, the 26-year-old son of Marty Brennaman, the Cincinnati Reds' longtime radio voice. Thom, who had been broadcasting Reds games on television with partner Johnny Bench, would spend six years in the Cubs' broadcast booth. The radio analyst role formerly held by Nelson went to former Cubs third baseman Ron Santo and ex-MLB catcher Bob Brenly, who formed a three-man booth with either Brennaman or Caray. Brenly spent two seasons with the Cubs before leaving to become a coach with the San Francisco Giants. Santo, a beloved player during his 14-year career with the Cubs, would become an equally beloved broadcaster who would continue in that role until his death in 2010.

Interviewed for this book, both Brenly and Brennaman spoke positively about working with Harry Caray. Broadcasting games with Caray, said Brenly, felt comparable to playing in the company of great players when he was a young major-league catcher.

> When I first came to the major leagues as a ballplayer, I'd be squatting behind home plate, and Steve Garvey and Dusty Baker and Mike Schmidt and Pete Rose would come up to bat. I almost felt like, "What am I doing here? Do I really belong here?" And I kind of felt that same sensation in the booth: "I'm working with Harry Caray! This guy is one of the greatest of all time, one of the best ambassadors for the game of baseball for all time . . . what am I doing here?" Once I got over that initial feeling, it was great to listen to Harry do what he did so well for so many years, and just to be there beside him. It was a tremendous experience for a very inexperienced broadcaster.[14]

The son of a major-league broadcaster, Brennaman was quickly able to bond with Caray, whose son and grandson were broadcasting in major professional sports. Said Brennaman,

> After we started working together, Harry learned that I was very close to my grandfather, who was still alive at the time. When my grandfather passed away, although I'd never spoken about this verbatim to him, Harry took me under his wing like I was his own grandson. And that's what it felt like from that moment on. In the short time that I was there, I felt we became quite close, and I loved the guy. I just loved being around him.[15]

In 1990, Brennaman was 26 years old, and Brenly 36. Dewayne Staats was 37 in 1989, his last year with the Cubs. Yet, all three marveled at the energy of Caray, who turned 76 in 1990, and had suffered a stroke three years earlier. "I'm in my 50s now, and I know how much the grind of a baseball season, with all the traveling and late hours, affects me," said Brennaman. "I can't imagine what it must have been like for Harry, who was in his 70s and 80s when we were working together. And then you add in his night life behind it . . . he had friends in every city, and he went out every night. The guy was just a machine. He just kept going, and never slowed down."[16]

Caray's late-night hours, even after his stroke, were legendary. Brenly recalled a night in Philadelphia when "Harry stuck his head in the radio booth on his way out and said, 'Kid—tonight you're going with me.'" After the game, Caray whisked Brenly down to the limousine that was still being provided by WGN. They went off to visit several haunts that, to Brenly, resembled the "speakeasies" of the Prohibition era. "Harry knocked on the door, there was a little sliding panel that opened up, and we walked into these various social clubs on our way to the airport. It was like Norm coming into 'Cheers'; everybody knew who he was. 'Harry! Hey, Harry!'"[17]

Caray, who came of age during a time when heavy drinking was not unusual, was unabashed about his alcohol consumption. "Harry always talked about how much he drank," Grant DePorter, CEO of Harry Caray's restaurant group, said in an interview. DePorter continued,

> He said he would go to about six bars a night. Based on that, we figured out that he had consumed 300,000 alcoholic drinks in his lifetime. I always thought that was an exaggeration, but about four years ago, Harry's accountant and lawyer, Marty Cohn, went through some files in the storage room that no one had looked at since the 1970s. They were all of Harry's "drinking diaries" . . . who he was with, what bar he was at, how much he spent. He did that for about a decade. . . . So we have proof that 300,000 is actually a realistic number. Keith Olbermann of ESPN did a big story on it. Harry lived to almost 84 years of age, and if you look at his lifestyle . . . it was superhuman. He just loved being with people, loved the fans.[18]

❋ ❋ ❋

For the Chicago Cubs, the 1990 season was a major disappointment: One year after winning the National League Eastern Division title, the Cubs finished a distant fourth, with a 77–85 record. For the Cubs franchise, the season highlight was likely the Major League All-Star Game at Wrigley Field on July 10. It was the first All-Star Game played at Wrigley since 1962, and of course the first-ever night All-Star Game at the North Side ballpark. The contest, a 2–0 victory for the American League, was hampered by rain: a 17-minute delay at the start of the game and a 68-minute interruption in the top of the seventh inning. The second delay came prior to what the *Chicago Sun-Times* called the "best-sounding moment" of the night: Caray leading the crowd in "Take Me Out to the Ball Game" during the seventh-inning stretch.

Caray made other headlines during the 1990 All-Star break. On the morning of the game, the *Sun-Times* released a poll of major-league players on such subjects as best player, best pitcher, best manager, and the like. Caray was selected as the players' "favorite TV announcer." The other bit of news involving Caray was not so pleasant. White Sox team president Jerry Reinsdorf had spent the All-Star Game in WGN-TV's Wrigley Field skybox as a guest of the station. According to press reports, Caray walked over to Reinsdorf's table, and said—in reference to the comments Reinsdorf had addressed to Caray and Jimmy Piersall after the White Sox clinched the 1983 American League West title—"I ought to knock you right on your (bleep). You called me scum." The report said WGN-TV officials quickly interceded and escorted Caray out of the skybox.

Contacted about the incident, Reinsdorf said, "I don't think it was any big deal. I had a great time at the game." Caray begged to differ. "Imagine this guy asking me why I wouldn't just say hello," Caray said. "I didn't forget what he said." Caray also denied that he'd been asked to leave the skybox. "[WGN executive] Jim Dowdle said. 'Hey, Harry, please stop it,'" Caray said. "But I left on my own terms."[19]

The incident was not the first time since Reinsdorf's "scum" comment that Caray had openly expressed negative feelings about the White Sox. In spring training prior to the 1984 season, Sox designated hitter Greg Luzinski reported that when he was opening his mail from the winter, he found a note from Caray. It said, "Hi, Greg. For a guy who was on stage before the [1983] playoffs, you sure were conspicuous by your absence after them! Some of us stand out in the open and take the heat. Others, like you, hide out in the showers or players' lounge when things get tough." Caray was referring to the fact that Luzinski had been unavailable to the media following the Sox' 3–0 loss in the final playoff game against the Baltimore Orioles. When asked about Caray's note, Luzinski, who said he'd been consoling teammates after the playoff loss, said, "I think it's funny."[20]

In 1985, when Reinsdorf was the subject of a largely laudatory profile by Phil Hersh in the *Chicago Tribune*, Caray was one of the few people who spoke negatively about the White Sox president. "I have never liked him from the time I met him and never trusted him," Caray said to Hersh. "I really don't want to talk about the guy."[21]

In November 1990, Caray was at it again. This time, with the White Sox preparing to open their new Comiskey Park the following April, Caray reflected on how Reinsdorf almost moved the White Sox to St. Petersburg, Florida, in the late 1980s. It wasn't Reinsdorf who saved the White Sox for Chicago, Caray insisted; it was superstar basketball player Michael Jordan of the Chicago Bulls, a team also owned by Reinsdorf.

> Jerry Reinsdorf [said Caray] was set to move the White Sox to that new stadium in St. Petersburg. A done deal, in my opinion. But then he realized, or was made to realize by his partners, that he never could keep ownership of the Bulls in Chicago if he also owned the Florida White Sox. Why? Because he'd have been run out of town. Couldn't have set foot in Chicago Stadium for a basketball game.
>
> Now if you have a lousy basketball team, so what? You sell it. But Reinsdorf's got a cash cow in the Bulls, and he's also got maybe the greatest player and goodwill ambassador in NBA history. No way Reinsdorf is going to let go of Jordan, and that's the reason the White Sox stayed.

Reinsdorf fired back, "Mr. Caray is wrong again. One thing had nothing to do with the other. If we'd have been forced to move the White Sox to St. Petersburg, I was fully prepared to sell the Bulls."[22] Fortunately for Reinsdorf, he kept the Bulls, who were about to embark on a run of six NBA championships in the next eight seasons. His White Sox were improving, also, and about to open Chicago's first new major-league ballpark since 1914. The North Side–South Side battle was getting interesting again.

21

NORTH SIDE VERSUS SOUTH SIDE

Harry's career gives the lie to the propaganda we've heard for ages about the relation of clean living to longevity.

Asked to explain his tenure, he said, "I'm sure it was the clean, healthy, wholesome, normal life I lead."

Then he joined heartily in my laughter. In my own baseball travels, I'd been continually amazed at his ability to stay late at so many oases, drink as much as a camel who'd spent a week in the desert, and show up for work next day as chipper as though his nectar had been milk.

He has leaned more toward moderation since his stroke, he said, but not because any doctor has curbed his thirst.

"As you get older, you can't drink as much. But I have two or three martinis, a bottle of Budweiser (a sponsor), a glass of wine with dinner, an after-dinner drink, maybe a couple of other drinks if I'm with convivial company. Instead of six or eight drinks a day, it used to be 80. Nature says I can't drink as much as I used to. Still, it's such a part of my life I'd rather die than not be able to have a cocktail."— Ray Sons, *Chicago Sun-Times*, September 1992[1]

On April 17, 1991, the Chicago White Sox lost to the Detroit Tigers, 16–0, in their home opener. It was one of the worst losses in Sox franchise history—but the defeat couldn't erase the feeling of euphoria on the South Side. After a battle that had taken several years, the White Sox had opened their new Comiskey Park before a sellout crowd of 42,191. "What we have now is a great park," said team president Jerry Reinsdorf. "The fans are going to love it."[2]

Reinsdorf and Sox vice chairman Eddie Einhorn had been talking about a new park since 1984, due to the deteriorating shape of the old Comiskey Park, the team's home since 1910. After meeting resistance for funding help from the city of Chicago, the Sox bought a parcel of land in suburban Addison as a possible site for a new stadium; however, voters in Addison's DuPage County rejected a stadium proposal in a nonbinding referendum in November 1986, effectively killing the Sox-to-Addison idea. The White Sox then turned to the state of Illinois, hoping to get funding for a new park to be built on the south side of 35th Street across from the old Comiskey. Progress was slow, and by June 1988, the Sox seemed likely to relocate to St. Petersburg, Florida. Finally, on June 30, with the clock running out on the final night of the Illinois General Assembly's legislative session, Governor James R. Thompson was able to round up enough votes to approve a stadium-funding package.

The new park, which would be renamed U.S. Cellular Field in 2003, and then changed to Guaranteed Rate Field in 2016, ultimately would not be popular among critics of baseball stadium design; for example, in 2017, *Washington Post* baseball writer Thomas Boswell ranked the Sox' ballpark 27th among the 30 Major League Baseball stadiums. But in 1991, Chicago fans reacted positively to the new park. "It's mind-boggling," said one season ticket holder who was checking out Comiskey II's bleacher seats and outfield concourse. "These seats have backs on them. They're among the best in the park. This concourse is wide enough to give people a feeling of room."[3]

For the 1991 season, 2,934,154 fans attended games at the new Comiskey Park—a Chicago baseball record by more than a half-million and over 600,000 more fans than attended games at Wrigley Field that year (2,314,250). While the Cubs and Harry Caray continued to rule the airwaves, the Sox were making progress there as well. On television, White Sox games were now available on either WGN-TV (52 games) or SportsChannel (107), which—unlike Einhorn's old SportsVision model—was available on basic cable in most of the Chicago area. Sports-Channel, which also carried the Chicago Bulls and Blackhawks, along with a variety of high school and college sports, had more than 2 million subscribers and was Chicago's first 24-hour-a-day sports channel. "[SportsChannel] is an adult now," said Sox television play-by-play voice Ken Harrelson. "The growing pains are gone."[4] The White Sox broadcasts on WGN Channel 9 were giving the Cubs a run for their money; in August, Steve Nidetz reported that Sox broadcasts on WGN had averaged a 9.5 rating during the summer sweeps period, compared to an 11.2 rating for the Cubs.

* * *

While the White Sox were offering strong competition to the Cubs in 1991, the North Siders managed to increase their home attendance to 2.3 million—at the time, the second-highest figure in team history— despite a 77–83 record and another fourth-place finish (the Sox were second in the American League West, with an 87–75 mark). Caray, who turned 77 in 1991, was drawing more and more comments about his on-air mistakes; however, his energy and enthusiasm continued to amaze the much-younger colleagues who traveled and worked with him. Bob Verdi recalled an East Coast road trip from Caray's poststroke years.

> I remember one time when the Cubs were in New York playing the Mets, and their next series was in Philadelphia. I saw Harry in the press box, and he asked me how I was getting to Philly. I said I was taking the train. He said, "Don't worry about doing that; I've got the limo for four days and we'll take it down to Philly." So I rode down with him. We were staying in different hotels, and the driver dropped him off and then took me to my hotel, which was about two or three miles away. On the way, just to make conversation, I said to the driver, "How's it going? You've had Harry for four or five days in New York." He looked back at me in the mirror and just rolled his eyes and said, "This guy is killing me." So it wasn't Harry who needed sleep; it was his driver.[5]

One of the personal highlights of Caray's life came on May 13, 1991, when the Cubs hosted the Atlanta Braves. That night Harry was broad-casting the game for the Cubs; his son Skip was working the Braves broadcast; and grandson Chip was joining his dad as a fill-in for Skip's usual partner, Pete Van Wieren. It was the first time in major-league history that three generations of broadcasters from the same family were covering a game in the same ballpark. The three appeared togeth-er on camera prior to the game, and Harry was obviously touched.

Skip: This is something, huh?

Harry: It certainly is. This is the thrill of my life. . . . If the good Lord said to me right now, "Harry, this is your last moment on earth," I'd die a happy man.

Skip: We don't want that to happen. Chip, what are the pitching matchups for today's game?

Chip: Well, the Braves will have their big left-hander, Tom Glavine, going today against the Cubs' Shawn Boskie.

Harry: That's all?

Skip: That's it. (All three laugh in unison.)[6]

"After 47 years of broadcasting baseball," Harry told Steve Nidetz, "everything I've done seems to be relegated to the background at the thought, almost the frightening thought, that I'm one of three generations to broadcast Major League Baseball at the very same time."[7]

"Looking back on that night, it was really cool to see how many people thought it was a big deal," Chip Caray said in a 2018 interview. He continued,

> For my dad and I at least, it was the family business; it was what we did. My dad, who was an extremely shy person, was not at all comfortable with the attention. But I think that for my grandfather this was probably a huge source of familial pride for him. He was a guy that didn't have family, didn't have much of a legacy other than what he had created. To see his son doing what he did, to see his grandson doing what he did, to see two people who had his name doing what he did and spending that day with him, I think for him that was one of the crowning achievements of his life. And whatever role I played in that continues to be a real highlight.[8]

Chip candidly admits he was not close to his grandfather when he was growing up. He once related a painful story about a time when he was playing in a Little League game, and Harry, who stopped by, had no idea that he was watching his grandson. "He really had trouble being Dad," Chip said. "He had no trouble being Harry Caray."[9] Yet, Chip understands how Harry's own background left him untrained for dealing with a family. "When it came to family, Harry hadn't been trained," he told me, adding,

> He didn't have any experience. His mom died when he was young, his father abandoned him, and he wound up being raised by his mother's sister-in-law in St. Louis. So he really didn't have family as a touchstone. He really didn't know how to be a dad or a grandfather, and how to relate to me or my family. He just didn't know how to do it. [10]

✵ ✵ ✵

As the 1991 season was coming to a close, Barry Cronin of the *Chicago Sun-Times* asked, "Is this Harry Caray's last at-bat?" He recited a litany of Caray's on-air gaffes, like referring to Cubs outfielder George Bell as "George Bush" and calling San Diego Padres catcher Benito Santiago "Benito San Diego," or discussing a triple play while referring to it as a double play. "It's not the significance of the errors but their sheer numbers that upsets Caray's critics," wrote Cronin. Yet, he also mentioned the adulation Caray still constantly received from fans: "All of the criticism—even though it's justified—can't outweigh the kind of love, humor, enthusiasm, and style Harry Caray brings to every game he broadcasts."

As for his mistakes with names, Caray said, "For 47 years I've kicked around names. I was an 'A' student in Spanish and you hit me with a Spanish name cold and I'll butcher it. Irish names. Italian names. I'm half-Italian myself. I butcher Italian names. But that's been going on forever." While Cronin wrote about the "fine line between a few butchered names and the dissolution of a living legend before our eyes," it was apparent Caray wasn't ready to retire. "Enjoy this man for what he is while he's here because there will never be anyone like him," said Caray's partner Steve Stone. "And when he's gone, there will be a lot of people who will miss the love he brought to this game." [11]

✵ ✵ ✵

In 1992, their second season in the new Comiskey Park, the White Sox again outdrew the Cubs by more than a half-million fans: 2,681,156 attended Sox home games, compared to 2,126,720 for the Cubs at Wrigley. Having a better team helped: The White Sox finished third in the American League West, with an 86–76 record, while the Cubs ranked fourth in the National League East, with a 78–84 mark. It was the third-straight season that the Cubs finished the year with either 77 or 78 wins.

But White Sox home attendance was almost 300,000 lower than in 1991, and a drumbeat of criticism about their new ballpark was starting to be heard. "The new Comiskey Park enjoyed a short, sweet honeymoon with the public," wrote Sox historian Richard Lindberg. "By the middle of the second year, however, the critics changed their minds." One of the major complaints was the steep, 35-degree slope of the park's upper deck. "To get an idea of what it is like in the higher elevations of the upper deck," wrote one critic, "think of Glacier National Park and think Himalayas."[12] The White Sox eventually bowed to the criticism, and the park underwent extensive renovation in the early 2000s, including the removal of more than 6,000 seats from the upper deck.

While Cubs' home attendance trailed the White Sox by a considerable margin in 1992, the nationwide popularity of the Cubs franchise continued to be immense—thanks to the magic of Caray and the WGN superstation. In July, Jack Craig of the *Boston Globe* reported that while WGN was available nationally in 38.1 million homes, far less than the 60 million homes that received Atlanta Braves games via Ted Turner's WTBS, the Cubs' $32 million in TV revenue was the highest for any major-league team. "The Tribune Co.'s decision in 1988, to have lights for night games installed at Wrigley Field, carried out against a firestorm of complaints, was directly linked to TV revenue," wrote Craig.[13]

Although no one was questioning Caray's personal popularity, criticism of his on-air mistakes reached a new level in 1992. In the *Chicago Sun-Times*, Dan Cahill and Mark Gaffney's weekly coverage of sports media now featured a "Harry-o-Meter" (Sammy Sosa was "Sammy Scioscia," Bret Saberhagen was "Bret Sobberhoggen"). Caray's malapropisms were also the subject of frequent mockery on Chicago's new all-sports radio station, WSCR.

In July, one of Caray's most vocal critics, Milo Hamilton, received the Ford C. Frick Award from the National Baseball Hall of Fame—the same award given to Caray in 1989. While saying that he was a "little teary-eyed" when he'd heard that he was being given the award, Hamilton remained bitter about his experience with the Cubs and Caray in the early 1980s. "The headlines were as big as World War III when they brought me back," Hamilton said in describing his amazement when he heard that the Cubs were pushing him aside in favor of Caray. He talked of how fans wrote to him about turning down Caray's voice on their TV sets so they could listen to Hamilton's radio descriptions. "That was one of the reasons I was let go here," Hamilton said. "That was something [Caray] couldn't live with."[14]

"When fans would get up for the seventh-inning stretch in Houston, Milo would toss out peanuts and Cracker Jacks to the fans sitting below the booth," said Bill Brown, who broadcast Astros games from 1987 to 2016. Brown continued,

> But when Harry was in town, it got ugly because a lot of Cub fans were looking up to *their* booth. That was the last thing Milo wanted to see or hear. He sometimes would go off on a tirade off the air about Harry. If a fan came up to him and said something about loving Harry, Milo would find it very hard to restrain himself from saying something derogatory.[15]

Caray, who said he congratulated Hamilton on the Frick Award, remained defiant in the face of criticism, whether from Hamilton or the Chicago sports media. For him, retirement was still out of the question. He wasn't even ready to consider cutting down on his work schedule. "I have 12 boxes of mail I haven't gotten to yet," he told the *Sun-Times* at the end of the 1992 season. "The mail is so positive, it's embarrassing. If I'm really that bad, they'll let me know."[16]

Caray knew he couldn't last forever, but he wanted to go out doing what he loved. "One day it's going to be over," he said in September. "I hope I die with my boots on, yelling: 'Cubs win!' Keel over and die. Lug Caray away."[17]

❊ ❊ ❊

In 1993, the Chicago White Sox had one of the best seasons in franchise history. With 94 wins, the Sox won the American League West by an eight-game margin, reaching the postseason for only the third time since 1920. In a familiar refrain for Chicago's baseball teams in the divisional-play era, the Sox lost to the eventual World Series champion Toronto Blue Jays in the American League Championship Series; however, the club—with a talented roster than included Most Valuable Player Frank Thomas, Cy Young Award winner Jack McDowell, and multisport star Bo Jackson, among others—seemed poised to remain a dominant franchise for the next several years. For the season, the Sox again drew more than 2.5 million fans to the new Comiskey Park.

Yet, despite the division title, White Sox attendance actually *declined* in 1993, by more than 100,000 fans. Even worse, the Sox were outdrawn by the crosstown Cubs, 2,653,763 to 2,581,091. It wasn't a particularly good Cub team; the North Siders were barely over .500, with an 84–78 record, and finished fourth in the seven-team National League East.

Boston Globe columnist Dan Shaughnessy, who came to Chicago for the series against Toronto, wrote that he was "struck by the lukewarm anticipation for the playoffs. There was little evidence that a big event was about to take place." He noted that there still were seats available for American League playoff games six and seven, and that the lead story in both Chicago newspapers that morning was not about the White Sox, but the National Football League's Chicago Bears. "This would be unthinkable in a place like . . . Boston," he wrote. "When the Red Sox have a chance to get to the World Series, they infiltrate every part of our lives. There is no escape."

Shaughnessy also noted the popularity of Chicago's other baseball team. "And of course, the Cubs are the official mascots of couch potatoes from Bangor to La Jolla," he wrote. "The Cubs are hip. Billy Murray is a Cubs fan. All hip people are Cubs fans. Even the Cub broadcaster, Harry Caray, has his own restaurant."[18]

No one knew it at the time, but the 1992 season was, through 2018, the last year the White Sox would draw more fans than the Cubs. While the Cubs, by most measures, certainly have been the more popular of the two Chicago MLB teams since the late 1960s, this was a major change. During the first 12 years of the Reinsdorf–Einhorn era (1981–1992), the White Sox outdrew the Cubs at home six times, and the Cubs' overall attendance edge was a little more than 150,000 fans per year; the Cubs had the advantage, but there was some competition. But for the 26-year span from 1993 to 2018, the Cubs not only outdrew the White Sox every year, but also in most seasons it wasn't even close. For that 26-year-period, the Cubs' average home attendance margin was more than 875,000 fans per season. In the final two years of that period (2017–2018), the Cubs outdrew the White Sox by more 1.5 million fans in each season, while nearly doubling the White Sox in total home attendance (6,380,651 to 3,238,287).

The battle for Chicago baseball supremacy was over: The Cubs—and Harry Caray—had won.

22

SLIPS, STRIKES, AND CONTROVERSIES

Harry Carabina, once an orphan in St. Louis, is entering his 50th year in broadcasting. The familiar voice known as Harry Caray seems like a longtime member of every Cub fan's extended family.

The remarkable legacy of the Hall of Fame announcer will continue to be scripted this season, and if the 70-something Caray has his way, for many more to come, contrary to retirement rumors.

"I hope to do 50 more," Caray said, clearing his throat between innings of a recent Cubs exhibition game broadcast on WGN radio. "But we know that isn't possible. Nobody is immortal. I want to broadcast as long as the good Lord accepts me."—Fred Mitchell, *Chicago Tribune*, April 1994[1]

Shortly before the 1994 baseball season began, Harry Caray received another major honor. On March 22, in Las Vegas, he was inducted into the National Association of Broadcasters Hall of Fame as the 1994 honoree for radio. Baseball broadcasters Mel Allen and Red Barber had been previous honorees in the NAB's radio division, which usually went to people and shows in the entertainment business (Jack Benny, Bing Crosby, and Red Skelton were among the previous radio honorees). At the ceremony, Jack Buck, Caray's partner for many years in St. Louis, narrated a video tribute to Caray, saying Harry was "more than just an announcer. He makes you feel like he's one of you sitting in the stands." (Buck himself would be honored by the NAB in 2005.) In accepting the award, Caray noted that his son Skip was broadcasting games for the Atlanta Braves, while grandson Chip was working for the Seattle Mariners. "If I'd had any imagination, I would have called myself Flip," Caray said. "Then there'd be Flip, Skip, and Chip." He finished by leading the audience in a chorus of "Take Me Out to the Ball Game."[2]

It was an appropriate time to be honoring Caray, who was about to begin his 50th season broadcasting major-league games. In an interview with Dave van Dyck of the *Chicago Sun-Times* as the season was about to begin, Caray admitted he wouldn't mind reducing his schedule of road games in future years. But he wasn't about to retire. "I love it," he said, adding,

> I can't conceive what I would do if I wasn't broadcasting baseball. You know it's not the money. I've got more money than I can ever spend. And my children will have much more money than I ever imagined making, much less leaving to other people. It isn't that. I really love the game. I get just as mad, just as angry, just as ecstatic, just as deliriously happy when something happens.[3]

Caray's broadcast partners remained supportive of him, despite the increased frequency of his on-air gaffes. "So what if he mangles a few words and gets some names wrong. In the end, what difference does it make?" said Caray's television partner, Steve Stone. "The object of baseball is for everyone to enjoy themselves. In the seventh inning, no matter where we go, everybody stands up and looks to the booth, looks to Harry." Caray's partners also continued to marvel at his energy and constant late-night hours. "I couldn't keep up with him," said Ron Santo, the veteran of the group but still 23 years younger than Caray. "Harry is bigger than anybody in the game—player, coach, manager, any of them," said Thom Brennaman.[4]

* * *

When the Cubs began their 1994 season against the New York Mets at Wrigley Field on April 4, Caray was part of the story. "Tuffy Rhodes. Hillary Rodham Clinton. And Harry Caray. In that order," wrote Brian Hewitt of the *Sun-Times*. "They were the stars of the surrealistic show Monday at the Cubs' home opener. All for different reasons."[5] Rhodes, a previously obscure outfielder, tied a major-league Opening Day record by hitting three home runs in the Cubs' 12–8 loss. First Lady Hillary Clinton, who grew up in suburban Park Ridge, was greeted with boos and derogatory placards (there were also some cheers) when she threw out the first ball prior to the game. Caray helped put things in a more positive vein for the first lady. He invited Mrs. Clinton to the broadcast booth and asked her to join him in singing "Take Me Out to the Ball Game" during the seventh-inning stretch—this time to "mostly cheers and waves," according to press reports. When they finished, Caray planted a kiss on Mrs. Clinton's cheek. (He got the first lady's name wrong at one point, referring to her as "Hillary Rodman Clinton.")[6]

The season-opening loss was the start of another long season for the Cubs, who lost their first three games, slipped into last place in the new five-team National League Central Division, and stayed there. It was exasperating for Caray. When Cubs pitcher Jose Guzman was struggling during an early season game against the Los Angeles Dodgers, Caray snapped. "Aw, get someone warmed up," he said. "This guy's got nothin.'" In the same game, Guzman surrendered a three-run homer to Dodgers pitcher Kevin Gross, prompting Caray to bark, "Just because we pay these pitchers these big salaries, does that mean we have to keep usin' 'em?" (Guzman and the Cubs managed to win the game, 6–3.)[7]

Early in the season, there were signs that Caray—a man known for his boundless energy—was starting to wear down. At the Montreal airport during the Cubs' first road trip in early April, Caray slipped and took a nasty spill on a freshly waxed floor. Two months later, in Philadelphia, Caray fell and crashed through a glass table in the visitors' clubhouse, a "scary moment but no harm done—except to the table, which was a pile of shards," according to the *Chicago Tribune*. Road trips were becoming difficult for Caray, who said in May that 1994 might be the last season he traveled full-time with the team. "If I can talk them into just doing home games, I'd consider that a victory," he said.[8]

In late June, the Cubs flew to Miami to play the Florida Marlins, who had joined the National League as an expansion team a year earlier. It was the last leg of a 12-day road trip in which the Cubs had traveled to San Diego and San Francisco before flying cross-country to play the Marlins. Prior to the second and final game of the series on a humid, 90-degree night, Caray stumbled and fell once again—this time on the concrete steps of the visitors' bullpen at Joe Robbie Stadium. He fell face-first on the steps, suffering bruises to his face, upper lip, and knee. According to press reports, "Paramedics who rushed to Caray's aid in Florida detected some fluttering of his heart, and he experienced several more instances of rapid heartbeats while in the hospital." Caray was taken to nearby Parkway Hospital. After two days in intensive care, he was flown to Chicago and admitted to Northwestern Memorial Hospital. "He was very pleasant and jovial," said a Parkway spokeswoman. "He was joking with our nurses. If I had fallen on my head and cut my head, I would be a lot more cranky." Recovering in Chicago, Caray told reporters, "I feel all right, but I look like I just stepped out of the ring from Mike Tyson."[9]

"I want the whole world to know two things," said Caray from his Chicago hospital bed. "I didn't have a heart attack, and I didn't have a stroke. I'm feeling good and I'll be back soon."[10] The mishap forced the Cubs to postpone Harry Caray Day, scheduled for Sunday, June 26, to celebrate his 50th year as a major-league broadcaster, but Caray said he hoped to return by July 4. According to WGN-TV executive producer Arne Harris, Caray was determined to finish out the year, including Cubs road trips.

Caray's hopes for an early return were overly optimistic. Treated for an irregular heartbeat, he remained in Northwestern Memorial Hospital until July 7. A hospital spokesman said Caray was "expected to return with little or no restrictions."[11] Ultimately, the Cubs decided to schedule Harry's return for Friday, July 22—the same day the team was enshrining former Cubs second baseman Ryne Sandberg, who had abruptly retired in June, to the team's Walk of Fame (Sandberg would return as an active player in 1996). In the meantime, Caray fans were treated to the July 11 airing of "When Harry Met Baseball," a WGN-TV special honoring Caray. The special was hosted by Bob Costas and featured appearances by Stan Musial, Tim McCarver, Jack Buck, and former president Ronald Reagan, among others.

The July 22 return of Sandberg and Caray—who had been inducted into the Cubs' Walk of Fame in 1993—was a festive occasion, especially when Caray led the Wrigley Field crowd in "Take Me Out to the Ball Game" during the seventh-inning stretch. "I've seen every game on TV, and I tell you, the fans have been terrific," said Caray. He said that the medication he was taking for an irregular heartbeat prevented him from consuming alcoholic beverages, but "I'm hoping that will change. Seems to me that once the medication settles things down, a guy could drink moderately. And you know, I never drank any way but moderately to begin with." Noting his serious car accident in 1968, his stroke in 1987, and his latest mishap, he said, "How many lives does a cat have? I have six to go."[12]

Caray had originally been scheduled to travel on a restricted number of road trips during the 1994 season, but he never got the chance. On August 12, the Major League Baseball Players Association went on strike, and Major League Baseball cancelled the remainder of the season, including the postseason. The Cubs kept Caray and Steve Stone in touch with WGN-TV viewers by featuring them in a 60-second promo for the station's reruns of the television series *Coach*. The promo, entitled "Killin' Time with Harry and Steve," featured Caray singing—but not the song that helped make him famous.

At the time the 1994 season was stopped, the Cubs were in last place in the National League Central Division with a 49–64 record. In the American League, the Chicago White Sox led the Central Division by one game with a 67–46 mark. Yet the Cubs, with a home attendance of 1,845,208, had outdrawn the White Sox (1,697,398) by almost 150,000 fans.

❖ ❖ ❖

In November, Caray was hospitalized again, this time for a possible bladder infection. The condition was not serious and he was released after a short stay; however, when the Cubs announced their broadcast plans for 1995 three months later, the schedule called for Caray to broadcast all home games but only selected road contests. "The road games are going to be more or less at my discretion, you know, places I want to go," Caray said. Meanwhile, major-league players and owners continued to be at loggerheads, with the owners attempting to install a salary cap or payroll tax, along with ending salary arbitration and adding new restrictions on free agency. The owners announced that, barring a new basic agreement with the players, they would play the season with "replacement players"—minor leaguers who were not members of the MLBPA. During his birthday celebration at one of his Chicagoland restaurants on March 1 (he was 81 but said he was "about 75"), Caray expressed his exasperation concerning the continued dispute. "Anything would be better than looking at guys whose names I don't know and can't place," he said. [13]

The strike finally ended on March 31, when U.S. District Court judge (and later, Supreme Court Justice) Sonia Sotomayor issued an injunction against the owners' attempt to unilaterally impose new work rules. Acting baseball commissioner Bud Selig announced the season would begin on April 25, with a reduced schedule of 144 games. But the labor dispute remained unsettled, and many fans kept their vow to stay away from the ballparks. "Major League Baseball returned to the playing field after a 234-day work stoppage," wrote Steve Gietschier in the *Sporting News Baseball Guide for 1996*, "but the full enthusiasm and affection of its fans lagged far behind. Attendance dropped 20 percent from 1994, despite discounted ticket prices, as many people once deeply attached to the game professed indifference." [14]

Harry Caray never stopped working to bring the fans back. "Harry was the only guy who still worked for the fans," recalled Caray's longtime friend, Minor League Baseball owner Pete Vonachen. Added Vonachen,

> Shaking hands, loving everybody. People could look at the ballplayers, who weren't playing. They could look at the owners, who were all fat, dumb, and happy. Or they could look at Harry. He's the one who carried the flag for baseball through all the tough times. This guy never knew a stranger. The strike was when Harry grew to legendary status. [15]

"I know there's bitterness, and that's understandable; the fan is the last person they thought about," said Caray a few days before the season opened. "But why should I change my broadcast? The sooner we forget about this, the better off the fans are. The owners and players all come and go. The only constant is baseball." [16] It was a tough sell, even for Caray. Despite posting a winning record (73–71) and moving up from fifth (last) place in 1994 to third place in 1995, Cubs home attendance declined by almost 5,000 fans per game (31,275 in 1994; 26,643 in 1995).

Caray was still restricted from drinking alcohol. It was not an easy adjustment for him, but he handled it with his usual good humor. "During that time Harry was drinking O'Doul's, the nonalcoholic beer that Anheuser-Busch made," Bob Verdi recalled. Verdi continued,

Now I don't know how many shares of Anheuser-Busch stock Harry had—it had to be thousands—but one day on the air he said, 'You know, I've been trying this O'Doul's . . . and it's not very good!' Where would you hear something like that anymore? Only Harry could get away with it. [17]

※ ※ ※

On September 12, the Cubs prepared to face the Los Angeles Dodgers and Japanese rookie sensation Hideo Nomo, who would win the Rookie of the Year Award in 1995. During the taping of his pregame show with Cubs manager Jim Riggleman, Caray and Riggleman were talking about Nomo when Harry jokingly asked, "Well, my eyes are slanty enough, how 'bout yours?" Riggleman quickly changed the subject, but the remark was not edited out of the broadcast; Caray, who insisted he was being lighthearted and intended no criticism, quickly found himself the object of criticism for his remark. "It's very unfortunate that something like that is said and I don't condone it," said WGN program director Tisa LaSorte. "I'm sure Harry didn't mean anything by it because everybody knows Harry's not a malicious person. But it's the kind of thing that makes people uncomfortable." [18]

Caray, however, felt no need to apologize for his words. "I'm never going to make an apology," he said three days after the incident. "I didn't do anything wrong. If I did, I'd be the first to apologize." He said he had nothing against Asians. "Anybody who knows me knows I go out of my way to make friends," Caray said. "People don't have a color to me. I don't care whether they're pink or white or black or what they are. If a guy's got slanty eyes, he's got slanty eyes, what the hell's wrong with it?" [19]

Although WGN general manager Dan Fabian also issued an apology, Bill Yoshimo of the Japanese American Citizens League wanted it to come from Caray. "I don't think he says these things with real malicious intent, but the fact is it goes out over the airwaves for public consumption and it reinforces the use of racial slurs to people who don't know better," Yoshimo said. Yoshimo said that about 10 years prior to the Nomo incident, Caray had used the word "Jap" on the air. Caray refused to back down and expressed astonishment that his words had created a stir. "This is ridiculous," he said. "That kind of stuff is said all the time. It's acceptable these days. Gee whiz, [Jay] Leno and [David] Letterman say it all the time, and everyone laughs. Now they're not laughing because I say it? C'mon!"[20]

The controversy continued for more than a week. Caray not only refused to apologize, but was upset that others had apologized on his behalf. Other broadcasters came to Caray's defense. "I've known Harry for 35 years, so maybe I'm prejudiced," said former Cubs broadcaster Jack Brickhouse. "Speaking as a guy who has been there with him, I know darn well he was simply making a statement in jest and for no other reason. Harry Caray is not a prejudiced guy."[21] Fox TV morning host Bob Sirott said, "I took it to mean Harry was making fun of himself. It was supposed to be self-deprecating, like, 'Look at my eyes, they're kind of slanty too. Ha ha ha.' I think that's what he meant. Assuming it had any meaning at all."[22]

Others felt some sort of apology was appropriate. "Whatever he might have meant, he surely meant no harm," wrote *Chicago Tribune* columnist Eric Zorn. He continued,

> So the apology he owes people of Asian descent is the apology he'd owe a person he bumped into while taking a step back for a better look at the shelves in a supermarket. The situation calls for an 'I'm sorry' not in the 'I've been wicked, forgive my execrable person' sense, but in the 'I didn't mean to hurt anyone, please excuse me' sense. . . . If you mean no harm, apologize. If your heart's in the right place, I'll bet they forgive you.[23]

Caray stuck to his guns, stating,

> You know what would hurt my image? If I did what [the media] and friends of mine and people in our business have all recommended— to say some words, to apologize, say you're sorry. But how phony would that be? They want me to say something that I don't believe. I never said anything that could possibly make anybody mad. I've only had a couple of phone calls, both from Orientals [*sic*], and they were laughing about it. For me to go on and be so insincere as to give a phony explanation is ridiculous. I am what I am. You either like me or you don't like me.[24]

Ultimately, WGN officials announced that they were taking full responsibility for Harry's remarks and that they would not insist that

Caray make his own apology. "It was the radio station's responsibility," said Dan Fabian. "I've apologized, and Tisa LaSorte apologized on the air Friday night. Both of us had our say. I don't see any sense in refocusing on this again." Fabian said he would talk with Caray about "tightening up," but he added, "The odds on me asking him to apologize are not terrific. If you ad-lib every day for 50 years, you're going to say something that offends someone."[25]

"The Nomo incident hurt Harry quite a bit," said Caray's broadcasting colleague, Thom Brennaman, in a 2018 interview. Brennaman further stated,

> Everyone who knew him—white, black, Hispanic—knew that Harry didn't have a racist bone in his body. When he made his comment, it sounds terrible today in the more politically correct atmosphere we live in, but he really didn't mean anything nasty by it. There was no internet back then, no cell phones like we have today, and news traveled much more slowly. It got more and more absurd. And that really bothered Harry a lot. He acted like it didn't bother him, but he talked a lot about it off the air, and he was not happy about it.[26]

A few days after the incident, *Chicago Sun-Times* columnist Rick Telander wrote that he had been standing next to Caray during the taping of the show in which Harry had made his comments about Nomo. Telander was convinced that Harry, who "was smiling the entire time he interviewed Riggleman," was no racist. Nonetheless, he felt that Caray's words "showed a lack of understanding of modern times, of the pain that members of minority groups carry with them," and that an apology for his comments was appropriate.[27] "Harry was not a guy who would go very far with political correctness," Telander said in a 2018 interview. Telander added,

> He didn't take his words [about Nomo] back, but I think everyone could sense that something had gone wrong here. He didn't think he had done anything wrong. In the old days people used to do things like that. Howard Cosell would say, "Look at that little monkey run." They probably thought, "Well, I used to say stuff like that and nobody minded," but times change. Harry broadcast for more than 50 years, and what was seen as okay at the start of a career that long is going to be looked at differently by the end.[28]

❖ ❖ ❖

The controversy about Caray's comments eventually subsided, and in November the news about Cubs broadcasters involved not Harry, but his grandson Chip. Thom Brennaman had decided to leave the Cubs broadcast crew after six seasons, and there was a vacancy on the staff—actually two vacancies, since the Cubs planned to hire both a broadcaster to work radio only and one who would work with Harry and Steve Stone on television. The new TV broadcaster would take Harry's place on road trips when Caray was not traveling. Brennaman and WGN-TV had talked about a deal that would have made him Harry's successor, but negotiations had stalled concerning WGN's insistence that he give up his secondary job as a FOX NFL broadcaster on autumn Sundays when the Cubs were also playing.

Chip Caray, who at the time was broadcasting NBA games for the Orlando Magic and Turner Broadcasting, emerged as the favorite for the WGN radio spot. "It's a great job," said Chip. "I'm very excited about the opportunity. It's very flattering to be considered."[29] After the WGN radio opening went to Pat Hughes, who had been broadcasting Milwaukee Brewers games, Chip continued to talk with WGN officials about the vacant spot on the television crew. But WGN-TV officials and Chip were unable to come to an agreement, and the job went to Wayne Larrivee, who had filled in for Harry Caray in 1994–1995, when Harry was unavailable.

"Not being able to go to the Cubs after the 1995 season was a big disappointment," Chip Caray said in an interview, continuing,

> I was doing Orlando Magic basketball at the time, but I made no bones about it: I wanted to do baseball. And I would have loved to come to Chicago; however, the offer I was made was for less money than I was making in Orlando doing 82 basketball games. I was married, and the economics of it just made no sense.

Chip's failure to work out an acceptable deal with WGN was extremely disappointing to Harry. "When I turned down the offer, my grandfather and I didn't speak for a while," said Chip. "I tried to make him understand that this wasn't me rejecting him; I would be moving from a very small town with a reasonable cost of living to a place that I wouldn't be able to survive on that salary."[30]

When Harry remained upset, Chip asked his father Skip to talk to Harry, who said that working in Chicago was the greatest opportunity in the world. "My dad finally said to him, 'If you think that's right, why don't you make up the difference between what they're offering and what he should be paid?' And very quickly Harry said, 'Well, I guess I understand that.'" Turning down the WGN offer in 1995–1996 worked out well for Chip, who spent two seasons as a studio host and play-by-play broadcaster for FOX network baseball before finally coming to Chicago. "I think as hard as it was for my grandfather to accept, in his heart of hearts he knew I was right," Chip said. "I wanted the job, but I didn't want the job at all costs. I had to stand up for what I thought was right, and ultimately I was proven right."[31]

Nonetheless, Harry was extremely disappointed that he would not be able to work with his grandson. "It broke my heart," Caray said in spring training in 1996. "It was his job if he wanted it, but I guess he didn't want to give up his other broadcasting. It's no knock on Wayne Larrivee, because he's very talented, but it would've been a wonderful experience for me to share the booth with Chip."[32]

23

LAST CALL

Harry Caray may not be broadcasting Cubs games in the 21st century, but then again, who knows? Caray says he'll be back next year, but for home games only.

Let's see, that's 81 renditions of "Take Me Out to the Ball Game" and 107 mispronunciations of Andres Galarraga.—Joe Knowles, *Chicago Tribune*, September 1996[1]

After raising hopes with a winning record (73–71) in 1995, the Chicago Cubs had another losing season in 1996. With a 76–86 record, the Cubs finished below .500 for the 11th time in Harry Caray's 15 seasons as the team's lead broadcaster. At least they were consistent: 1996 marked the seventh time in those 15 years that the Cubs had posted between 76 and 78 victories.

For Caray personally, it was a year largely free of both controversy and medical issues. Although he was disappointed that he would not be working with his grandson Chip, Caray developed a smooth relationship with both Wayne Larrivee, who shared television work with Harry and Steve Stone, and Pat Hughes, the team's new lead radio broadcaster. Larrivee, who had filled in for Caray in 1994–1995 when Harry was not traveling with the team or unavailable for medical reasons, took one of the jobs that might have gone to Chip Caray in 1996: working the middle three innings on television when Harry was broadcasting on radio, and the entire game when Harry was off. Harry was magnanimous about the decision. "Wayne's hiring might not have the romance that Chip's would have," he said, "but they couldn't have hired a better guy."[2]

Larrivee, a versatile broadcaster who was the play-by-play voice of the NFL Chicago Bears and NBA Chicago Bulls, while also working Big Ten football and basketball games, was born in Lee, Massachusetts, and grew up idolizing Marv Albert, a New York-based broadcaster who also did play-by-play in several different sports. Like Albert and unlike Caray, Larrivee believed in an impartial broadcast. "You try to be fair on each play," he said. "I know some people criticize me for that. I feel that the play, the athletic play, deserves a good call."[3]

Larrivee has fond memories of working with Caray. "Harry was great to me," he said in an interview. "I think he appreciated that I did other sports, and I had no problems whatsoever with him. I know he could be a little crusty with some people, but with me it was great. The whole Cubs broadcasting crew was great to work with. We had a lot of laughs off the air."

Larrivee recalled Caray's adjustment to a life without alcoholic beverages. "I remember being with him and Dutchie in spring training, and we went out to dinner at a restaurant," he said. "He was drinking nonalcoholic wine, and he asked me to tell him what I thought about it. I took a sip and said, 'I think it's fine, Harry.' He looked at me and said, 'It sucks. It's awful, isn't it?' So I knew he wasn't too happy with the fact that they weren't going to allow him to drink anymore."[4]

Pat Hughes, the Cubs' new radio voice, had spent the previous 12 years working with another broadcasting icon, Bob Uecker of the Milwaukee Brewers. Like Larrivee, Hughes had taken a job that might have gone to Chip Caray, but Hughes and Harry hit it off from the start. "He treated me like a king," Hughes said in an interview. "He went out of his way to come into the booth about a month into my time, and he said, 'Pat, I want you to know that people really love what you're doing and just keep on doing it.' It was very gracious of him. I loved the guy."[5]

With the Cubs consciously trying to reduce Caray's workload, Harry no longer worked the middle three innings on radio. But he couldn't seem to stay away from the broadcast booth—even on days when he wasn't scheduled to work. "One of my fondest memories of Harry would be Saturday afternoon games where the WGN telecast would be preempted because a network telecast was going on," said Hughes. He continued,

Even though he was not working the game, he would still come out to the ballpark. So I would invite him into the radio booth with Ron Santo and myself, and he absolutely loved being there. He did a little play-by-play, not much . . . he was over 80 years old at the time. It was a great memory for me, and I know he enjoyed it also."[6]

＊ ＊ ＊

In August 1996, Caray took time out from his Cubs duties to appear at the Democratic National Convention at Chicago's United Center, where Bill Clinton was being nominated for a second term as U.S. president. In what the *Chicago Tribune* called an "inspired touch" on the part of city officials, Caray led the delegates in singing "Take Me Out to the Ball Game."[7]

In September, Caray—still traveling on occasional Cubs road trips—returned to Miami's Joe Robbie Stadium, scene of his nasty fall two years earlier. Reflecting on the mishap, Caray was lighthearted but also aware of the fact that his hospital stay had revealed an irregular heartbeat, which might have resulted in a heart attack or stroke if left untreated. There was one obvious downside to the medication he continued to take: His drinking days were over. Asked by broadcast partner Steve Stone if he remembered his last drink on June 22, 1994, Caray recalled only that it had taken place at legendary coach Don Shula's restaurant in Miami. "If I had only known, I would've ordered a punch bowl full of martinis," he quipped. "Every time I go in to get my heart checked I ask the doctor if I can have a drink, and the doctor always says no," Caray said. "Last time I asked him, he said, 'Harry, I tell you what. You can have two drinks the day the Cubs win the pennant.' Well, I've been broadcasting for 52 years, but I hope don't have to wait another 52 years for that or I'm going to be pretty old."[8]

Although the 1996 season ended with no pennant for the Cubs and no drinks for Harry, it was a positive season overall for Caray. In October, Ted Cox of the *(Chicago Suburban) Daily Herald* announced the winners of awards in his "annual baseball award banquet—Chicago TV and radio division." Cox's Comeback of the Year Award went to Caray. "After a season in which he came under harsh attack," Cox wrote, "he trimmed his schedule, cut down on the errors, and proved, once again, that he is the city's most dependable announcer when it comes to pointing out the shortcomings of both players and management—in short, to telling it like it is. Overall, Caray enjoyed his best season since his stroke."[9]

In November, Caray put a capper on a satisfying personal year. The Des Plaines-based Maryville Academy, a residential facility for abused and neglected children, which Caray had supported for years, honored his generosity by giving him its Standing Tall Award at a banquet attended by more than 650 people. Attendees included former Cardinals great Stan Musial and present and former Cubs broadcasters Jack Brickhouse, Ron Santo, and Pat Hughes.

Caray, whose own childhood had helped make him keenly aware of the plight of children growing up in difficult circumstances, had annually treated the children of Maryville—almost 1,000 of them—to Thanksgiving dinner, along with making frequent visits to the home. Father John Smyth, president of Maryville, said in an interview, "Harry came out here many times. He was sincere, he was open, he was welcoming to the kids. The kids, of course, were mesmerized by him." Caray added a personal touch to his visits. "He would often play baseball with the kids," said Father Smyth. "When Harry came to bat, he would deliberately swing and miss. They would get excited and say, 'Oh, we struck him out! We struck out Harry Caray!' He would be so down to earth with them, so friendly, so open with them. He was just a big friend to these kids."[10]

"I don't think most people have a grasp for just how generous Harry is," said Cubs director of marketing John McDonough. "But every time he makes an appearance for me, or for WGN, he directs nearly all the money he makes back to Maryville." As an example, McDonough said Caray had donated his fee for singing "Take Me Out to the Ball Game" at the Democratic National Convention to Maryville. "He's always mentioning Maryville and Father Smyth on his broadcasts," said Maryville spokeswoman Clare Conerty. "You can't buy that kind of support or publicity."[11]

✸ ✸ ✸

In December, WGN-TV announced that Caray would have a new broadcasting partner in 1997. Josh Lewin, who had been broadcasting games for the Baltimore Orioles radio network, along with weekend telecasts for the Fox Sports network, would work with Steve Stone on Cubs road games (Caray was no longer traveling), plus the middle innings of games at Wrigley Field—essentially the role previously handled by Wayne Larrivee. Lewin, a 28-year-old graduate of Northwestern University, had grown up in Rochester, New York. As a child, Lewin said, "I didn't hear that much of Harry because we didn't get WGN that clearly. I didn't really get the full essence of Harry until I got to NU. Then he blew me away." Lewin spoke glowingly of Caray and Steve Stone: "I've got to be careful, because it might sound like I'm blowing smoke, but they really are a big reason why I decided to pursue this business. I can't say it was an epiphany, because I sort of always knew I'd like to do this someday, but it was the hammer that drove it home."[12]

Despite the glowing words, the Lewin–Caray relationship was strained from the start by most accounts. Like Chip Caray, Lewin was a young broadcaster who could be seen a possible successor to Harry at some point. But the Cubs and WGN, who had failed to work out an agreement with Chip two years earlier, had now added Lewin—even agreeing to allow Josh to work national network broadcasts, a major sticking point in their negotiations with Chip (and earlier, in renewal talks with both Dewayne Staats and Thom Brennaman).

Although Lewin made an effort to build a relationship with Caray, Harry seemed indifferent to the idea. "Harry was not an angel," said Bob Verdi. "He did not exactly embrace Josh Lewin, who is a tremendous broadcaster. Harry was expecting that the Cubs would hire Chip; instead, Josh showed up, a complete pro, a wonderful broadcaster, and Harry was very cool to him."[13]

"Caray didn't much like what Lewin brought to a broadcast. . . . Suffice it to say, Harry thought Lewin prepared himself too much with endless anecdotes and stories rather than being spontaneous and reacting to what was happening on the field," wrote Mike Kiley of the *Chicago Sun-Times*.[14] "The underlying plot is that Chip originally turned down the WGN offer before Lewin was hired for 1997. Harry always thought his grandson was a superior talent and held Lewin to a standard no one could match."[15]

Lewin remained deferential toward Caray, to a fault. When the 1997 season began, Caray decided to work all nine innings of the Cubs' home games, reducing Lewin's role to pre- and postgame studio host. Lewin didn't set foot in the WGN broadcast booth at Wrigley Field until May 15, six weeks into the season. "Lewin, acutely aware of understudy protocol after 14 home games, did not take crossing this important threshold lightly," wrote Phil Rosenthal of the *Chicago Sun-Times*. "He paused outside the door of the booth for a moment and took a deep breath. 'May I come in?' he asked WGN analyst Steve Stone."[16]

Lewin's deference and courtesy did not help his relationship with Caray. At one point during the 1997 season, Steve Stone wrote, Lewin's grandmother, a big Harry Caray fan, passed away. Hoping to bond with Caray, Lewin approached Harry after attending his grandmother's funeral. He told Caray about his grandmother's death and how much she had enjoyed Harry's work, and then thanked him for making her life a little more enjoyable. Stone wrote that Caray, who had been writing in his scorebook without looking up while Lewin spoke, threw down his pen and gazed out toward the field without making eye contact with Lewin.

"Yeah, Levine," Caray said to Lewin, "all my fans are dying." He then went back to writing in his scorebook.[17]

Unlike Milo Hamilton, who held a lifelong grudge against Caray for what he perceived as mistreatment, Lewin took the high road and refused to speak negatively about his experiences with Harry. After Caray died in 1998, Bob Verdi said, "I went to the memorial for Harry in Chicago and the memorial in Palm Springs. Josh Lewin was in the front row. That shows you what a class act Josh is."[18]

✿ ✿ ✿

Caray, who turned 83 on March 1, 1997, continued to bring in big business for the Cubs. "We have more, or certainly as many, endorsement requests for Harry than any of our marquee players," said Cubs marketing director John McDonough. "Harry is the Pied Piper of Wrigley Field. Despite the fact we are accused of selling ivy and sunshine and bleachers and bricks . . . what goes on on the field is the most important thing that we have. But boy, Harry's involvement is huge." Of Caray, whose salary for broadcasting Cubs games was said to be in the neighborhood of $500,000 a year, Fred Mitchell of the *Chicago Tribune* wrote, "In an era of $11-million-a-year ballplayers, who is to say that

Caray doesn't put more fans in Wrigley Field and bring more viewers nationwide to Cubs telecasts than any player?"[19]

On the field, it was another long season on the North Side. When the Cubs opened their home season against the Florida Marlins on April 8, the team had an 0–6 record. The temperature at game time was 29 degrees, and with 31-mile-per-hour winds whipping off the lake, the wind chill was minus-one. Nonetheless, 35,393 fans packed into Wrigley Field to see the Cubs lose once again, 5–3. "It looked like the Cubs were going to have a terrible year," said Grant DePorter, CEO of Harry Caray's Restaurant Group. "So I tried thinking, what would Harry do, since he always wanted to do his best for the fans."

> We decided to start selling 45-cent Budweisers [in honor of 1945, the year of the Cubs' last World Series appearance] at the restaurant until the Cubs finally won a game. The fans loved it. They knew the Cubs didn't have a shot that year, so why not just have some fun, be together, and drink some Buds. The Cubs ended up starting the year 0–14, which was a National League record. It became a national news story. Every time the Cubs lost, ESPN would update how many Buds we had served—10,000 Buds, 15,000, 20,000 . . . it went all the way up to 50,000. When the Cubs finally won their first game against the Mets on April 20, we made the headlines; the *New York Times* said, "Mets Raise the Price of Beer in Chicago." Harry loved it; he kiddingly told [Cubs manager] Jim Riggleman in front of all the news media that Riggleman was going to bankrupt him because he was selling all this cheap beer. Harry even got behind the bar to help serve the fans their 45-cent beers. He really liked being with the fans. That was his thing.[20]

The fans may have been enjoying their beers with Harry, but at least one Chicago sportswriter was not enjoying Caray's work. In a story on April 11, entitled "Let's Be Frank: Channel 9 Has Duty to Recast Harry," Jim O'Donnell of the *Chicago Sun-Times* compared Caray's work in the Cubs' home opener to "others on the pop lines who refused to acknowledge the final gong," including Muhammad Ali, Joe Namath, Willie Mays, and Frank Sinatra.

> After three hours of random thoughts, guttural coughing, and occasional phonetic ramblings, Harry Caray's Opening Day 1997 was complete. And when the play-by-play mess had mercifully ended,

242   **CHAPTER 23**

the feeling on this side of the television was hauntingly similar to the poignancy and melancholy felt after exiting a Frank Sinatra concert a few years ago back in Aurora. . . . It was nothing but sad, stark testimony to the inherent pathos and self-parody awaiting even the greatest star nearing the end of the line who refuses to get off the trolley when the clanging is done.

O'Donnell suggested that WGN change Caray's role "into a more appropriate, venerated role," for example, spending the game wandering around the ballpark greeting fans and interviewing celebrities. "And yes, he could even shake the webs every seventh inning with his one-note wonder, 'Take Me Out to the Ball Game.'"[21]

Caray would not be changing his role, however, and there wasn't much support for him to do so—even at O'Donnell's own newspaper. "The best reason for Cubs announcer Harry Caray not to step aside on WGN-TV (Ch. 9)," wrote Phil Rosenthal of the *Sun-Times* three days after O'Donnell's column, "is there's no evidence most fans want him gone. After all, no one refuses to watch Cubs telecasts because he's calling play-by-play, and some people tune in just because of him."[22]

With the Cubs heading for last place and 94 losses, their worst performance since Caray had come to the team, his role as one of the franchise's major attractions was arguably stronger than ever. When Major League Baseball inaugurated interleague play in June 1997, Paul Sullivan of the *Chicago Tribune* noted for the benefit of fans of the Milwaukee Brewers, then a member of the American League and the first American League team to visit the North Side, "The ballpark and Harry Caray are the two main draws here, and no one from the Cubs really bothers to hide the fact." When the Cubs visited Comiskey Park later in the month to play the first-ever regular-season games between the Chicago baseball teams, a major news story involved whether the White Sox would allow Caray to sing "Take Me Out to the Ball Game" during the seventh-inning stretch. To the disappointment of many, they did not. "They didn't give me a microphone," said Harry.[23]

The Cubs' final home game was an 11–3 victory against the Philadelphia Phillies on September 21, in front of a Wrigley Field crowd of 29,992. It was the last game at Wrigley for Ryne Sandberg, who had announced his retirement effective at the end of the season. Sandberg had a double and single before being removed for a pinch-runner, and the Cubs hit four home runs—the last by Jose Hernandez in the bottom of the seventh, after Caray had sung "Take Me Out to the Ball Game" for the final time in 1997. After the game, Cubs players and manager Jim Riggleman stayed on the field and interacted with the fans. Then Harry Caray signed off.

> The ballpark is still filled with people. What a wonderful way to end a season. The players . . . it had to be just something they felt like doing. Riggleman was the first man to start running toward the stands. That was really great.
>
> And I think this man [Sandberg] did it all. I think maybe he ushered in a new feeling, a new relationship between the players and the fans, rather than just the fans toward the players.
>
> Well, Harry Caray speaking from Wrigley Field. God willing, hope to see ya next year. Next year maybe will be the year we all have been waiting for forever.
>
> So long, everybody. [24]

✿ ✿ ✿

On December 18, WGN-TV made a major announcement: Chip Caray would be joining the Cubs broadcast crew to work alongside his grandfather Harry beginning with the 1998 season. "It's a wonderful, overwhelming opportunity. He's my hero," said Chip. "Naturally, I'm tickled," said Harry. "Holy cow! What a Christmas present." WGN would also allow Chip to keep doing his work for Fox Saturday baseball, a major sticking point in his previous negotiations with the station. [25]

Caray was much less pleased on January 28, when the Cubs made another major announcement: In 1998, only 92 Cubs game would be broadcast on WGN-TV, 47 fewer than in 1997. The 62 remaining broadcasts would be shown on CLTV, the Tribune Company-owned cable station, which had aired only a handful of Cubs games in the past (12 games in 1997). WGN officials said that the change was being driven by economics. Cubs ratings on WGN had fallen from 11.7 in 1989, the last time the team had reached the postseason, to 5.5 from 1995 to 1997. The station pointed out that two Warner Bros. network shows featured at night on WGN, *Buffy the Vampire Slayer* and *Dawson's Creek*, were drawing much higher ratings than the Cubs.

Reached at his winter home in Palm Springs, California, Caray expressed his disappointment. "Everybody out here was telling me how much they enjoy hearing me [on WGN's superstation broadcasts]. Now, maybe they're not going to hear me as often."[26]

24

A LONG GOODBYE

"He did well wherever he went," said St. Louis Cardinals great Stan Musial, Caray's all-time favorite player. "The Cubs fans loved him, the White Sox fans loved him, the Cardinals fans loved him. He loved life and he loved people."—Ed Sherman, *Chicago Tribune*, February 1998[1]

On Saturday, February 14, 1998—Valentine's Day—Chicago Cubs pitchers and catchers reported to the team's spring training headquarters in Mesa, Arizona. That evening, Harry Caray and his wife Dutchie had dinner at Basin Street West, a nightclub in Rancho Mirage, California, near their winter home in Palm Springs. The headliner, singer Tony Martin, knew Caray from a previous meeting and came over to greet him. "I first met him in back in the '80s, and we talked about that meeting," Martin said. "He seemed to be having a good time, and I told him we will see each other again."

When a member of the audience noticed Caray's presence, he stood up to acknowledge the crowd. As he rose, Caray leaned on a nearby table. "He simply put his hand on the table, just for balance," said Dutchie, "and the table was not secured, and it came up and knocked him." The table struck Caray's head, and he fell to the floor, unconscious. Martin said that after speaking with Caray, "I headed back to the stage, and the next thing I know I look over and there is this man laid out on the floor. It was him. It couldn't have been more than five minutes later."

Two Basin Street West employees, waiter Bobby Wehrle and bartender Chris Boni, performed cardiopulmonary resuscitation on Caray, who remained unconscious. "I did everything I could to assist him until the paramedics arrived," said Wehrle, who did not realize at first that the man he was trying to help was Caray.[2]

Caray was rushed to Eisenhower Medical Center in Rancho Mirage. He remained unconscious for the next few days as he underwent tests for a sudden change in his heart rhythm, and was listed in critical but stable condition. Caray's son Skip and grandson Chip monitored developments from Atlanta, Skip's hometown, where Chip was scheduled to broadcast a Monday night NBA game between his team, the Orlando Magic, and the Atlanta Hawks. "There is nothing we can do there," Chip said about his decision to keep working. "If the situation were turned around, I would want my grandfather to keep doing what he's doing. Broadcasting is what we do."[3]

By Tuesday, doctors had determined that Caray had suffered extensive brain damage and that the "prognosis for functional recovery is poor." Dr. Brian Olshansky, director of the Loyola (Illinois) University Medical Center, said Caray's condition could remain unchanged for weeks or months. "But if he doesn't start responding soon, then there has to be discussion of whether to withdraw him from the respirator."[4] On Wednesday, February 18, Skip Caray flew in from Atlanta and received an update on his father's condition. The end came quickly: Caray died at 4:10 Pacific Time that afternoon. The cause of death, in laymen's terms, was cardiac arrest with resultant brain damage. Family spokesman and longtime Caray friend Bill Wills would not comment on whether Harry had been taken off life support before he died.

Chip Caray recalled how he received the news.

> I'll never forget it. I was doing an NBA game in Orlando, and my wife was home with our three-month-old daughter. I think it was the second or third quarter of the game, and my wife came in sobbing, and I said, "What are you here for?" She said, "Your grandfather died." And I'm in the middle of a game. It was a commercial timeout, and I just sat there stunned and the game went back on. My partner, Jack Givens, said, "You need to go home." And I said, "Nope, I'm going to do what my grandfather would do: Just do your job and finish the game." So I finished the game.

And yeah, it was horrible. As I said before, we were a family very, very much looking forward to closing some open circles. I didn't know Harry, I didn't know him as a grandfather. I would have loved to have found out the family history, I would have loved to find out what it was like growing up in downtown St. Louis, what my dad was like as a kid, what was it like being on a train with Stan Musial, what was it like watching Jackie Robinson play, all the baseball history, not to mention the family history. When he died, that was an awful, awful loss.[5]

Caray's death was a major news story throughout the country. First Lady Hillary Rodham Clinton, who had sung "Take Me Out to the Ball Game" with Caray at the Cubs' home opener in 1994 (and who had been serenaded by Caray with the same song at her 50th birthday celebration in 1997), said in a statement, "Harry was one of a kind, and nobody could sing 'Take Me Out to the Ball Game' like he could. And I hope he's doing a seventh-inning rendition in heaven." Legendary broadcaster Vin Scully said, "People in the bleachers, as well as the man in the box seat, knew they shared their love of baseball with a true fan. Harry will be sorely missed." Cubs first baseman Mark Grace said, "No one wanted the Cubs to win more than he did. He didn't make any bones about it. Harry was probably the greatest announcer of all time."[6]

"Mr. Caray cut a humorous, opinionated, and sometimes controversial figure, whether his loud and pungent voice was calling (and rooting for) the St. Louis Cardinals, the Oakland A's, the Chicago White Sox, or the Chicago Cubs," wrote Richard Sandomir in Caray's *New York Times* obituary. Sandomir further elaborated,

A short man with oversized glasses, Mr. Caray punctuated home team home runs by shouting: "It might be! It could be! It is!" He made "Holy cow!" his on-air trademark of astonishment long before Phil Rizzuto adopted it. And after a victory for the Cubs, who were perennial losers during his tenure at Wrigley Field, he roared in delight: "Cubs win! Cubs win! Cubs win!"[7]

Broadcaster Curt Gowdy, a contemporary of Caray who had received the Hall of Fame's Ford C. Frick Award in 1984, recalled his first meeting with Harry at an Italian restaurant in St. Louis in 1948. Gowdy was dining with Hank Iba, one of the country's most famous college basketball coaches; however, when Caray—"already a legend" in only his fourth season broadcasting St. Louis Cardinals games—came over to pay his respects to the coach, Gowdy said, "I had my mouth open about a foot." Gowdy told *Boston Globe* writer Howard Manly,

> It's a funny thing about radio and TV. People have you on in their living rooms and in their ears, and the announcers get to be a part of their experience watching and listening to their favorite teams. Imagine those people in the Midwest listening to this guy with a hoarse voice getting all excited about every play, every pitch. Nobody can copy him nor should they try. That was a big mistake. He was unique.[8]

While fond words about Caray came forth from numerous sources, there was one notable exception. Asked for a comment on Caray's death by a reporter, Harry's old rival, Milo Hamilton, was quoted as follows:

> Harry felt that he was bigger than the game. I don't think there's any doubt about it. He told me one time, "The only reason they come out to the ballpark is to hear me sing in the seventh inning." So I said, "I'll tell you what I'm going to do. Thursday is an open date. Let's announce that you're going to sing at three o'clock and see how many people buy a ticket."

Hamilton's comments were roundly criticized, with Skip Caray leading the way. "What kind of man says that about a colleague two days after he died?" Skip said. "A very sick man. . . . This says more about the kind of person Milo Hamilton is than the kind of person Harry Caray was." In response, Hamilton said that his quote about Harry had come from an old magazine article. "I said it again yesterday. . . . A guy from the internet called and was prodding me about us not getting along. I have made no attempt to harangue or discredit Harry. I have even been telling people what a big influence he was on me in my career."[9]

In his autobiography, *Making Airwaves*, published in 2006, Hamilton wrote that the "internet reporter was grilling me over the phone, trying to get me to bite and talk negatively about Harry." He said he told the reporter to "look up that magazine article from 13 years ago" and then hung up. Hamilton wrote that he tried to approach Skip Caray in spring training in 1998, to explain his side of the story, but Skip "waved me away, which didn't surprise me. Skip is much like his father. He treats people around him like crap, a real chip off the old block. Just ask folks at Turner Broadcasting, WSB, or the ballpark in Atlanta; they'll tell you what he's like."[10]

* * *

Caray's family chose to have two ceremonies to remember his life and say goodbye: a wake for friends and colleagues in Palm Springs and a larger funeral ceremony and Mass in Chicago a week later. The Palm Springs ceremony, which took place at St. Theresa Church on Friday, February 20, was attended by almost 300 people, including Caray's widow Dutchie, broadcasters Jack Buck and Ron Santo, and comedian George Wendt. "I remember when the Cubs asked me if I wanted to do the games," Santo said. "I said I would try, and the only reason was because of Harry. He was so good and the same in and out of the booth. He loved baseball more than life itself." Jack Buck said, "He was the most unique broadcaster ever. It was an honor to work with him. I've lost a friend. I feel like I've lost an older brother." The half-hour prayer service, conducted by Rev. David Andel, concluded with the playing of "Take Me Out to the Ball Game."[11]

Caray's funeral Mass took place on Friday, February 27, at Chicago's Holy Name Cathedral. Among the more than 1,000 mourners were Illinois governor Jim Edgar; Chicago mayor Richard M. Daley; former congressman Dan Rostenkowski; Cubs manager Jim Riggleman; and Cubs players Mark Grace, Sammy Sosa, and Scott Servais. Former Cubs stars Billy Williams, Ryne Sandberg, and Rick Sutcliffe were also in attendance. Rev. John Smyth of Maryville, who performed the funeral Mass, invited the congregation to applaud in appreciation of Caray. Harry's friend Pete Vonachen, who delivered a humorous and heartfelt eulogy, quipped, "With all that clapping, I thought he'd jump out." Vonachen, Caray's friend for 48 years, said, "Harry never knew a stranger. He was forever young at heart." (Caray's grandson Chip called Vonachen's eulogy the "best tribute to a friend I've ever heard.") As the coffin was being carried out of the cathedral, Holy Name organist Sal Soria played a slowed-down version of "Take Me Out to the Ball Game." Soria admitted that he needed to borrow sheet music for the song.[12]

Caray's friend Grant DePorter, CEO of Harry Caray's Restaurant Group, recalled the rest of the day.

Afterward there was a procession. The hearse drove past the restaurant, where there were Clydesdales in front of the restaurant so
Harry could see the Clydesdales and his friends and fans for the last
time. Then they went to All Saints Cemetery [in suburban Des
Plaines], where he was buried. Afterward the restaurant was closed
to the public, but all of Harry's friends were here: Bob Costas, Rick
Sutcliffe, Greg Maddux, Sammy Sosa, anyone you could think of. It
kept on going and going. Late in the evening, these friends of Harry
would all raise a glass. It wasn't a sad event; it was more a case of
people toasting Harry and celebrating his life. At one point in the
evening maybe 40 people were standing on top of the bar toasting
Harry and just telling one Harry story after another.[13]

"The thing that came across at Caray's funeral Friday morning," wrote
Rick Telander, "then was reassessed and respun at the ensuing wake at
his restaurant, was that this man was somehow bigger than life and yet
absolutely a part of it. He was large, yes. But he was us."[14]

✿ ✿ ✿

With Harry gone, the Cubs prepared for the 1998 season, and Chip
Caray prepared for the daunting task of taking over for his grandfather
as the team's television play-by-play announcer. "And in Chicago with
Harry's partner Steve Stone," Chip recalled. He continued,

Harry's great producer Arne Harris. Harry's microphone. Harry's
booth. Harry's team. Harry's town. With Harry's last name. There
were a lot of traps and minefields there. I'm so glad I had Steve
Stone and Arne Harris to guide me through some of those tricky
spots, because if they hadn't helped me I'm not sure I would have
made it.[15]

The Cubs opened the season in Miami, where they took two of three
games from the Florida Marlins before returning to Chicago for their
April 3 home opener against the Montreal Expos. It was a frigid day—
temperatures in the low 40s with strong winds—but a sellout crowd of
39,102 was on hand. The game was only part of the attraction, as the
Cubs were also honoring Caray, celebrating Harry's life a little more
than six weeks after his passing. Throngs of people, hoping to buy

standing room tickets, lined up outside Wrigley Field several hours before the game was scheduled to start.

Chip Caray had gone to Mass at Holy Name Cathedral early that morning, arriving at Wrigley at around 8 a.m. with Dutchie and Pete Vonachen. It was only the fourth time Chip had been to Wrigley Field for a game. "When I stepped into the booth, it was eerie," Chip said. "The enormity of it was too much. . . . I had to get out of the booth for a while and do things elsewhere before I went back."[16]

In honor of Caray, the Cubs' uniforms were adorned with sleeve patches featuring Harry's face in his trademark oversized glasses. After a moment of silence for Caray prior to the start of the game, a large version of the same caricature of Caray was unfurled above the television broadcast booth. The day's most anticipated event would come during the seventh-inning stretch, when Dutchie was scheduled to lead the crowd in singing Harry's trademark song, "Take Me Out to the Ball Game." Mrs. Caray admitted she was so nervous she hadn't slept for days.

The sellout crowd could hardly bear to wait for the seventh-inning stretch. The Cubs were leading, 5–1, with two out in the top of the seventh inning when the chants of "Harry! Harry!" began ringing through the ballpark. Soon almost everyone in the park was standing and joining in the chant. "It felt eerily like a World Series game in late October," wrote Skip Bayless. "The anticipation rose as the temperature fell."[17] Cubs pitcher Steve Trachsel, anxious to get the final out in the half-inning, said, "I lost it mentally for a few pitches. I was thinking about getting in the dugout, knowing what the fans wanted."[18] First baseman Mark Grace, a close friend of Harry's, said he had chills when the fans began cheering. "Nobody understands how big that man was," said Grace. "He's bigger than anyone who played the game, bigger than any Cub."[19]

When Expos second baseman Mark Grudzielanek—fittingly, a player whose last name Harry always struggled to pronounce—grounded out to end the top of the seventh, the stadium erupted. Dutchie's first words were drowned out by the cheering, but then she called Harry's familiar "A one! A two! A three!" and began the song. Just like Harry, she waved the microphone to the crowd as the song continued. "It was just great, a great feeling to know how much they loved Harry," said Dutchie, who hugged Chip after finishing the song. "I was just overwhelmed."[20] The tribute to Harry was not quite over. After the finish of "Take Me Out to the Ball Game," blue and white balloons were released and the stadium sound system played a somber rendition of "Amazing Grace" on bagpipes as the crowd grew silent. Many people were in tears.

WGN-TV director of production Bob Vorwald remembered the day, a 6–2 Cubs victory.

> Opening Day in 1998 after Harry passed away was a raw, cold day. The Cubs were not supposed to be very good that year, and at the start of the game there were like 3,000 people in the ballpark. But by the seventh inning, the place was packed. Then Chip and Dutchie did the seventh-inning stretch, and they played "Amazing Grace" and let the balloons go. It was an electric, wonderful moment. By the time there were two outs in the eighth inning, there was nobody left in the ballpark. Everybody was there for that moment; nobody was there for the baseball.[21]

Pete Vonachen commented, "It's still the same. Nothing's changed. After the seventh inning, the fans were leaving the ballpark like rats leaving a sinking ship. Vrroom. Out the door."[22]

✧ ✧ ✧

Along with the Opening Day tributes to Caray, the Cubs announced that they would be keeping Harry's tradition of singing "Take Me Out to the Ball Game" by inviting "guest conductors" to lead the Wrigley Field crowd in song throughout the 1998 season. Among those invited were Stan Musial, Vin Scully, Walter Payton, Jay Leno, Joe Mantegna, and Rev. John Smyth. Some thought the continued tributes to Caray a bit much. "No doubt Mr. Caray would have been embarrassed and chagrined if he could have somehow known his death would create such a months-long fuss," wrote Richard Roeper of the *Chicago Sun-Times*.[23] But the "guest conductor" tradition was still being continued in 2018, two decades after Caray's death, with Harry himself leading the crowd on many days, via video on the Wrigley Field scoreboard.

One unfortunate tradition from the Harry Caray years that the Cubs were *not* keeping in 1998 was putting a losing team on the field. The club got off to a 6–1 start, cooled off a bit, then caught fire in May, a month in which Cubs rookie Kerry Wood pitched one of the greatest games in major-league history: a one-hit shutout against the Houston Astros in which he struck out 20 batters (tying a major league record), while walking none. The National League Most Valuable Player, Sammy Sosa, waged a season-long duel with the Cardinals' Mark McGwire to break Roger Maris's single-season home run record of 61. Sosa wound up with 66 home runs, four fewer than McGwire, including a single-month record 20 in June. The Cubs finished the season with 90 wins and won the National League wild card by defeating the San Francisco Giants in a one-game playoff. Unfortunately, the North Siders were swept by the Atlanta Braves in the National League Division Series, but it was still a special year. Being able to broadcast games for a winning team was a relief to Chip Caray in his first season as the successor to his grandfather. "When you have a good team, all your sins are seemingly forgiven as a broadcaster, and the 1998 Cubs were one of them," Chip said. "One of the great Cinderella stories in Chicago sports history, and I got to be there for every single game of it."[24]

In August, the Cubs held a Harry Caray Day at Wrigley Field, something they were unable to do in 1994–1995, due to Harry's medical issues and the baseball strike. Dutchie Caray threw out the first pitch prior to the game, and Chip Caray led the crowd in "Take Me Out to the Ball Game" during the seventh-inning stretch. At the same time, the Cubs announced that a statue of Harry would be erected outside Wrigley Field prior to the start of the 1999 season. No Cubs player had ever been honored with a statue, and the decision was questioned in some quarters—particularly after Jack Brickhouse, the Cubs' lead broadcaster for 39 years, died on August 6. Many people thought that if Caray merited a statue, so did Brickhouse. Richard Roeper of the *Sun-Times* thought the whole notion questionable.

> As children growing up in this country, we were taught that only great men and women of brave and lasting accomplishment were immortalized in statues that might dominate a park or plaza for decades. Saints, presidents, war heroes, Native American chiefs, martyrs, pioneers and explorers, scientists and astronomers, doctors who invented cures for killer diseases, Greek gods.
>
> People who get statues get multi-page entries in encyclopedias.[25]

Nonetheless, Caray got a statue; Brickhouse did not (the Cubs would subsequently dedicate statues outside Wrigley Field to former players Ernie Banks, Billy Williams, and Ron Santo). Caray's statue would, in fact, not be the first by a team to honor a broadcaster. In late August 1998, the St. Louis Cardinals unveiled a statue of Jack Buck, Caray's successor as the Cardinals' lead broadcaster, outside Busch Stadium. Buck, who was still active in his 45th season broadcasting Cardinals games, quipped that there appeared to be no hurry to dedicate his statue until Caray's death. "I said we'd better get that sucker up there," observed Buck.[26]

The Caray statue, which showed Harry with his left hand outstretched and his right hand reaching out while holding his microphone—as he usually did when leading the crowd in "Take Me Out to the Ball Game"—was dedicated at the Cubs' home opener against the Cincinnati Reds on April 12, 1999. The principal sculptor was Omni Amrany, a native Israeli who had lived in Chicago for 10 years and was the creator of the Michael Jordan statue outside Chicago's United Center. Dutchie Caray was on hand with her four-year-old grandchildren, Jenna Johnson and Brendan Newell. Asked what his grandfather would have thought about the statue, Chip Caray laughed and said, "Probably something like, 'Hey, I'm a lot better looking than that.' But he also would feel as honored as the rest of the family was, because his fans were there."[27]

As was often the case during Harry's life, the dedication of the statue was not without controversy. Along with unveiling the statue of Caray, the Cubs paid tribute to Jack Brickhouse by displaying his trademark home run call—"Hey Hey"—on the left- and right-field foul poles. Some writers and fans complained that Brickhouse was being slighted. "To call it a slight is being kind," wrote Jay Mariotti in the *Chicago Sun-Times*. "Consider it blatant favoritism, Tribune Co.'s way of honoring its own beloved Caray while dissing a similarly beloved broadcaster who happened to precede its ownership." Nonetheless, Pat Brickhouse, Jack's widow, refused to be drawn into the controversy. "There was no competitiveness between these two men," she said of her husband and Caray. "They loved each other."[28]

The Cubs lost to the Reds that day, 7–2, on their way to a 67–95 record and a last-place finish in the six-team National League Central

Division. For the Cubs, the magic of 1998 was gone, at least for a while. Harry Caray's magic would live on.

25

EPILOGUE

Harry Caray's Lasting Impact

Time doesn't really march on, much as we'd be comforted if true.

It's more like time races by at 90 mph while we try to get out of the left lane and avoid getting run over by an unforgiving, undefeated calendar.

Witness the 20 years it's already been since Harry Caray left us in February 1998.

It sure doesn't feel like it.

Maybe it's because he is so dearly missed, those summer days and nights of entertaining the faithful even in years when the Cubs offered so little of the same.—Barry Rozner, (*Chicago Suburban*) *Daily Herald*, February 2018[1]

As the world began a new millennium in 2000, Harry Caray was gone, and the sports world that he worked in was undergoing major changes. While Caray would never be forgotten, many of the broadcasters he worked with were passing on, and the teams and stations he worked for were entering a new era.

* * *

In June 2002, Jack Buck, who had worked with Caray for 15 years before succeeding him as the Cardinals' main play-by-play voice, died at age 77. Buck had worked for the Cardinals for 48 years, and his obituary in the *St. Louis Post-Dispatch* called him the "voice of St. Louis"—a title that had once belonged to Caray. "He had a simple rule, but it was Golden," the obituary stated. "Treat other people the way you want them to treat you."[2] More than 2,000 fans responded to the question, "What's your favorite Jack Buck radio call?" on the newspaper's website, stltoday.com. The winner: "Go crazy folks! Go crazy!" after Ozzie Smith's walk-off homer against the Los Angeles Dodgers in Game 5 of the 1985 National League Championship Series.[3]

❉ ❉ ❉

In 2003, the Cubs finished in first place in the National League Central Division, then defeated the Atlanta Braves—Skip Caray's team—in the Division Series. It was the Cubs' first win in a postseason series since 1908. As the Cubs took on the Florida Marlins in the National League Championship Series, Paul Sullivan wrote, "The ghost of Harry Caray hovers over Wrigley Field come playoff time. Or at least that's been the legend since a giant helium balloon of his head appeared on Sheffield Avenue outside the park during the 1998 wild-card tiebreaker game against San Francisco."[4] The Cubs won that 1998 game, but Harry's ghost was no help in 2003. After winning three of the first four games against the Marlins, leaving them a victory away from the World Series, the Cubs dropped the final three games to lose the series.

❉ ❉ ❉

In 2004, the Cubs drew more than 3 million fans to their home games—the first time either Chicago baseball team had topped the 3 million mark. During the next 14 seasons, the Cubs would top 3 million in home attendance 10 times and never draw fewer than 2.6 million fans.

In October 2004, Chip Caray left the Cubs after seven seasons as the team's lead television broadcaster. Caray chose to take a position with the Atlanta Braves, where he was reunited with his father, Skip. Cubs' analyst Steve Stone left the team as well; he spent several years working for Chicago sports radio station WSCR before becoming the Chicago White Sox' television analyst in 2008.

Caray and Stone did not leave the Cubs quietly. In something reminiscent of incidents during Chip's grandfather's career, Caray and Stone were under fire from Cubs players and manager Dusty Baker for their blunt criticism of the team during the late stages of the 2004 season. "The Cubs still had a chance in September, but they just tripped all over themselves and played poorly," Chip recalled. He continued:

> And unfortunately it was very, very easy and very convenient for the players to point to the broadcast booth as the reason that they weren't winning. I really thought that was a horrible copout. . . . When you're doing a national TV broadcast like Steve and I were, I wasn't about to sacrifice my credibility and tell 100 million baseball fans that chicken shit was chicken salad.

But Caray said that the friction with Baker and Cubs players—particularly pitcher Kent Mercker—was not a factor in his decision to leave. "I've long since made up with Dusty Baker and Kent Mercker," he revealed. The bottom line was that the Braves simply made him a better offer. "The Cubs offered me a two-year contract that was almost laughable," he said, "and the Braves offered me a much longer and more lucrative contract than the Cubs, and the Tribune Company chose not to exercise."[5]

* * *

In 2005, the Chicago White Sox won the World Series, becoming the first Chicago baseball team to do so since the 1917 Sox. It was a triumph for Jerry Reinsdorf and Eddie Einhorn in their 25th season running the team. "Jerry would say that though he had the six NBA championships with the [Chicago] Bulls, the World Series in 2005 was worth more to him and his legacy," said Chicago broadcaster Mike Leiderman. "I always thought Jerry got a bad rap. He was the best owner this town has seen. Jerry took a really bad, needy team, stuck with it, did the best he could with it, and took the heat."[6]

Even with a championship team in 2005, the White Sox (home attendance 2,342,833) were outdrawn by the Cubs (3,099,992), who had a losing record (79–83) and finished fourth in a six-team division, by more than 750,000 fans. The next year, with a 90-win team, the White Sox drew a franchise record 2,957,414 fans to their South Side ballpark. The Cubs, with a last-place team that lost 96 games, had a home attendance of 3,123,215.

✿ ✿ ✿

In 2006, Milo Hamilton's autobiography, *Making Airwaves*, was published. Hamilton, who had clashed with Harry Caray for most of his life, "appropriates a portion of his autobiography to defame his fellow Hall of Famer [*sic*]," wrote Bob Verdi, who called it an "uncomfortable read, but perhaps an inevitable occurrence." Among other things, Hamilton referred to Caray as a "miserable human being." That was not a path Caray had taken in his own autobiography, *Holy Cow!* Verdi—who collaborated with Caray on *Holy Cow!*—said in an interview that when they were putting together the book, Caray deliberately avoided the subject of his difficult relationship with Hamilton.

> I was in spring training when I took over working on Harry's book with him. We would go out to dinner, and Harry would start telling me all these great stories, including some about Milo; I'd be writing them down on cocktail napkins because we were having dinner and I wasn't prepared for doing an interview. The next morning he'd call me at about 7:30 and say, "You know that stuff we talked about last night. . . . I don't want any of that in the book." So you'll notice that there's very little mention of Milo in the book.[7]

Hamilton, who would retire as a broadcaster prior to the 2012 season and die in 2015, at age 88, would soften a bit in his later years on the subject of Caray. "That's behind me, and I settled that in my book," he said in 2007. "I felt it was something I had to say, and I haven't said anything about it since. I've had too good a career to keep that going. . . . I don't even think about it anymore." He even complimented Caray's broadcasting style, saying, "Sure, he was different. . . . But with his abilities and the way he did his job, he would find a place today."[8]

✿ ✿ ✿

In August 2008, Skip Caray died at age 68—his father's age when Harry began broadcasting for the Cubs in 1982. Skip had been working with his son Chip on Atlanta Braves broadcasts since 2005, and although Skip's health had been failing in recent years (in 2008, he was broadcasting only Braves home games), it had been a good time for both. "We've probably had more in-depth conversations on the way to and from the park, laughed more, and enjoyed each other more than at any time in the last 35 or 40 years," Chip said.

"In an industry predicated on likeability, he really didn't care if you liked him or not," Mark Bradley wrote in an appreciation of Skip Caray. "He said what he thought . . . and if he happened to ruffle the tender sensibilities of listeners or management, well tough." Skip may have paid a price for his honesty: Unlike his father and many of his broadcasting contemporaries (one of whom was Milo Hamilton), he never received the National Baseball Hall of Fame's Ford C. Frick Award. It bothered him. Cincinnati Reds broadcaster Marty Brennaman—Thom's father and the Frick Award winner in 2000—once commented, "You don't talk to Skip about the whole Hall of Fame thing. That'll really gets him going. He's never gotten over it."

Skip Caray's most famous call came in the seventh game of the 1992 National League Championship Series. With two out in the bottom of the ninth, the bases loaded, and Caray's Braves trailing the Pittsburgh Pirates, 2–1, Skip described Francisco Cabrera's game-winning hit, which drove in slow-footed Sid Bream for the winning run, with his customary humor.

> A lot of room in right center. If he hits one there, we can dance in the streets. The 2–1. Swung, line drive to left field! One run is in! Here comes Bream! Here's the throw to the plate! He is . . . safe! Braves win! Braves win! Braves win! Braves win! Braves win! They may have to hospitalize Sid Bream; he's down at the bottom of a huge pile at the plate. [9]

*　*　*

In August 2009, the Tribune Company sold a 95 percent interest in the Cubs to the Ricketts family, led by Chicago-based investment banker Tom Ricketts. The purchase price of about $800 million was almost 40 times the $20.5 million the Tribune Company had paid for the team in 1981. With circulation and ad revenue in steep decline for the *Chicago*

Tribune, the *Los Angeles Times*, and the company's other newspapers, the Tribune Company had filed for bankruptcy in December 2008. Shortly thereafter, the company had solicited bids for the team, and the Ricketts family had been selected as the company's targeted buyer.

The Ricketts family's ability to improve the Cubs on the field was met with skepticism at first—on the day of the sale, the Tribune Company-owned *Los Angeles Times* had called the Cubs a "team known as lovable losers." But during the next several years the family hired Boston Red Sox executive Theo Epstein, who had led the Red Sox to Boston's first World Series championships since 1918; put money into developing one of baseball's best farm systems; made major renovations to Wrigley Field and its environs; and set the team on the path toward its World Series championship in 2016.

* * *

In September 2010, Caray's statue outside Wrigley Field was moved from the corner of Addison and Sheffield to a new location outside the bleachers entrance at Waveland and Sheffield. A statue of Cubs great Billy Williams was placed at the former location of the Caray statue.

Dutchie Caray, Harry's widow, said she was a little sad at first when she learned of the relocation but that she was happy with the outcome. "Well here we go again—Harry is on the move," she said outside the new location of the statue, adding that Harry always needed to be where the action was. "How many drinks [Harry and friend Pete Vonachen] left on bars because Harry couldn't stay in one place." She then led the small crowd gathered near the statue in a rendition of "Take Me Out to the Ball Game."[10]

* * *

In May 2014, WGN America announced that WGN-TV would be converting from a superstation to a basic cable channel. A major ramification of the move was that WGN would no longer offer nationwide broadcasts of games featuring the Chicago Cubs, White Sox, Bulls, or Blackhawks. Unlike the years in which Caray was broadcasting Cubs games on the WGN superstation with little nationwide competition from other teams, almost every major-league game was now available for viewing via video streaming through subscription services marketed by mlb.com. Even in Chicago, the Cubs and White Sox were broadcasting more games on Comcast Sportsnet Chicago (now known as NBC Sports Chicago), an all-sports cable station jointly owned by the Cubs, White Sox, Bulls, and Blackhawks, than on WGN-TV. This was essentially the baseball broadcasting world envisioned by Eddie Einhorn when he launched SportsVision with the White Sox in 1982—only with more games available at cheaper prices. "The fact that you're now paying hundreds of dollars for what you used to get for free is a testament to Eddie Einhorn and Jerry Reinsdorf's vision," said Mike Leiderman. "Like many other things, SportsVision came a little too soon. Wrong time, wrong place."[11]

In March 2014, the Cubs had announced the end of another era: Beginning in 2015, the Cubs were ending their 90-year relationship with WGN radio, shifting their broadcasts to WBBM. The contract allowed the Cubs an opt-out after one year, and, since 2015, Cubs radio broadcasts have been heard on all-sports station WSCR. But WGN radio wasn't finished with baseball broadcasting: In 2018, WGN became the radio home of the Chicago White Sox. That news might have merited a "Holy Cow!" from Harry Caray.

* * *

In February 2016—the year the Cubs finally won the World Series after an 108-year drought—Chicago White Sox vice chairman Eddie Einhorn died at age 80, after complications from a stroke. One month later, Caray's former St. Louis Cardinals broadcasting partner, Joe Garagiola, died at age 90.

Garagiola, the winner of the National Baseball Hall of Fame's Ford C. Frick Award in 1991—two years after Caray—was one of the few broadcasting contemporaries of Harry's who had arguably become more famous than Caray. The two had never really reconciled since their last years together with the Cardinals, when Garagiola's fame began to spread and Caray, his former mentor, had considered Joe unappreciative.

Caray also had a strained relationship with Einhorn, concerning his move from the White Sox to the Cubs in 1982. But in his last recorded interview in January 1998, several weeks before his death, with *Chicago*

Tribune writer Paul Sullivan, Caray expressed warm feelings toward Einhorn—although not toward Jerry Reinsdorf, who had once referred to Caray and Jimmy Piersall as "scum." "I liked Einhorn all right, because you knew where he was coming from," he told Sullivan. "Reinsdorf was one of the tricky guys who you better look at the last line of the contract in very small print."[12]

* * *

In April 2018, *Forbes* magazine issued its yearly list of the current values of major-league franchises. The Cubs, with a value of $2.9 billion, were ranked as MLB's third most-valuable franchise after the New York Yankees ($4 billion) and Los Angeles Dodgers ($3 billion). Jerry Reinsdorf's Chicago White Sox ranked 14th among the 30 MLB franchises with a value of $1.5 billion.

It is worth recalling that, during a fairly short time period in 1980–1981, both the White Sox and Cubs were sold for approximately the same price, $20 million—and also worth noting that 1981 was Harry Caray's last season broadcasting games for the White Sox before moving to the Cubs. There are certainly many factors involved in the amazing increase in the value of the Cubs franchise since 1981. Credit should properly go to the national impact of the WGN-TV superstation during the 1980s and 1990s; the enduring charm of Wrigley Field, one of baseball's most hallowed stadiums; the Tribune Company and the Ricketts family, for their work in marketing the team as a national franchise and helping make the park a destination for baseball fans; and Theo Epstein and his management team, for their work in turning the Cubs from lovable losers into World Series champions.

But almost everyone associated with the Cubs in the last four decades would give major credit to Harry Caray for his work in popularizing the team from coast to coast. "Harry's impact on the Cubs franchise was immeasurable," said writer Ron Rapoport. "He was the face of the franchise in a way that no player could have been, because the players didn't stay that long; they came and went, especially in that era. But Harry was there forever. He was like the great player, the lovable player that everyone wanted on their team, and he never left."[13]

In criticizing the Cubs' decision to erect a statue of Caray in 1998, Richard Roeper wrote, "We were taught that only great men and women of brave and lasting accomplishment were immortalized in stat-ues."[14] Harry Caray may or may not have deserved a statue—but he was certainly a man of lasting accomplishment.

❋ ❋ ❋

In his 2005 book *Voices of Summer*, sports broadcasting historian Curt Smith ranked baseball's 101 greatest announcers using a 10-point sys-tem for each of the following criteria: longevity, continuity, network coverage, kudos, language, popularity, persona, voice, knowledge, and miscellany. Smith ranked Vin Scully first, with a perfect score of 100 (10 in every category). Then came Mel Allen (99), Ernie Harwell (97), Jack Buck (96), Red Barber (95), and Harry Caray (94). Smith gave Caray perfect 10s in each category except for eights in continuity, network coverage, and miscellany, which includes work in other sports.[15]

Whatever one thinks of this system or the resulting rankings, it puts Caray near the top of his profession. And the system perhaps slights some of Harry's greatest strengths. One difference between Caray and the men Smith ranked above him was that the others arguably had a greater impact on the national stage, often working network radio and television postseason broadcasts viewed and heard by millions. By contrast, Caray's network experience was more limited and not always well-received; in particular, the reviews of his work in national broad-casts of the Cardinals' 1960s World Series were pretty harsh. But Ca-ray's strength was always based on his deep connection to a *local* team, even when his WGN-TV superstation broadcasts were available to a national audience. Disregarding his brief experience with the St. Louis Browns and Oakland Athletics, he worked for three different franchises and made an indelible impact on all of them. For fans of the Cardinals, White Sox, and Cubs, he was a trusted and greatly loved voice—*their* voice. That is an amazing accomplishment.

"How many people did Harry meet in his life . . . 10 million?" said WGN-TV's Bob Vorwald, who added,

> But he made everyone who met him feel like they were the most important person in the world in that moment. How many people could create the magic that Harry did, for three different franchises? He was beloved with the Cardinals, and then beloved with the White Sox, and then he went to the Cubs, and he was the most beloved

there as well. He was a Hall of Fame broadcaster for three different teams.[16]

❊ ❊ ❊

Could Caray's style—personal, honest, and often harshly critical of the players, managers, and even the owners of the teams he was covering—work today? Even people who admired Caray have their doubts. "Back then the players didn't like it; now it would be even worse," said one of Caray's former broadcast partners, Rich King. Added King,

> I don't think the station would put up with it, and I don't think management would either. You don't see that much anymore. You see guys criticize individual plays—if a guy makes an error, he makes an error—but if you start getting on a guy constantly, or getting on management's case, saying they're bringing in the wrong players or something, I think you'd get in big trouble.[17]

"The landscape has changed; the pressure that broadcasters are under to understand that they are employees of the ballclub is great," said Ed Randall of New York sports radio station WFAN. "So they're not going to be as critical as Harry was."[18] Rick Telander, who began working for the *Chicago-Sun Times* when Caray was broadcasting White Sox games in the 1970s, agreed. "I'm afraid Harry's style wouldn't work today," said Telander. "All his rough edges would get sanded off. Too much controversy, management is too tight. These days, a broadcaster is employed by the team. You can criticize things up to a point, but Harry would sometimes go over the top with his criticism."[19]

Yet, two decades after his death, Caray's memory remains largely undiminished. "People always say that Harry is larger than life," said Grant DePorter of Harry Caray's Restaurant Group. "He's the spirit of the Cubs, and people felt like he was pulling strings when the Cubs finally won the World Series." Every year on the anniversary of his death, the Caray restaurants celebrate a worldwide toast to Harry. "We've had people doing this in bars and restaurants in over 120 countries, and over 5 million fans have toasted Harry over those years," said DePorter. "This last year [2018] we had people toasting Harry in Antarctica; people toasted Harry at NASA; the year before last we had 80 sets of identical twins dressed in Cubs gear toasting Harry. Fans just come out strong."[20]

"How many people in this business so long after their passing have the kind of presence that he still has?" said Caray's former broadcast partner, Dewayne Staats. "When you mention Harry, people know who you're talking about 20 years after he passed away. He's always had this bigger than life presence, and I think that has transcended his death. And he still has that presence. It's really amazing."[21]

"Twenty years after Harry's death," said Bob Verdi, "he's remembered like it happened yesterday. He's got his mug on the press box. There's a statue of him outside the park. People still talk about him on the radio. People still imitate him. I think he is so beloved 20 years later not because he was great at what he did, but because as the years go by we realize how unique, how different he was. You will not replace him."[22]

* * *

Asked how he remembered his grandfather, Chip Caray recalled a complicated man who tried hard to work past the scars he received as a child.

> I think I remember Harry as most fans do, as this lovable Falstaffian kind of character without the monk's robes and the beard, the guy that wanted to be the life of the party, a guy that sought acceptance because as a child he didn't have any, and had no idea or knowledge of all these things that are sort of automatically in our DNA when it comes to family and friendships. Harry was fiercely loyal, fiercely independent. He was a guy you did not cross, not the old turn-the-other-cheek kind of person, He loved his beer, he loved his baseball, he loved his wife Dutchie. Steve Stone and Thommy Brennaman were kind of like sons that he could nurture while he was there. I guess baseball was his family in lieu of the one that he really had.
>
> Dutchie, at the end of his life, really started to help him understand the importance of family. As I said before, I only had meals with my grandfather a handful of times; one was a Christmas celebration that Dutchie had him put together in Chicago. That was the only time I ever saw him cry, because he saw his extended family, his

grandchildren, his great grandchildren, he saw the enormity of what he accomplished in life, from penniless and an orphan in St. Louis to be the toast of Chicago, and a famous person who never had to worry about what color pants he wore—because that was how he was taunted as a kid—and to see all these people coming to pay homage to him, I think that was probably humbling for him and maybe the only time in his life that he ever had been.[23]

Ned Colletti, who began his long career working for major-league teams with the Cubs in 1982—Harry's first year on the North Side—summed up his feelings about Caray, in a sentiment shared by many. "I know a thousand people in the game," he said. "I only knew one like Harry."[24]

NOTES

INTRODUCTION

1. Dan Caesar, "To Jack Buck, Caray Was Independent, Confrontational, Unique," *St. Louis Post-Dispatch*, February 19, 1998, A9.

2. Dick Miller, "Melton, Bonds Fill Angels' Need for More Muscle," *Sporting News*, January 3, 1976, 42.

3. Author interview with Bob Verdi, March 1, 2018.

4. Author interview with Bob Costas, May 24, 2018.

5. Rick Telander, "Harry Caray Retrospective Offers Honest Look at Beloved Figure," *Chicago Sun-Times*, January 30, 2016.

6. E-mail from Len Kasper to author, January 17, 2018.

1. THE MAN WHO WASN'T THERE

1. Audio from WGN Chicago Cubs broadcast, October 6, 1991. Available at https://www.youtube.com/watch?v=iPaACIEnQMg&t=68s (February 22, 2018).

2. I. E. Sanborn, "Cubs Supreme in Baseball World," *Chicago Tribune*, October 15, 1908, 1.

3. Audio from Pat Hughes's WSCR Chicago Cubs radio broadcast, November 3, 2016. Available at http://www.youtube.com/watch?v=-SprKzChpyc (February 23, 2018).

4. Author interview with Ned Colletti, January 19, 2018.

5. Audio from Harry Caray Budweiser commercial, November 3, 2016. Available at http://www.dailymail.co.uk/news/article-3902434/Now-lives-

complete-Budweiser-pulls-epic-ad-overnight-featuring-legendary-sportscaster-Harry-Caray-announcing-Cubs-World-Series-champions.html (February 22, 2018).

    6. Author interview with Dutchie Caray, March 22, 2018.

2. EARLY DAYS

    1. "Back Home at KXOK," in "On the Air Lanes," *Sporting News*, January 13, 1944, 9.

    2. Joe Goddard, "Holy Halls of Fame! Two in One Day for Harry," *Sporting News*, February 6, 1989, 29.

    3. Rich Wolfe and George Castle, *I Remember Harry Caray* (Champaign, IL: Sports Publishing, 1998), xxviii.

    4. Audio from DVD *"Hello Again Everybody": The Harry Caray Story*. JLT Films, 2006.

    5. Jerome Holtzman, "He Had Many Loves: People, Baseball, Chicago—and Life," *Chicago Tribune*, February 19, 1998, 51.

    6. *"Hello Again Everybody": The Harry Caray Story*.

    7. Richard Dozer, "Harry Caray! Holy Cow!" *Chicago Tribune Magazine*, August 13, 1972, 26.

    8. Ted Patterson, *The Golden Voices of Baseball* (Champaign, Ill.: Sports Publishing, 2000), 110.

    9. Patterson, *The Golden Voices of Baseball*, 110.

    10. Curt Smith, *Voices of the Game: The First Full-Scale Overview of Baseball Broadcasting, 1921 to the Present* (South Bend, Ind.: Diamond Communications, 1987), 97.

    11. Harry Caray, with Bob Verdi, *Holy Cow!* (New York: Villard, 1989), 51.

    12. Stew Thornley, *Holy Cow! The Life and Times of Halsey Hall* (Minneapolis, Minn.: Nodin Press, 1991), 7.

    13. Dozer, "Harry Caray! Holy Cow!" 27.

    14. "Browns Put on Air," in "On the Air Lanes," *Sporting News*, August 17, 1944, 8.

    15. Dozer, "Harry Caray! Holy Cow!" 27.

    16. "Broadcaster Dean Tells Folks What He Seen," *Sporting News*, August 7, 1946, 11.

    17. J. G. Taylor Spink, "Dean Tops Play-by-Play Aircasters; Commentator Prize to Wismer Again," *Sporting News*, November 2, 1944, 4.

    18. Stuart Shea, *Calling the Game: Baseball Broadcasting from 1920 to the Present* (Phoenix, Ariz.: Society for American Baseball Research, 2015), 209.

19. J. G. Taylor Spink, "Down Memory Lane with the Old Sarge," in "Looping the Loops," *Sporting News*, August 20, 1947, 2.

20. "Neat Feat, Street," *St. Louis Star-Times*, May 25, 1945, 20.

21. "Dizzy' Dean Rides 'em Again!" Falstaff ad, *St. Louis Star-Times*, April 16, 1945, 19.

22. Caray, with Verdi, *Holy Cow!* 77–82.

23. "Complaints about Series Broadcasts Prompt Survey of Listeners' Desires," *Sporting News*, October 16, 1946, 25.

24. J. G. Taylor Spink, "Allen and Caray Top Play-by-Play Announcers," *Sporting News*, November 27, 1946, 19.

25. Peter Golenbock, *The Spirit of St. Louis: A History of the St. Louis Cardinals and Browns* (New York: Avon Books, 2000), 375.

3. VOICE OF THE CARDINALS

1. Charles Menees, "Popular Recordings," *St. Louis Post-Dispatch*, September 6, 1950, 38.

2. Ray Gillespie, "DeWitt's Rent Hike Hopes Grow with Cards' Crowds," *Sporting News*, August 17, 1949, 14.

3. "Caray and Allen Named Top Play-by-Play Broadcasters," *Sporting News*, October 3, 1951, 2.

4. "Fans Flock from Far Points to See Redbirds Play Dodgers," *Sporting News*, September 3, 1952, 11.

5. Curt Smith, *Voices of the Game: The First Full-Scale Overview of Baseball Broadcasting, 1921 to the Present* (South Bend, Ind.: Diamond Communications, 1987), 458.

6. Rich Wolfe and George Castle, *I Remember Harry Caray* (Champaign, Ill.: Sports Publishing, 1998), 118.

7. Bill Fleischman, "It Might Be! It Could Be! It Is!" *St. Louis Star-Times*, July 6, 1949, 27.

8. "Caray Makes Ticker Talk Sound Like Park Aircast, *Sporting News*, July 20, 1947, 18.

9. John Snyder, *Cardinals Journal: Year by Year and Day by Day with the St. Louis Cardinals since 1882* (Cincinnati, Ohio: Emmis Books, 2006), 359.

10. "Caray and Street Jabber Way through Long Game," *Sporting News*, May 26, 1948, 24.

11. J. G. Taylor Spink, "Broadcasting Awards Won by Allen and Caray," *Sporting News*, October 6, 1948, 13.

12. Smith, *Voices of the Game*, 458.

13. John Crosby, "Dean's Wit and 'Prose' Earn Him Choice Spot," *Washington Post*, September 28, 1947, 1.1.

14. Bill Fleischman, "Voice from the Sidelines," *St. Louis Star-Times*, October 12 (26), 17 (23), 18 (21), 21 (39), 24 (20).

15. Lee Baker, "Baker's Dozen," *Alton (Illinois) Evening Telegraph*, August 16 and 23, 1952, 9.

16. "FBI Probes Threat to Cardinals and Harry Caray," *St. Louis Star-Times*, July 29, 1949, 1.

17. Harry Caray, with Bob Verdi, *Holy Cow!* (New York: Villard, 1989), 107.

18. John Smith, "Holy Cow, It's Caray, Baseball's No. 1 Fan," *Florida Today*, March 30, 1975, 6C.

4. CHANGING TIMES

1. Merle Jones, "Egypt Sport Talk, *(Carbondale) Southern Illinoisan*, July 1, 1950, 9.

2. "Boos for Making Good 'Hard Way,'" *Sporting News*, September 18, 1946, 7

3. Scott Ferkovich, "Sportman's Park (St. Louis)," *Society for American Baseball Research*, 2014, https://sabr.org/bioproj/park/sportsmans-park-st-louis (December 11, 2017).

4. Stanley Woodward, "Views of Sport," *New York Herald Tribune*, May 9, 1947, reprinted in *Sporting News*, May 21, 1947, 4.

5. Warren Corbett, "The 'Strike' against Jackie Robinson: Truth or Myth," *Baseball Research Journal* 46, no. 1 (2017): 88–92.

6. Harry Caray, with Bob Verdi, *Holy Cow!* (New York: Villard, 1989), 98.

7. "Harry Christopher Caray (baseball commentator)," *Broadcasting and Cable*, March 14, 1994.

8. Richard Goldstein, "Fred Saigh, Who Helped Cardinals Stay Put, Dies at 94," *New York Times*, January 2, 2000.

9. Bob Broeg, "Sports Comment," *St. Louis Post-Dispatch*, July 9, 1961, 66.

10. Bing Devine, with Tom Wheatley, *The Memoirs of Bing Devine: Stealing Lou Brock and Other Winning Moves by a Master GM* (Champaign, Ill.: Sports Publishing, 2004), 85.

11. Peter Golenbock, *The Spirt of St. Louis: A History of the St. Louis Cardinals and Browns* (New York: Avon Books, 2000), 391.

12. "Card Broadcaster Absent When Dyer Quit as Pilot," *Sporting News*, October 25, 1950, 14.

13. Ed Alsene, "Quotes and Notes," *(Bloomington, Illinois) Pantagraph*, November 7, 1950, 14.

14. "Harry Caray's Wife Wins Divorce, Calls Him 'Cold, Indifferent,'" *St. Louis Star-Times*, November 11, 1949, 20.

15. Tony Silvia, *Fathers and Sons in Baseball Broadcasting: The Carays, Brennamans, Bucks, and Kalases* (Jefferson, N.C.: McFarland, 2009), 91–92.

16. "Harry Caray's Tribute to One of Baseball's Greats—Gabby Street," *(Sikeston, Missouri) Daily Standard*, March 2, 1951, 8.

17. (Advertisement) "Broadcasting Opportunity for 'Big Name' Baseball Man," *Sporting News*, April 11, 1951, 30.

18. Stuart Shea, *Calling the Game: Baseball Broadcasting from 1920 to the Present* (Phoenix, Ariz.: Society for American Baseball Research, 2015), 210.

19. Bill Veeck, with Ed Linn, *Veeck—as in Wreck: The Chaotic Career of Baseball's Incorrigible Maverick* (New York: G. P. Putnam's Sons, 1962), 222.

20. Veeck, with Linn, *Veeck—as in Wreck*, 222.

21. "Players Who Cheered His Ouster Also May Be Dropped by Browns, Rog Says," *Sporting News*, June 18, 1952, 3.

22. "Not Amusing, But Confusing, Caray Says of Veeck's Moves," *Sporting News*, November 5, 1952, 2.

5. NEW PARTNERS

1. "Many Applicants for Job of Airing Cardinal Games," *Sporting News*, October 14, 1953, 32.

2. "Cardinals Ball Club Sold to Anheuser-Busch Inc. by Fred Saigh for $3,750,000," *St. Louis Post-Dispatch*, February 20, 1953, 1, 4.

3. "Cardinals Ball Club Sold to Anheuser-Busch Inc. by Fred Saigh," 4.

4. Peter Hernon and Terry Ganey, *Under the Influence: New Edition of the Unauthorized Story of the Anheuser-Busch Dynasty* (New York: Simon & Schuster, 2012; Kindle edition), chapter 41, location 3538.

5. Harry Caray, with Bob Verdi, *Holy Cow!* (New York: Villard, 1989), 140.

6. Stuart Shea, *Calling the Game: Baseball Broadcasting from 1920 to the Present* (Phoenix, Ariz.: Society for American Baseball Research, 2015), 211.

7. Caray, with Verdi, *Holy Cow!* 145.

8. Richard Dozer, "Harry Caray! Holy Cow!" *Chicago Tribune Magazine*, August 13, 1972, 30.

9. Milo Hamilton and Don Schlossberg, with Bob Ibach, *Making Airwaves: 60 Years at Milo's Microphone* (Champaign, Ill.: Sports Publishing, 2006), 39.

10. Jack Buck, with Rob Rains and Bob Broeg, *That's a Winner* (Champaign, Ill.: Sagamore, 1997), 83.

11. Buck, with Rains and Broeg, *That's a Winner*, 84.

12. Joan Niesen, "The Spirit of St. Louis," *Sports Illustrated*, September 22, 2014, 64.

13. Niesen, "The Spirit of St. Louis," 64.

14. Tony Silvia, *Fathers and Sons in Baseball Broadcasting: The Carays, Brennamans, Bucks, and Kalases* (Jefferson, N.C.: McFarland, 2009), 85.

15. Roy Holliman, "Jack Not One to Pass Buck," *Florida Today*, March 30, 1975, 1C.

16. Steve Nidetz, "Finally, It's Buck's Turn in Limelight," *Chicago Tribune*, April 13, 1990, 44.

17. Herb Heft, "Garagiola Ace Reporter Doing Things Naturally," *Sporting News*, July 6, 1955, 13.

18. Dan Hall, "Spring Training Is Different Now," *Tampa Bay Times*, April 1, 1956, 110.

19. Joe Garagiola, *Baseball Is a Funny Game* (New York: Bantam, 1962), 149.

20. Warren Corbett, "Joe Garagiola," *Society for American Baseball Research*, www.sabr.org/bioproj/person/ba3bd453 (January 7, 2018).

21. Heft, "Garagiola Ace Reporter Doing Things Naturally," 13–14.

22. Robert L. Burnes, "Garagiola Sees Good Humor Side," *Sporting News*, November 14, 1956, 11

23. "Caray Still First in 'Holy Cow' Loop, Says Pal Joey," *Sporting News*, July 20, 1955, 18.

24. "Tribute to 'Harry and Joe' in Rhyme by St. Louis Fan," *Sporting News*, November 14, 1956, 12.

25. Al Abrams, "Sideline on Sports," *Pittsburgh Post-Gazette*, June 7, 1957, 21.

26. Corbett, "Joe Garagiola."

27. Curt Smith, *Pull Up a Chair: The Vin Scully Story* (Washington, D.C.: Potomac Books, 2009), 152.

28. Buck, with Rob Rains and Bob Broeg, *That's a Winner*, 88.

29. Jimmy Claus, "Sporting Around," *Terre Haute (Indiana) Tribune*, December 8, 1961, 22.

30. Clifford Terry, "Fans It's So Hot on the Field Today That Our Third Baseman Is Melton!" *Chicago Tribune Magazine*, August 3, 1975, 141.

31. Richard Sandomir, "DOG SHOW; Action! When Arf Imitates Life," *New York Times*, February 12, 2001, D7.

32. Caray, with Verdi, *Holy Cow!* 70.

6. KMOX

1. Bill Fleischman, "Caray Right at Home in Hot Water," *St. Louis Globe-Democrat*; reprinted in *Sporting News*, November 15, 1961, 14.

2. Joan Niesen, "The Spirt of St. Louis," *Sports Illustrated*, September 22, 2014, 62–63.

3. Bill James, *The Bill James Historical Baseball Abstract* (New York: Ballantine, 1985), 184.

4. Ed Sherman, "Caray Part of Cubs, Cards Lore," *Chicago Tribune*, October 13, 2015, 1.

5. Bob Costas, "Harry Caray: A Baseball Life," *Chicago Tribune*, February 27, 1998, Section 9, 7.

6. Transcribed from Lou Brock's Hall of Fame acceptance speech, July 28, 1985, available at https://video.search.yahoo.com/search/video?fr=mcafee&p=lou+brock+hall+of+fame+speech+1985#id=1&vid=5e56263dd3cb0765de8f395822eedb6e&action=click (January 11, 2018).

7. Skip Bayless, "The Best Summer Love: Harry and Baseball," *Chicago Tribune*, April 2, 1998, 47–48.

8. Costas, "Harry Caray," Section 9, 1, 7.

9. Peter Golenbock, *The Spirit of St. Louis: A History of the St. Louis Cardinals and Browns* (New York: Avon Books, 2000), 515–16.

10. Richard Rothschild, "St. Louis Years Paved Way to Hall," *Chicago Tribune*, February 27, 1998, 205.

11. Harry Mitauer, "Cards Rib Kasko, Haze Caray on Dugout Show," *Sporting News*, August 7, 1957, 9.

12. Bob Broeg, "Redbirds Try Wings, Enjoy Trip to Coast," *Sporting News*, April 30, 1958, 13.

13. Bill Kerch, "Kibitzers 'Help Out' Caray in Broadcast from Bleachers," *Sporting News*, June 18, 1958, 41.

14. Dan Daniel, "Duke Finds That Bavasi Beef Can Be Pretty Tough"; "An Interview with Caray Touched Off Bavasi's Blast"; "Bavasi Claims Dove of Peace Has Landed in Snider Dispute," *Sporting News*, May 28, 1958, 1, 8.

15. Neal Russo, "Hemus, Dascoli Hurl Brickbats on Caray's Radio Show," *Sporting News*, May 24, 1961, 8, 10.

16. Les Biederman, "Buc Bench-Rider Stuart Ready for Switch in Uniform," *Sporting News*, May 31, 1961, 10.

17. Clark Nealon, "Farrell Drops Bomb in Spitter Confession," *Sporting News*, August 4, 1962, 26.

7. UP AND DOWNS

1. Oscar Ruhl, "From the Ruhl Book," *Sporting News*, December 14, 1955, 15.

2. Gerald Holland, "Gussie Busch's Kind of Day," *Sports Illustrated*, May 20, 1957, 65–67.

3. Curt Flood, with Richard Carter, *The Way It Is* (New York: Trident, 1971), 67, 70.

4. David Halberstam, *October 1964* (New York: Villard, 1994), 25–26.

5. Bing Devine, with Tom Wheatley, *The Memoirs of Bing Devine: Stealing Lou Brock and Other Winning Moves by a Master GM* (Champaign, Ill.: Sports Publishing, 2004), 27.

6. John Smith, "Holy Cow, It's Caray, Baseball's No. 1 Fan," *Florida Today*, March 30, 1975, 6C.

7. Milo Hamilton and Dan Schlossberg, with Bob Ibach, *Making Waves: 60 Years at Milo's Microphone* (Champaign, Ill.: Sports Publishing, 2006), 40.

8. "Stanky, at Luncheon Quiz Session, Ribbed about 'Board of Strategy,'" *Sporting News*, January 19, 1955, 11.

9. Myron Cope, "When Harry Caray Was a Rebel with a Microphone," *Deadspin.com*, April 1, 2015, https://thestacks.deadspin.com/when-harry-caray-was-a-rebel-with-a-microphone-1695031810 (January 20, 2018).

10. Peter Hernon and Terry Ganey, *Under the Influence: New Edition of the Unauthorized Story of the Anheuser-Busch Dynasty* (New York: Simon & Schuster, 2012; Kindle edition), chapter 48, location 4118.

11. Cope, "When Harry Caray Was a Rebel with a Microphone."

12. Rich Wolfe and George Castle, *I Remember Harry Caray* (Champaign, Ill.: Sports Publishing, 1998), 170–71.

13. "'Hemus Worships Stan, Too,' Chirps Caray, Voice of Birds," *Sporting News*, June 1, 1960, 15.

14. E-mail from Rick Hummel to the author, January 24. 2018. Reprinted with permission.

15. Bill White, with Gordon Dillow, *Uppity : My Untold Stories about the Games People Play* (New York: Grand Central Publishing, 2011), 80–81.

16. White, with Dillow, *Uppity*, viii.

17. Halberstam, *October 1964*, 259.

18. Cope, "When Harry Caray Was a Rebel with a Microphone."

19. Author interview with Tim McCarver, January 27, 2018.

20. Flood, with Carter, *The Way It Is*, 93.

21. Jim Brosnan, *The Long Season: An Inside Chronicle of the Baseball Year as Seen by Major League Pitcher Jim Brosnan* (New York: Harper & Brothers, 1960), 105.

22. Brosnan, *The Long Season*, 132.

23. Peter Golenbock, *Wrigleyville: A Magical History Tour of the Chicago Cubs* (New York: St. Martin's, 1996), 455.

8. GLORY DAYS

1. Myron Cope, "When Harry Caray Was a Rebel with a Microphone," *Deadspin.com*, April 1, 2015, https://thestacks.deadspin.com/when-harry-caray-was-a-rebel-with-a-microphone-1695031810 (January 20, 2018).

2. Harry Caray letter to "Voice of the Fan," *Sporting News*, April 4, 1964, 18.

3. "Stan Musial the Final At-Bat.Mov," *YouTube*, https://video.search.yahoo.com/search/video?fr=mcafee&p=harry+caray+stan+musial+final+hit#id=1&vid=9d58e12d7a4fa897a74fe374a4140af5&action=click (January 22, 2018).

4. Transcribed from audio of Cardinals' radio broadcast, October 4, 1964 (author's collection).

5. Vince Leonard, "Cardinals Colorful on Screen," *Pittsburgh Post-Gazette*, October 8, 1964, 66.

6. Don Page, "Sportslook," *Los Angeles Times*, October 10, 1964, 34.

7. Bob Wolf, "Carays Set a Big-Time First as Father-and-Son Aircasters," *Sporting News*, June 12, 1965, 27.

8. Bruce Weber, "Skip Caray, 68, Atlanta Braves Voice Known for His Biting Wit, Is Dead," *New York Times*, August 5, 2008, http://www.nytimes.com/2008/08/05/sports/baseball/05caray.html (January 27, 2018).

9. Dick Kaegel, "'Holy Cow!' the Voice of Caray Has a Tight Grip on Card Fans," *Sporting News*, July 2, 1966, 19.

10. Al Flint, letter to "Voice of the Fan," *Sporting News*, September 16, 1967, 4; Bob Laurie, letter to "Voice of the Fan," *Sporting News*, September 30, 1967, 10.

11. Don Page, "World Series Fans Take Dip in Pool," *Los Angeles Times*, October 7, 1967, 34.

12. Don Page, "Sportslook: A Linescore on the Cliché Series," *Los Angeles Times*, October 5, 1968, 39.

13. Vince Leonard, "Hoot Gibson Stars on NBC," *Pittsburgh Press*, October 3, 1968, 58.

14. Bettelou Peterson, "The TV Set: Booo! To Gowdy, Caray: Why Did NBC Do This?" *Detroit Free Press*, October 12, 1968, 14.

9. END OF AN ERA

1. Bob Fallstrom, "Once Over Lightly: Cardinals without Caray Like Namath without Girls," *Decatur (Illinois) Herald*, September 9, 1969, 11.

2. Clifford Terry, "Holy Harry! The Ol' Ballgame Is Just One of the Many Bases 'Ol Caray Covers," *Chicago Tribune Sportsweek*, August 18, 1978, 45.

3. "Harry Caray's Condition Serious; Struck by Car," *St. Louis Post-Dispatch*, November 4, 1968, 12. Details of accident obtained from Metropolitan Police Department—City of St. Louis Vehicular Accident Report, November 3, 1968 (courtesy Jessica Luna, Sunshine law coordinator).

4. Associated Press, "Harry Caray Off Critical List," *Boston Globe*, November 5, 1968, 27.

5. United Press International, "Harry Caray Wants Out," *Orlando Evening Star*, November 9, 1968, 10.

6. Jimmy Mann, "Wheel Chair Can't Hide Caray Smile," *Sporting News*, January 25, 1969, 26.

7. Ed Levitt, "Harry Caray Nets New Job as Voice of Athletics," *Sporting News*, February 7, 1970, 46.

8. Ed Wilks, "Digs Leave Caray Limp, but Not Wholly Cowed," *St. Louis Post-Dispatch*, April 8, 1969, 31.

9. Ron Fimrite, "The Big Wind in Chicago," *Sports Illustrated*, September 18, 1978, 40.

10. Neal Russo, "Redbird Express Blew Boiler Early," in *Sporting News Official Baseball Guide for 1970* (St. Louis, Mo.: Sporting News, 1970), 133.

11. John Smith, "Holy Cow, It's Caray, Baseball's No. 1 Fan," *Florida Today*, March 30, 1975, 1C.

12. "Pirates' Prince Confirms Bid from St. Louis Station," *Pittsburgh Post-Gazette*, August 19, 1969, 18.

13. "Cards Make Big Offer to Prince," *Pittsburgh Press*, August 19, 1969, 50.

14. "Report on Hiring of Prince Denied," *St. Louis Post-Dispatch*, August 19, 1969, 27.

15. "Ouster Report Amuses Caray," *St. Louis Post-Dispatch*, September 21, 1969, 107.

16. "Caray Hunting Job after Dismissal," *St. Louis Post-Dispatch*, October 10, 1969, 1.

17. "Caray Hunting Job after Dismissal," 1.

18. William Knoedelseder, *Bitter Brew: The Rise and Fall of Anheuser-Busch and America's King of Beers* (New York: HarperBusiness, 2012), 107; Chad Garrison, "Busch Unbottled: Divulging Secrets from the Sudsy to the Sordid, a New Book Pops the Top Off the St. Louis Beer-Brewing Dynasty,"

Riverfronttimes.com, November 8, 2012, www.riverfronttimes.com/stlouis/busch-unbottled-divulging-secrets-from-the-sudsy-to-the-sordid-a-new-book-pops-the-top-off-st-louis-beer-brewing-dynasty/Content?oid=2501601 (June 15, 2018).

19. Smith, "Holy Cow, It's Caray, Baseball's No. 1 Fan," 1C.

20. "Harry Caray Tells His Side of Story," *Mattoon (Illinois) Journal-Gazette*, December 9, 1969, 9.

21. Richard Dozer, "Harry Caray! Holy Cow!" *Chicago Tribune Magazine*, August 13, 1972, 34.

22. Jerry Berger, "Near Beer," *St. Louis Post-Dispatch*, June 13, 1995, 41.

23. Myron Cope, "When Harry Caray Was a Rebel with a Microphone," *Deadspin.com*, April 1, 2015, https://thestacks.deadspin.com/when-harry-caray-was-a-rebel-with-a-microphone-1695031810 (January 20, 2018).

24. Peter Hernon and Terry Ganey, *Under the Influence: New Edition of the Unauthorized Story of the Anheuser-Busch Dynasty* (New York: Simon & Schuster, 2012; Kindle edition), chapter 48, location 4118.

25. Hernon and Ganey, *Under the Influence*, chapter 48, location 4162.

26. "Caray Hunting Job after Dismissal," 15.

27. Tom Gettel, letter to "Voice of the Fan," *Sporting News*, November 1, 1969, 8.

28. Robert L. Nussbaumer (letter to the editor), "Never Again the Same," *St. Louis Post-Dispatch*, October 15, 1969, 78.

10. SIBERIA

1. "A's, Caray Discussing Radio Jobs," *St. Louis Post-Dispatch*, November 13, 1969, 30.

2. Mark Armour, "Charlie Finley," *Society for American Baseball Research*, https://sabr.org/bioproj/person/6ac2ee2f (June 15, 2018).

3. Ed Levitt, "Harry Caray Nets New Job as Voice of Athletics," *Sporting News*, February 7, 1970, 46.

4. Perry Phillips, "Night Sounds," *Oakland Tribune*, January 20, 1970, 34.

5. Bill Rose, "A's Monte Moore Happy in New Role," *Oakland Tribune*, February 14, 1970, 2-E.

6. John Wiebusch, "Holy Cow! Caray, Finley to Play as Team for Coming Season," *Los Angeles Times*, April 1, 1970, 67.

7. Jack Craig, "SporTView: Caray Finley's Voice, but He's Still a Card," *Boston Globe*, May 3, 1970, 92.

8. Lowell Hickey, "Neutral Corner: Voice of A's Really Torrid in Chicago," *Fremont (California) Argus*, July 3, 1970, 13.

9. Jerome Holtzman, weekly column, *Sporting News*, July 11, 1970, 6.

10. Bob Addie, "Addie's Atoms," *Sporting News*, August 22, 1970, 16.

11. Jim Scott, "Oakland Is A-Okay, Claims a Contented Caray," *Sporting News*, June 27, 1970, 37.

12. Jerome Holtzman, "Give Caray the Valor Award," *Sporting News*, May 9, 1970, 18.

13. Scott, "Oakland Is A-Okay," 16.

14. Jack Craig, "The Improbable Team: Chicago and Harry Caray," *Boston Globe*, April 1, 1971, 91.

15. Hickey, "Neutral Corner," 13.

16. Don Merry, "Angels Win, Eye Twins' Showdown," *Long Beach (California) Independent*, July 6, 1970, 21.

17. Ron Bergman, "Charge! Ex-GI Monday Fires at .300," *Sporting News*, August 29, 1970, 10.

18. Ed Levitt, "Reggie & Mudcat," *Oakland Tribune*, August 20, 1970, 35.

19. Gary Deeb, "Waller: Out of the Frying Pan into the Fire," *Chicago Tribune*, January 28, 1975, 45.

20. Bill Soliday, "Caray Believed in Freedom of Airwaves," *Fremont (California) Argus*, October 17, 1970, 13.

21. Curt Smith, *Voices of the Game: The First Full-Scale Overview of Baseball Broadcasting, 1920 to the Present* (South Bend, Ind.: Diamond Communications, 1987), 329.

22. Ron Fimrite, "The Big Wind in Chicago," *Sports Illustrated*, September 18, 1978, 40.

23. Deeb, "Waller," 45.

24. Brian Hewitt, "Harry Caray: Survivor of More Than Stroke, He's Set to Rally Again," *Chicago Sun-Times*, May 17, 1987, 2.

25. Pete Rahn, "Rumors Send Caray to Cincy: 'I Hope It's True,' Says Harry," *Sporting News*, October 31, 1970, 53.

26. Rahn, "Rumors Send Caray to Cincy," 53.

27. Ad for "Harry Caray's School of Broadcasting," *Sporting News*, October 31, 1970, 36.

11. NEW MAN IN TOWN

1. David Condon, "In the Wake of the News," *Chicago Tribune*, January 9, 1971, 71.

2. Eleanor Page, "More Gals to Watch!" *Chicago Tribune*, April 9, 1971, 1.

3. Richard Dozer, "Unbeaten Sox (2–0) to Open Here Today," *Chicago Tribune*, April 9, 1971, 44.

4. Edgar Munzel, "White Sox' Severe Anemia Causes Head Shakes," in *Sporting News Official Baseball Guide, 1971* (St. Louis, Mo.: Sporting News, 1971), 59.

5. Dozer, "Unbeaten Sox (2–0) to Open Here Today," 44; Marc Okkonen, *Baseball Uniforms of the 20th Century: The Official Major League Baseball Guide* (New York: Sterling, 1991), 29.

6. Stuart Shea, *Calling the Game: Baseball Broadcasting from 1920 to the Present* (Phoenix, Ariz.: Society for American Baseball Research, 2015), 69.

7. Shea, *Calling the Game*, 69.

8. Author interview with Bob Verdi, March 1, 2018.

9. Ed Sherman, "Expos' Silence Has a Precedent: Sox Fans Can Remember '71," *Chicago Tribune*, April 24, 2000, 30.

10. Bob Logan, "Holy Cow! Newcomer Wows Baseball Diners," *Chicago Tribune*, January 11, 1971, 58.

11. Richard Dozer, "44,250 See Sox Beat Twins, 3 to 2," *Chicago Tribune*, April 10, 1971, 71.

12. Bob Vanderberg, "Sox Lure a Standout to Broadcast Booth, Bleachers," *Chicago Tribune*, February 27, 1998, 206.

13. Harry Caray, with Bob Verdi, *Holy Cow!* (New York: Villard, 1989), 185.

14. Jack Craig, "The Improbable Team: Chicago and Harry Caray," *Boston Globe*, April 25, 1971, 91.

15. Jack Craig, "Few Qualified to Judge Baseball Announcers' Bias," *Boston Globe*, June 20, 1971, 86.

16. Larry Everhart, "Holy Cow! Caray Is Here, Tra-La," *(Chicago Suburban) Daily Herald*, July 20, 1971, 8.

17. "Dyamic Duo Spurs Chisox (AP)," *Washington Post*, August 15, 1971, 42.

18. Shea, *Calling the Game*, 70.

19. Richard Dozer, "Harry Caray! Holy Cow!" *Chicago Tribune Magazine*, August 13, 1972, 25.

20. "Robert Markus," *Chicago Tribune*, May 18, 1972, 58.

21. David Condon, "In the Wake of the News," *Chicago Tribune*, July 7, 1972, 48.

22. Dozer, "Harry Caray! Holy Cow!" 25.

23. "Major Flashes," *Sporting News*, September 9, 1973, 24.

12. SOUTH SIDE BLUES

1. "Harry Caray Captures Some More Fans," *(Chicago Suburban) Daily Herald*, January 18, 1973, 19.

2. C. C. Johnson Spink, "Spink Picks Red Sox in Closest Division Race," *Sporting News*, April 14, 1973, 4, 10.

3. Paul Logan, "Bob Waller—Making His Mark with a Mic," *(Chicago Suburban) Daily Herald*, July 19, 1973, 44.

4. Ed Sherman, "33 Seasons: You Can Put It on the Board," *Chicago Tribune*, March 23, 2018, 3.

5. Rich Wolfe and George Castle, *I Remember Harry Caray* (Champaign, Ill.: Sports Publishing, 1998), 129.

6. Bob Logan, "Egan Calls Sox Fans Front-Runners," *Chicago Tribune*, May 18, 1972, 62.

7. Edgar Munzel, "Allen's Leg Fracture Gives Sox New Case of Staggers," *Sporting News*, July 14, 1973, 5.

8. Gary Deeb, "Caray a Clear-Headed Judge of Pro Character," *Chicago Tribune*, July 22, 1975, 39.

9. Munzel, "Allen's Leg Fracture Gives Sox New Case of Staggers," 5.

10. Dan Helpingstine, *The Cubs and the White Sox: A Baseball Rivalry, 1900 to the Present* (Jefferson, N.C.: McFarland, 2010), 99–100.

11. "Harry Caray and Wife Agree to End Marriage," *St. Louis Post-Dispatch*, January 18, 1974, 5.

12. John Smith, "Holy Cow, It's Caray, Baseball's No. 1 Fan," *Florida Today*, March 30, 1975, 6C.

13. George Langford, "It's Wild! Sox Opener Ruined 8–2," *Chicago Tribune*, April 6, 1974, 21.

14. Dick Allen and Tim Whitaker, *Crash: The Life and Times of Dick Allen* (New York: Ticknor & Fields, 1989), 149–50.

15. Author interview with Jim Kaat, February 1, 2018.

16. Richard Lindberg, *Who's on 3rd? The Chicago White Sox Story* (South Bend, Ind.: Icarus Press, 1983), 155.

17. Gary Deeb, "Caray—'Having a Better Year Than Most Sox,'" *Chicago Tribune*, September 24, 1974, 41.

18. Smith, "Holy Cow, It's Caray, Baseball's No. 1 Fan," 6C.

19. George Langford, "Caray Won't Quit over Tanner Feud," *Chicago Tribune*, June 12, 1974, 85.

20. Ed Fowler, "Peace Play: Tanner–Caray 'Feud' Turns into a Real Love-in," *Chicago Daily News*, June 12, 1974, 37.

21. David Condon, "Harry Sounds Off on Tanner," *Chicago Tribune*, November 5, 1974, 39.

22. Paul Logan, "Tanner–Caray Feud Signals End for Sox' Popular Voice," *(Chicago Suburban) Daily Herald*, January 23, 1975, 21.

23. Wolfe and Castle, *I Remember Harry Caray*, 86–87.

24. Condon, "Harry Sounds Off on Tanner," 39.

25. Deeb, "Caray's Sidekick Still Waiting for White Sox Call," *Chicago Tribune*, October 22, 1974, 43.

26. Condon, "Harry sounds Off on Tanner," 39.

27. Curt Smith, *Voices of the Game : The First Full-Scale Overview of Baseball Broadcasting, 1920 to the Present* (South Bend, Ind.: Diamond Communications, 1987), 469.

28. Gary Deeb, "Holy 'Q'! Caray to Return to Sox Mic," *Chicago Tribune*, October 16, 1974, 60.

13. A TUMULTUOUS YEAR

1. Tom Fitzpatrick, "Melton the Giant and Why He Cries," *Chicago Sun-Times*, July 24, 1975, 138.

2. C. C. Johnson Spink, "Spink Sees Yankees Back on Throne," *Sporting News*, April 12, 1975, 4.

3. Photo caption from "Rangers Ruin Sox Opener 6–5 in 13th," *Chicago Tribune*, April 16, 1975, 13.

4. "Harry Caray Married to Ballwin Woman," *St. Louis Post-Dispatch*, May 12, 1975, 34.

5. Fred Mitchell, "Harry's Persistence Won Dutchie's Heart," *Chicago Tribune*, February 27, 1998, 60.

6. Mark Liptak interview with Bill Mercer, *Whitesoxinteractive.com*, 2010, www.whitesoxinteractive.com/rwas/index.php?category=11&id=3890 (March 14, 2018).

7. Stuart Shea, *Calling the Game: Baseball Broadcasting from 1920 to the Present* (Phoenix, Ariz.: Society for American Baseball Research, 2015), 71.

8. Liptak interview with Mercer.

9. Mark Liptak interview with J. C. Martin, whitesoxinteractive.com, 2002. www.whitesoxinteractive.com/rwas/index.php?category=11&id=935 (March 14, 2018).

10. Gary Deeb, "Mercer, Martin Act More Pathetic Than Sox' Play," *Chicago Tribune*, September 16, 1975, 45.

11. Curt Smith, *Voices of the Game: The First Full-Scale Overview of Baseball Broadcasting, 1920 to the Present* (South Bend, Ind.: Diamond Communications, 1987), 469.

12. Shea, *Calling the Game*, 70.

13. Barry Rozner, "Bill Melton, the '72 Sox, and What Might Have Been," *(Chicago Suburban) Daily Herald*, June 13, 2012, 5.

14. Bob Frisk, "Sharks, Sox, and Other Things . . .," *(Chicago Suburban) Daily Herald*, July 18, 1975, 29; Gary Deeb, "Caray a Clear-Headed Judge of Pro Character," *Chicago Tribune*, July 22, 1975, 39; Armand Schneider, "Tempest in a Sox-Pot," *Chicago Daily News*, July 22, 1975, 41.

15. Bob Verdi, "Fed Up, Melton Blasts Caray for 'Harping,'" *Chicago Tribune*, July 23, 1975, 43.

16. Dick Miller, "Melton, Bonds Fill Angels Need for More Muscle," *Sporting News*, January 3, 1976, 42.

17. Dick Miller, "Vet Brewer Rescues Angel Bullpen," *Sporting News*, June 5, 1976, 49.

18. Bob Vanderberg, "Sox Lure a Standout to Broadcast Booth, Bleachers," *Chicago Tribune*, February 27, 1998, 206.

19. "Allyn Supports Caray," *Sporting News*, August 9, 1975, 29.

20. Richard Lindberg, *Stealing First in a Two-Team Town: The White Sox from Comiskey to Reinsdorf* (Champaign, Ill.: Sagamore, 1994), 162.

21. Bob Verdi, "Sox HAVE to Drop Bill," *Chicago Tribune*, September 30, 1975, 44.

22. John Hillyer, "Caray Gets Bad Mouth from Sox," *Chicago Daily News*, October 2, 1975, 27.

23. Richard Dozer, "Caray Fired, Calls Allyn Stupid Man," *Chicago Tribune*, October 2, 1975, 85.

14. HARRY, JIMMY, AND BILL

1. Jerome Holtzman, "Doc Veeck to Try His New Theories on an Old Patient," *Sporting News*, October 18, 1975, 25.

2. Warren Corbett, "Bill Veeck," *Society for American Baseball Research*, https://sabr.org/bioproj/person/7b0b5f10 (March 15, 2018).

3. Author interview with Rick Telander, January 18, 2018.

4. David Condon, "Dear Mr. Veeck: Rehire Harry Caray," *Chicago Tribune*, December 21, 1975, 61.

5. David Condon, "'He Appreciates My Style': Caray," *Chicago Tribune*, January 14, 1976, 47.

6. David Condon, "Holy Cow!! Caray Hired as Sox Voice," *Chicago Tribune*, January 14, 1976, 45.

7. Bob Logan, "Skip Caray Won't Join Dad on Sox," *Chicago Tribune*, February 2, 1976, 51.

8. Richard Lindberg, *Stealing First in a Two-Team Town: The White Sox from Comiskey to Reinsdorf* (Champaign, Ill.: Sagamore, 1994), 169–70.

9. Corbett, "Bill Veeck."

10. "Chisox Announcing: A 'Harry' Situation (AP)," *Detroit Free Press*, July 20, 1979, 51.

11. Jerome Holtzman, "Gossage Feeling Electricity of Chisox Switch to Youth," *Sporting News*, February 7, 1976, 36.

12. Jerome Holtzman, "Shaken Bart Thanks Caray for His Biting Criticism," *Sporting News*, July 17, 1976, 10.

13. David Condon, "Sox Seeking Players—and Fans," *Chicago Tribune*, October 29, 1976, 55.

14. Corbett, "Bill Veeck."

15. Mark Liptak interview with Jimmy Piersall, *Whitesoxinteractive.com*, 2005, www.whitesoxinteractive.com/rwas/index.php?category=11&id=2852 (March 19, 2018).

16. Author interview with Bob Verdi, March 1, 2018.

17. Clifford Terry, "The Mellowing (Sort of) of Jimmy Piersall," *Chicago Tribune Magazine*, June 5, 1977, 33.

15. DEMOLITION

1. Cooper Rollow, "Cosell Labels Caray's Act Cheerleading," *Chicago Tribune*, April 8, 1978, 228.

2. Gary Deeb, "Richer Caray Will Return to Sox Booth," *Chicago Tribune*, January 10, 1978, 41.

3. Dennis Breo, "Holy Cow! It Might Be . . . It Could Be . . . It Is! It's Sportscaster Harry Caray!" *People*, August 7, 1978, https://people.com/archive/holy-cow-it-might-be-it-could-be-it-is-its-sportscaster-harry-caray-vol-10-no-6 (March 21, 2018).

4. Ron Fimrite, "The Big Wind in Chicago," *Sports Illustrated*, September 18, 1978, 36.

5. "Garr Rips Sox Radio-TV Crew," *Chicago Tribune*, May 18, 1978, 51.

6. Fimrite, "The Big Wind in Chicago," 36.

7. Rick Talley, "Money's on Rose—Even at 3–1 Odds," *Chicago Tribune*, August 1, 1978, 43.

8. Gary Deeb, "Namedropping Dropped: WGN's Sportscasters Finally Pull the Plugs," *Chicago Tribune*, June 2, 1978, 51.

9. David Condon, "Believe It or Not, Cubs Are Not the Only Game in Town," *Chicago Tribune*, May 22, 1979, 49.

10. Author interview with David Israel, March 5, 2018.

11. Richard Dozer, "Sox Promotion Ends in a Mob Scene," *Chicago Tribune*, July 13, 1979, 13.

12. Dave Hoekstra, "The Night Disco Died," *Chicago Magazine*, July 2016, www.chicagomag.com/Chicago-Magazine/July-2016/The-Night-Disco-Died/ (March 25, 2018).

13. Gary Deeb, "Disco Demolition Widens Cosell–Caray Rift," *Chicago Tribune*, July 20, 1979, 75.

14. "Chisox Announcing: A 'Harry' Situation (AP)," *Chicago Tribune*, June 25, 1979, 53.

15. David Israel, "Caray a Treasure for Weary Sox Fans," *Chicago Tribune*, June 25, 1979, 53.

16. Bob Verdi, "Brown Bids Caray a Fond Farewell," *Chicago Tribune*, January 29, 1980, 41; Mark Liptak, "Flashing Back with Joe McConnell," *Whitesoxinteractive.com*, 2009, www.whitesoxinteractive.com/rwas/index.php?category=11&id=3734 (March 25, 2018).

17. Author interview with Rich King, January 11, 2018.

18. Dave Nightingale, "Piersall Attacks Suburban Sportswriter," *Chicago Tribune*, July 3, 1980, 43.

19. Nightingale, "Piersall Attacks Suburban Sportswriter," 43.

20. Jimmy Piersall, with Richard Whittingham, *The Truth Hurts* (Chicago: Contemporary Books, 1984), 148.

21. Bob Verdi, "Jimmy Wrong, but Don't Discard Him," *Chicago Tribune*, July 4, 1980, 45.

22. Mark Liptak interview with Jimmy Piersall, *Whitesoxinteractive.com*, 2005, www.whitesoxinteractive.com/rwas/index.php?category=11&id=2852 (March 19, 2018).

23. Gerald Eskenazi, *Bill Veeck: A Baseball Legend* (New York: McGraw-Hill, 1988), 168.

24. David Condon, "Offers for White Sox Have Veeck Listening," *Chicago Tribune*, July 23, 1980, 51.

25. David Condon, "Holy Cow! Caray Wants in on Sox Deal," *Chicago Tribune*, August 5, 1980, 47.

26. Paul Dickson, *Bill Veeck: Baseball's Greatest Maverick* (New York: Walker & Company, 2012), 323; "AL Vote Anti-Veeck: Steinbrenner (AP)," *Chicago Tribune*, December 17, 1980, 65.

27. Bob Markus, "Caray Edgy Over Chisox Delay," *Sporting News*, January 17, 1981, 43.

28. Dave Nightingale, "Sox Buyers OK'd, Await Veeck's Plans," *Chicago Tribune*, January 30, 1981, 54.

16. EDDIE AND JERRY AND HARRY AND JIMMY

1. Jack Mabley, "Reagan's Speech the Most Sensible since Roosevelt," *Chicago Tribune*, February 23, 1981, 5.

2. Ron Alridge, "Einhorn Wants Sox TV Package to Be More of a Money-maker," *Chicago Tribune*, March 27, 1981, 56.

3. Alridge, "Einhorn Wants Sox TV Package to Be More of a Moneymak-er," 56.

4. Robert Markus, "Irate Caray Vows He Never Agreed to Sox Contract," *Chicago Tribune*, February 17, 1981, 49.

5. Paul Dickson, *Bill Veeck: Baseball's Greatest Maverick* (New York: Walker & Company, 2012), 327.

6. Bob Logan, "Piersall in No Danger: Sox Bosses," *Chicago Tribune*, May 9, 1981, 17.

7. Bob Verdi, "Piersall–Ump 'Fun' No Comedy," *Chicago Tribune*, June 1, 1981, 51.

8. Author interview with Mike Leiderman, November 27, 2017.

9. Author interview with Ron Rapoport, January 25, 2018.

10. Linda Kay, "Sox Add Brock in TV 'Experiment,'" *Chicago Tribune*, June 21, 1981, 51.

11. Robert Markus, "Luzinski Takes Out Anger on Unsuspecting Blue Jays," *Chicago Tribune*, September 4, 1981, 65.

12. Richard Dozer, "Sox Suspend Piersall after Insult to Players' Wives," September 10, 1981, 59.

13. Mike Kiley, "Caray Won't Quit over Piersall," *Chicago Tribune*, September 17, 1981, 63.

14. Neil Amour, "Chicago Cubs Are Sold by Wrigley to Tribune Co. for $20.5 Million," *New York Times*, June 17, 1981, 1.

15. Robert Markus, "Cubs Will Have Sox Fan as Chairman of the Board," *Chicago Tribune*, June 17, 1981, 69.

16. Dave Nightingale, "Cubs: Team Total Turmoil," *Sporting News*, August 1, 1981, 34.

17. Ron Alridge, "Brickhouse to Leave Cub Telecasts after Season," *Chicago Tribune*, August 6, 1981, 61.

17. HARRY HEADS NORTH

1. David Condon, "Caray Won't Alter His Style for Cubs," *Chicago Tribune*, November 17, 1981, 77.

2. Bob Logan, *Miracle on 35th Street: Winnin' Ugly with the 1983 White Sox* (South Bend, Ind.: Icarus Press, 1983; New York: Avon Books, 2000), 148.

3. Linda Kay, "City's Teams Plug in to Pay TV," *Chicago Tribune*, October 11, 1981, 61.

4. David Condon, "Einhorn Sells His New SportsVision Like Hadacol or Snake Oil," *Chicago Tribune*, October 13, 1981, 59.

5. Kay, "City's Teams Plug in to Pay TV," 66.

6. Linda Kay, "Drysdale May Do Sox Games," *Chicago Tribune*, October 10, 1981, 17.

7. Ron Alridge, "Caray, Sox to Meet," *Chicago Tribune*, October 15, 1981, 65.

8. Linda Kay, "Caray, Sox Clear Air," *Chicago Tribune*, October 17, 1981, 22.

9. Linda Kay, "Sox and Caray Near Deal; Pay-TV Lures Brickhouse," *Chicago Tribune*, October 28, 1981, 59.

10. Ron Alridge, "Sox and Caray Need Each Other," *Chicago Tribune*, November 6, 1981, 111.

11. Jerome Holtzman, "Two Unsung Men Made Caray a Chicago Name," *Chicago Tribune*, February 22, 1998, 36.

12. Rich Wolfe and George Castle, *I Remember Harry Caray* (Champaign, Ill.: Sports Publishing, 1998), 77–78.

13. Robert Markus, "Holy Cow! Caray's Going, Going, Gone to the Cubs," *Chicago Tribune*, November 17, 1981, 78.

14. Markus, "Holy Cow!" 78.

15. Ron Alridge, "A Stunned Milo Plans to Stay On," *Chicago Tribune*, November 17, 1981, 75.

16. Robert Markus, "Cub Fans Unhappy, but Sox Fans Go with Caray," *Chicago Tribune*, November 22, 1981, 56; "Voice of the People," *Chicago Tribune*, November 27, 1981, 37.

17. Author interview with Bob Verdi, March 1, 2018.

18. Peter Gammons, "Hype Strikes Out: The White Sox Ballyhoo Turns to Boo, Boo, Boo," *Boston Globe*, July 31, 1982, Sports 1; Peter Gammons, "White Sox Sideshow Is 'Veeck Legacy," *Sporting News*, August 16, 1982, 22.

19. Ron Alridge, "Caray–Hamilton Team Airs Professionalism, Not Differences," *Chicago Tribune*, September 14, 1982, 28.

20. Milo Hamilton and Dan Schlossberg, with Bob Ibach, *Making Airwaves : 60 Years at Milo's Microphone* (Champaign, Ill.: Sports Publishing, 2006), 102.

18. SUPERSTAR OF THE SUPERSTATION

1. George Will, "Critique of Pure Baseball," *Washington Post*, August 11, 1985, L7.

2. James R. Walker and Robert V. Bellamy Jr., *Center Field Shot: A History of Baseball on Television* (Lincoln: University of Nebraska Press, 2008), 242.

3. Linda Kay and Skip Myslenski, "Sox Owners Claim Piersall Broke His Promise," *Chicago Tribune*, April 7, 1983, 83.

4. Linda Kay, "Owners Bask in Success," *Chicago Tribune*, September 19, 1983, 62.

5. Mark Liptak, "The Legacy of SportsVision," *SoxNet*, January 17, 2016, www.chicagonow.com/soxnet/2016/01/the-legacy-of-sportsvision/ (March 19, 2018).

6. Mike Kiley, "Reinsdorf Has One Regret, No Retraction," *Chicago Tribune*, September 19, 1983, 52.

7. Mike Kiley, "So Ordered to Make Up Game," *Chicago Tribune*, September 21, 1983, 64.

8. Skip Myslenski, "Red Ink's Gone at SportsVision," *Chicago Tribune*, November 29, 1983, 54.

9. Author interview with Mike Leiderman, November 27, 2017.

10. Dan Helpingstine, *The Cubs and the White Sox: A Baseball Rivalry, 1900 to the Present* (Jefferson, N.C.: McFarland, 2010), 106.

11. Robert Markus, "Elias Swings for the Seats," *Chicago Tribune*, April 30, 1983, 17.

12. Stan Isle, "Caught on the Fly," *Sporting News*, May 30, 1983, 12.

13. Rich Wolfe and George Castle, *I Remember Harry Caray* (Champaign, Ill.: Sports Publishing, 1998), 80.

14. Author interview with Ron Rapoport, January 25, 2018.

15. Wolfe and Castle, *I Remember Harry Caray*, 101.

16. Author interview with Ned Colletti, January 19, 2018.

17. Author interview with Bob Verdi, March 1, 2018.

18. Author interview with Dan Schlossberg, January 11, 2018.

19. Skip Myslenski, "Stone Has Right Pitch on TV, Too," *Chicago Tribune*, June 7, 1983, 30.

20. Kevin Klose, "After 39 Lean Years, Chicago Cheers Cubs," *Washington Post*, September 26, 1984, B5.

21. "CHC@PIT: Sutcliffe Seals It, Cubs Clinch 1984 NL East," *YouTube*, September 22, 2015, www.youtube.com/watch?v=HXizF4nwZKM (March 19, 2018).

22. Author interview with Al Lerner, December 7, 2017.

23. Ian Thomsen, "The Master's Voice: Harry Caray's Whiskey Baritone Is the Sound of Chicago Baseball," *Boston Globe*, June 22, 1984, Sports 1.

24. Bob Ryan, "Einhorn's Minor Folly," *Boston Globe*, June 24, 1984, Sports 1.

25. "Voice of the Fan," *Sporting News*, May 28, 1984, 6; June 18, 1984, 6; August 6, 1984, 6; September 10, 1984, 6; September 17, 1984, 6; October 15, 1984, 6; November 26, 7; Bill James, *The Bill James Baseball Abstract* (New York: Ballantine, 1985), 184.

26. Skip Myslenski, "WGN Dumps Milo," *Chicago Tribune*, November 8, 1984, 83.

27. Milo Hamilton and Dan Schlossberg, with Bob Ibach, *Making Airwaves: 60 Years at Milo's Microphone* (Champaign, Ill.: Sports Publishing, 2006), 112.

28. Gordon Edes, "Caray, Hamilton Still Voicing Their Differences," *Los Angeles Times*, September 8, 1985, 64.

29. Author interview with Bob Vorwald, February 8, 2018.

30. Peter Golenbock, *Wrigleyville: A Magical History Tour of the Chicago Cubs* (New York: St. Martin's, 1996), 474.

31. Fred Mitchell, "Harry Caray: He's a Cub Fan and a Letterman," *Chicago Tribune*, August 1, 1986, 41.

32. Fred Mitchell, "Cub Notebook: Dernier Dropped in Batting Order," *Chicago Tribune*, August 20, 1986, 43.

19. STROKE AND RECOVERY

1. Bob Verdi, "To His Fans, 'New' Caray No Different from Old One," *Chicago Tribune*, May 17, 1987, 191.

2. Fred Mitchell, "Caray Eager to Return Home after Stroke," *Chicago Tribune*, February 20, 1987, 41.

3. Bob Verdi, "Is Harry Getting Better? He Might Be, He Could Be . . . He Is!" *Chicago Tribune*, March 1, 1987, 41.

4. Author interview with Ned Colletti, January 19, 2018.

5. Kevin Klose, "Mr. Cub of the Airwaves Goes Back on Active List," *Washington Post*, May 19, 1987, E1.

6. Ron Berler, "Holy Cow! Harry's Back Behind the Mic," *Los Angeles Times*, May 20, 1987, 36.

7. Author interview with Dutchie Caray, March 22, 2018.

8. "Six Chicago-Area Personalities Score Big as Pinch-Hitters for Harry," *Chicago Tribune*, May 19, 1987, 50.

9. Skip Myslenski, "Caray 'Can't Get Over' Call from Reagan," *Chicago Tribune*, May 20, 1987, 118.

10. Author interview with Bob Verdi, March 1, 2018.

11. Author interview with Colletti.

12. Author interview with Dutchie Caray.

13. "City to Shed Light on Cubs' Request," *Sporting News*, August 17, 1987, 17.

14. Linda Kay and Mike Conklin, "Odds & Ins," *Chicago Tribune*, April 15, 1988, 46.

15. Author interview with Al Lerner, December 7, 2017.

16. "Cubs," *Sporting News*, March 21, 1988, 37.

17. R. Bruce Dold and John Kass, "Storm Short-Circuits Cubs' Night of History," *Chicago Tribune*, August 9, 1988, 1; Jayson Stark, "Things Will Never Be the Same at Wrigley Field," *Chicago Tribune*, August 8, 1988, 71.

18. Bill Deane, *Baseball Myths: Debating, Debunking, and Disproving Tales from the Diamond* (Lanham, Md.: Rowman & Littlefield, 2015; Kindle edition), location 3675.

19. Steve Nidetz, "Too Bad Caray's Not in the Hall, Out of the Booth," *Chicago Tribune*, August 1, 1988, 24; Stan Isle, "Mr. Efficiency Reuschel Uses a First-Pitch Plan," *Sporting News*, May 9, 1988, 7.

20. "Voice of the Fan," *Sporting News*, May 23, 1988, 3; June 20, 1988, 3; August 15, 1988, 3; September 5, 1988, 3; October 17, 1988, 4; Nidetz, "Too bad Caray's not in the Hall, out of the booth," 24; Glen Cowing, "Work of Art" (letter to the editor, *Chicago Tribune*, August 11, 1988, 24; Felix Mlodzik, "Caray's lists" (letter to the editor), *Chicago Tribune*, August 15, 1988, 15.

21. Tom Shales, "Dutch Treat at Wrigley," *Washington Post*, October 1, 1988, C1; Charles M. Madigan, "Holy Cow! It's 'Dutch' Reagan Back on the Air," *Chicago Tribune*, October 1, 1988, 1–2.

22. Jerome Holtzman, "Hall Opens Its Door for Caray," *Chicago Tribune*, January 28, 1999, 28; Bob Verdi, "Caray Is Right Where He Belongs," *Chicago Tribune*, January 31, 1989, 27.

20. THE MAYOR OF RUSH STREET

1. Bill Modoono, "Caray Fans Fans' Love for Game," *Pittsburgh Press*, September 18, 1989, 17.

2. William Brashler, "'Holy Cow!' It's Harry on Caray, *Chicago Tribune*, March 10, 1989, 57.

3. Don McLeese, "Not the Whole 'Cow': Harry Caray Cuts Some Prime Parts from the Story of His Life," *Chicago Sun-Times*, March 29, 1989.

4. Paul Lomartire, "Book on Caray Won't Strike Out," *Palm Beach (Florida) Post*, April 2, 1989, 214.

5. Author interview with David Israel, March 5, 2018.

6. Bill Deane, *Baseball Myths: Debating, Debunking, and Disproving Tales from the Diamond* (Lanham, Md.: Rowman & Littlefield, 2015; Kindle edition), location 3649.

7. Jerome Holtzman, "Well, Here Harry Is: In the Hall of Fame," *Chicago Tribune*, July 24, 1989, 11.

8. Terry Boers, "Caray Should Call It Quits, End Slaughter," *Chicago Sun-Times*, July 26, 1989.

9. Author interview with Mike Leiderman, November 27, 2017.

10. William Gildea, "New Day May Dawn at Wrigley," *Washington Post*, September 21, 1989, B6.

11. Steve Nidetz, "Caray Steals the Show at His Latest Enshrinement," *Chicago Tribune*, December 15, 1989, 68.

12. Author interview with Dewayne Staats, April 19, 2018.

13. Steve Nidetz, "Nelson Works Hard to Stick with Cubs," *Chicago Tribune*, April 14, 1989, 56.

14. Author interview with Bob Brenly, March 20, 2018.

15. Author interview with Thom Brennaman, February 3, 2018.

16. Author interview with Brennaman.

17. Author interview with Brenly.

18. Author interview with Grant DePorter, March 22, 2018.

19. Bruce Levine, "Caray Loses No Love for Reinsdorf," *Chicago Sun-Times*, June 16, 1990.

20. Mike Kiley, "'Bull' Not Exactly Wild about Harry," *Chicago Tribune*, February 28, 1984, 46.

21. Phil Hersh, "Reinsdorf Moves to Head of His Class," *Chicago Tribune*, June 2, 1985, 41.

22. Bob Verdi, "Now a Few Words from Harry Caray," *Chicago Tribune*, November 28, 1990, 37–38; Bob Verdi, "McMahon Back to Throwing Strikes," *Chicago Tribune*, December 15, 1990, 40.

21. NORTH SIDE VERSUS SOUTH SIDE

1. Ray Sons, "Even Harry Caray Finds It's Time to Wine Down," *Chicago Sun-Times*, September 13, 1992.

2. Ed Sherman, "New Facility as Modern as Other Was Outdated," *Chicago Tribune*, April 17, 1991, 6.

3. Bill Jauss, "New White Sox Home Hits Homer with Fans," *Chicago Tribune*, April 19, 1991, 56.

4. Ed Sherman, "SportsChanel: Vision Fulfilled," *Chicago Tribune*, May 23, 1991, 56.

5. Author interview with Bob Verdi, March 1, 2018.

6. Tony Silvia, *Fathers and Sons in Baseball Broadcasting: The Carays, Brennamans, Bucks, and Kalases* (Jefferson, N.C.: McFarland, 2009), 89–90.

7. Steve Nidetz, "Now, Three Ways to Caray a Ballgame," *Chicago Tribune*, May 13, 1991, 35.

8. Author interview with Chip Caray, February 27, 2018.

9. Rick Telander, "Harry Caray Retrospective Offers Honest Look at Beloved Figure," *Chicago.suntimes.com*, January 30, 2016. https://chicago.suntimes.com/sports/harry-caray-retrospective-offers-honest-look-at-beloved-figure/ (April 28, 2018).

10. Author interview with Chip Caray.

11. Barry Cronin, "Holy Cows! And Sacred Cows: Unharried Caray Still Carrying On," *Chicago Sun-Times*, September 13, 1991.

12. Richard Lindberg, *Stealing First in a Two-Team Town: The White Sox from Comiskey to Reinsdorf* (Champaign, Ill.: Sagamore, 1994), 259–60.

13. Jack Craig, "WGN Fearing Bad-News Cubs? Team's Move to West May Also Shift Away Superstation's Newscast Viewers," *Boston Globe*, July 10, 1992, 86.

14. Steve Nidetz, "Next Stop for Hamilton: Cooperstown," *Chicago Tribune*, August 2, 1992, 38.

15. Author interview with Bill Brown, January 16, 2018.

16. Dave van Dyck, "Announcer Caray Hits Back, Says Critics' Blows Mean Little to Him," *Chicago Sun-Times*, October 2, 1992.

17. Sons, "Even Harry Caray Finds It's Time to Wine Down."

18. Dan Shaughnessy, "Sox' Following Isn't White-Hot: Comiskey Fans Cool on Pennant Fever," *Boston Globe*, October 6, 1993, 36.

22. SLIPS, STRIKES, AND CONTROVERSIES

1. Fred Mitchell, "Harry's Home in Hearts of Fans—for 50 Years," *Chicago Tribune*, April 3, 1994, 137.

2. "Caray Sings His Way into Broadcast Hall (AP)," *Northwest (Woodstock, Illinois) Herald*, March 24, 1994, 19.

3. Dave van Dyck, "Wild about Harry Caray's: 50th Year on Job Begins with a Look Back," *Chicago Sun-Times*, April 3, 1994.

4. Mitchell, "Harry's Home in Hearts of Fans," 137.

5. Brian Hewitt, "Tuff Earns Moniker, Respect," *Chicago Sun-Times*, April 5, 1994.

6. Ellen Warren, "Boo-tiful Day at Old Ballpark," *Chicago Tribune*, April 5, 1994, 41.

7. "High Fives/Low Lights," *Sporting News*, June 6, 1994, 6.

8. Joseph A. Reaves, "No Serious Injuries from Caray's Fall, but Tests Delay His Return Home," *Chicago Tribune*, June 24, 1994, 175; Joseph A. Reeves, "A Month Later, Dunston Has Respectably Raised Average," *Chicago Tribune*, June 10, 1994, 61; Joseph A. Reeves, "Caray Hopes to Become Home-Body Next Season," *Chicago Tribune*, May 12, 1994, 205.

9. "Fanfare: Caray Is Singing the Black-and-Blues," *Washington Post*, June 26, 1994, D2.

10. Joseph A. Reeves, "Caray Hopes to Be Back at Work Monday," *Chicago Tribune*, June 28, 1994, 165.

11. Joseph A. Reeves, "Caray May Return—with Sandberg," *Chicago Tribune*, July 8, 1994, 41.

12. Joseph A. Reeves, "Holy Cow! Harry Back, Ryno Visiting," *Chicago Tribune*, July 22, 1994, 187; Toni Ginnetti, "Recuperated Caray Returns to Wrigley," *Chicago Sun-Times*, July 23, 1994.

13. Joseph A. Reeves, "Birthday Boy Caray Turns . . . a Year Older," *Chicago Tribune*, March 1, 1995, 213.

14. Steve Gietschier, "Year in Review," in *Sporting News Baseball Guide, 1996* (St. Louis, Mo.: Sporting News, 1996), 150.

15. Rick Telander, "One Final Toast to Harry," *Chicago Sun-Times*, March 1, 1998.

16. Robert Kurson, "Local Baseball Announcers Facing New Challenge," *Chicago Sun-Times*, April 21, 1995.

17. Author interview with Bob Verdi, March 1, 2018.

18. Steve Nidetz, "WGN Apologizes for Caray's Remark in Interview," *Chicago Tribune*, September 15, 1995, 47.

19. Art Golab and Joe Goddard, "'I Didn't Do Anything Wrong': Caray Shrugs off Criticism Stemming from Racial Remark," *Chicago Sun-Times*, September 16, 1995.

20. Golab and Goddard, "'I Didn't Do Anything Wrong."

21. Steve Nidetz, "Still at the Mic: Broadcasting Colleagues Defend Caray," *Chicago Tribune*, September 19, 1995, 41.

22. Eric Zorn, "It Could Be, It May Be, but Intent of Caray's Comment Isn't Clear," *Chicago Tribune*, September 21, 1995, 225.

23. Zorn, "It Could Be, It May Be," 225.

24. Paul Sullivan, "In Caray's Eyes, He Owes No One Apology for Remark," *Chicago Tribune*, September 23, 1995, 46.

25. Steve Nidetz, "No Caray Apology Necessary: WGN," *Chicago Tribune*, September 18, 1995, 23.

26. Author interview with Thom Brennaman, February 3, 2018.

27. Rick Telander, "Harry's Apology Would Make All OK," *Chicago Sun-Times*, September 17, 1995.

28. Author interview with Rick Telander, January 18, 2018.

29. Steve Nidetz, "It Might Be, It Could Be . . . It Is, Another Caray, Chip, Joining Cubs Broadcast Team," *Chicago Tribune*, November 29, 1995, 50.

30. Author interview with Chip Caray, February 27, 2018.

31. Author interview with Chip Caray.

32. Barry Rozner, "Colangelo's Cash Lures Brennaman," *Arlington Heights Daily Herald*, March 7, 1996.

23. LAST CALL

1. Joe Knowles, "Hit & Run: Taking a Swing at the News," *Chicago Tribune*, September 27, 1996, 45.

2. Robert Kurson, "Bears' Larrivee is WGN-TV Pick for Cubs Games," *Chicago Sun-Times*, January 3, 1996.

3. Steve Nidetz, "Holy Cow! Now They'll Know Who Larrivee Is," *Chicago Tribune*, February 13, 1996, 183.

4. Author interview with Wayne Larrivee, May 11, 2018.

5. Author interview with Pat Hughes, May 3, 2018.

6. Author interview with Hughes.

7. Michael Tackett, "Dark Clouds Hover over Campaign," *Chicago Tribune*, August 30, 1996, 14.

8. Barry Rozner, "Harry Back at Scene of Fall—and Feeling Fine," *(Chicago Suburban) Daily Herald*, September 3, 1996, 13.

9. Ted Cox, "Rooney Earns Top Honors for WMVP and Fox Work," *(Chicago Suburban) Daily Herald*, October 3, 1996.

10. Author interview with Father John Smyth, May 9, 2018.

11. Eileen O. Daday, "Caray Lauded for Giving to Maryville Children," *(Chicago Suburban) Daily Herald*, November 3, 1996, 343.

12. Ted Cox, "Commuting Dues Pay off for Lewin," *(Chicago Suburban) Daily Herald*, January 30, 1997, 76.

13. Author interview with Bob Verdi, March 1, 2018.

14. Mike Kiley, "Cubs Planning to Caray on More Than Ever This Season," *Chicago Sun Times*, February 14, 1997.

15. Mike Kiley, "Despite Being Undermined, Lewin Praises Caray," *Chicago Sun Times*, February 16, 1997.

16. Phil Rosenthal, "Six Weeks Later, Lewin Sets Foot in Cubs Booth," *Chicago Sun-Times*, May 15, 1997.

17. Steve Stone, with Barry Rozner, *Where's Harry? Steve Stone Remembers His Years with Harry Caray* (Dallas, Tex.: Taylor, 1999), 55–56.

18. Author interview with Verdi.

19. Fred Mitchell, "Odds & Ins: Caray Set to Sing When Players Begin to Swing," *Chicago Tribune*, February 25, 1997, 201.

20. Author interview with Grant DePorter, March 22, 2018.

21. Jim O'Donnell, "Let's Be Frank: Channel 9 Has Duty to Recast Harry," *Chicago Sun-Times*, April 11, 1997.

22. Phil Rosenthal, "Cubs Are Definitely Laughable, Shawon," *Chicago Sun-Times*, April 14, 1997.

23. Paul Sullivan, "Sideshows Overshadow as Brewers Come to Wrigley," *Chicago Tribune*, June 13, 1997, 51; Paul Sullivan, "Inside the Cubs," *Chicago Tribune*, June 19, 1997, 63.

24. Michael Hirsley, "Harry's Final Sign off Sounded a Familiar Refrain for Cubs Fans," *Chicago Tribune*, February 27, 1998, 208.

25. Michael Hirsley, "Cubs Adding a Caray to the TV Booth," *Chicago Tribune*, December 18, 1997, 65.

26. Michael Hirsley and Tim Jones, "Forty-Seven Fewer Cubs Games on Ch. 9," *Chicago Tribune*, January 29, 1998, 43.

24. A LONG GOODBYE

1. Ed Sherman, "He Took Us out to the Ballgame," *Chicago Tribune*, February 19, 1998, 50.

2. Ed Castro, "Cubs' Caray Remained Hospitalized," *(Palm Springs, California) Desert Sun*, February 16, 1998, 1. Todd Henneman, "Doctors: Outlook Bleak for Caray," *(Palm Springs, California) Desert Sun*, February 18, 1998, 1.

3. Michael Hirsley, "Heart Irregularity Is Blamed for Caray's Fall," *Chicago Tribune*, February 17, 1998, 37.

4. Michael Hirsley, "Doctors Say Caray Prognosis 'Poor,'" *Chicago Tribune*, February 18, 1998, 1.

5. Author interview with Chip Caray, February 27, 2018.

6. Paul Sullivan, "The Voice—and the Man—Were Unique," *Chicago Tribune*, February 19, 1998, 54.

7. Richard Sandomir, "Harry Caray, 78, Colorful Baseball Announcer, Dies," *New York Times*, February 19, 1998, D25.

8. Howard Manly, "One of a Kind Caray's Zest for Life and Baseball Made Him a True Original," *Boston Globe*, February 20, 1998, D6.

9. I. J. Rosenberg, "Skip Caray's Reaction to Hamilton: 'Sick Man,'" *Atlanta Constitution*, February 21, 1998, 61.

10. Milo Hamilton and Dan Schlossberg, with Bob Ibach, *Making Airwaves: 60 Years at Milo's Microphone* (Champaign, Ill.: Sports Publishing, 2006), 115–16.

11. Ed Castro, "Caray Fans Bid Farewell," *(Palm Springs, California) Desert Sun*, February 21, 1998, 1.

12. Michael Hirsley and Mitch Martin, "It Was Harry's Kind of Funeral," *Chicago Tribune*, February 28, 1998, 1; "Pete Vonachen Tribute to Harry Caray," *YouTube*, March 4, 2011, www.youtube.com/watch?v=JgPmTXI99Es (May 13, 2018).

13. Author interview with Grant DePorter, March 22, 2018.

14. Rick Telander, "One Final Toast to Harry," *Chicago Sun-Times*, March 1, 1998.

15. Author interview with Chip Caray.

16. Michael Hirsley, "Harry Era Ends in Tears, Chants, Cheers," *Chicago Tribune*, April 4, 1998, 1.

17. Skip Bayless, "Hearing Sing-a-long Is Believing Anything Can Happen on North Side," *Chicago Tribune*, April 4, 1998, 45.

18. Mike Kiley, "Cubs Caray the Day: Warm Memories Help Trachsel Chill Expos," *Chicago Sun-Times*, April 4, 1998.

19. Toni Ginnetti, "Caray Tributes Amaze Grace," *Chicago Sun-Times*, April 4, 1998.

20. Mark Alesia, "Seventh Inning Packed with Emotions for Carays," *(Chicago Suburban) Daily Herald*, April 4, 1998.

21. Author interview with Bob Vorwald, February 8, 2018.

22. Paul Sullivan, "Inside the Cubs," *Chicago Tribune*, April 4, 1998, 47.

23. Richard Roeper, "Harry Is Irreplaceable, but Enough Is Enough," *Chicago Sun-Times*, April 6, 1998.

24. Author interview with Chip Caray.

25. Richard Roeper, "Remember Harry, Jack, but Forget the Statues," *Chicago Sun-Times*, August 10, 1998.

26. Patrick E. Gauen, "Cardinals Dedicate Stadium Statue to Jack Buck," *St. Louis Post-Dispatch*, August 31, 1998, 1.

27. Author interview with Chip Caray.

28. Jay Mariotti, "Cubs Drop the Ball with Brickhouse," *Chicago Sun-Times*, April 13, 1999; Bob Logan, "Caray, Brickhouse Tributes Stir Debate," *(Chicago Suburban) Daily Herald*, April 13, 1999.

25. EPILOGUE

1. Barry Rozner, "Two Decades Later, Still Missing Harry," *(Chicago Suburban) Daily Herald*, February 3, 1998.

2. "Jack Buck: The Voice of St. Louis," *St. Louis Post-Dispatch*, June 20, 2002, 28.

3. "Ask the Fans at stltoday.com," *St. Louis Post-Dispatch*, June 23, 2002, 38.

4. Paul Sullivan, "Perfect Alignment," *Chicago Tribune*, October 9, 2003, section 7, 9.

5. Author interview with Chip Caray, February 27, 2018.

6. Author interview with Mike Leiderman, November 27, 2017.

7. Bob Verdi, "Time to Wipe Away Bitterness of Caray–Hamilton Feud," *Chicago Tribune*, February 19, 2006, section 3, 14; author interview with Bob Verdi, March 1, 2018.

8. Fred Mitchell, "Former Cubs, Sox Announcer dies at 88," *Chicago Tribune*, September 18, 2015, section 3, 5.

9. Tony Silvia, *Fathers and Sons in Baseball Broadcasting: The Carays, Brennamans, Bucks, and Kalases* (Jefferson, N.C.: McFarland, 2009), 108, 110, 117–18; Bruce Weber, "Skip Caray, 68, Atlanta Braves Voice Known for His Biting Wit, Is Dead," *New York Times*, August 5, 2008, B8.

10. Alejandra Cancino, "Meet Me by the Harry Statue," *Chicago Tribune*, September 2, 2010, section 1, 3.

11. Author interview with Leiderman.

12. Paul Sullivan, "A Last Interview: Speaking of Past, Looking to Future," *Chicago Tribune*, February 19, 1998, 55.

13. Author interview with Ron Rapoport, January 25, 2018.

14. Richard Roeper, "Remember Harry, Jack, but Forget the Statues," *Chicago Sun-Times*, August 10, 1998.

15. Curt Smith, *Voices of Summer: Ranking Baseball's 101 All-Time Best Announcers* (New York: Carroll & Graf, 2005), 161, 391.

16. Author interview with Bob Vorwald, February 8, 2018.

17. Author interview with Rich King, January 11, 2018.

18. Author interview with Ed Randall, January 17, 2018.

19. Author interview with Rick Telander, January 18, 2018.

20. Author interview with Grant DePorter, March 22, 2018.

21. Author interview with Dewayne Staats, April 19, 2018.

22. Author interview with Verdi.

23. Author interview with Chip Caray.

24. Author interview with Ned Colletti, January 19, 2018.

BIBLIOGRAPHY

Allen, Dick, and Tim Whitaker. *Crash: The Life and Times of Dick Allen*. New York: Ticknor & Fields, 1989.

Alton (Illinois) Evening Telegraph, 1952.

Atlanta Constitution, February 1998.

Auletta, Ken. *Media Man: Ted Turner's Improbable Empire*. New York: W. W. Norton, 2004.

Baltimore Sun, 1989.

(Bloomington, Illinois) Pantagraph, 1950.

Boston Globe, 1946–1995.

Broadcasting & Cable, 1994.

Brosnan, Jim. *The Long Season: An Inside Chronicle of the Baseball Year as Seen by Major League Pitcher Jim Brosnan*. New York: Harper & Brothers, 1960.

Buck, Jack, with Rob Rains and Bob Broeg. *That's a Winner*. Champaign, Ill.: Sagamore, 1997.

Caray, Harry, with Bob Verdi. *Holy Cow!* New York: Villard, 1989.

(Carbondale) Southern Illinoisan, 1950–1954.

Chicago Daily News, 1974–1975.

(Chicago Suburban) Daily Herald, 1971–2018.

Chicago Sun-Times, 1975–2016.

Chicago Tribune, 1908–2018.

Chicago Tribune Magazine, 1972–1975.

Chicago Tribune Sportsweek, 1978.

Corbett, Warren. "The 'Strike' against Jackie Robinson: Truth or Myth." *Baseball Research Journal* 46, no. 1 (2017): 88–92.

Decatur (Illinois) Herald, 1969.

Des Moines Register, 1989.

Detroit Free Press, 1968–1979.

Devine, Bing, with Tom Wheatley. *The Memoirs of Bing Devine: Stealing Lou Brock and Other Winning Moves by a Master GM*. Champaign, Ill.: Sports Publishing, 2004.

Dickson, Paul. *Bill Veeck: Baseball's Greatest Maverick*. New York: Walker & Company, 2012.

Eskenazi, Gerald. *Bill Veeck: A Baseball Legend*. New York: McGaw-Hill, 1988.

Flood, Curt, with Richard Carter. *The Way It Is*. New York: Trident, 1970.

Florida Today, 1975.

Fremont (California) Argus, 1970.

Garagiola, Joe. *Baseball Is a Funny Game*. New York: Bantam, 1962.

Gibson, Bob, with Lonnie Wheeler. *Stranger to the Game: The Autobiography of Bob Gibson*. New York: Viking, 1994.

Golenbock, Peter. *The Spirit of St. Louis: A History of the St. Louis Cardinals and Browns*. New York: Avon Books, 2000.

———. *Wrigleyville: A Magical History Tour of the Chicago Cubs*. New York: St. Martin's, 1996.

Halberstam, David. *October 1964*. New York: Villard, 1994.

Hamilton, Milo, and Dan Schlossberg, with Bob Ibach. *Making Airwaves: 60 Years at Milo's Microphone*. Champaign, Ill.: Sports Publishing, 2006.

Helpingstine, Dan. *The Cubs and the White Sox: A Baseball Rivalry, 1900 to the Present*. Jefferson, N.C.: McFarland, 2010.

Hernon, Peter, and Terry Ganey. *Under the Influence: New Edition of the Unauthorized Story of the Anheuser-Busch Dynasty*. New York: Simon & Schuster, 2012. Kindle edition.

Houston Press, 2012.

Hughes, Pat, and Bruce Miles. *Harry Caray: Voice of the Fans*. Naperville, Ill.: Sourcebooks, 2008.

James, Bill. *The Bill James Historical Baseball Abstract*. New York: Ballantine, 1985.

Knoedelseder, William. *Bitter Brew: The Rise and Fall of Anheuser-Busch and America's Kings of Beer*. New York: HarperBusiness, 2012.

Lindberg, Richard. *Stealing First in a Two-Team Town: The White Sox from Comiskey to Reinsdorf*. Champaign, Ill.: Sagamore, 1994.

———. *Who's on 3rd? The Chicago White Sox Story*. South Bend, Ind.: Icarus Press, 1983.

Logan, Bob. *Miracle on 35th Street: Winnin' Ugly with the 1983 White Sox*. South Bend, Ind.: Icarus Press, 1983; New York: Avon Books, 2000.

Long Beach California Independent, 1970.

Los Angeles Times, 1964–1998.

Louisville Courier-Journal, 1972.

Mattoon (Illinois) Journal-Gazette, 1969.

New York Times, 2000–2001.

Oakland Tribune, 1970.

Okkonen, Marc. *Baseball Uniforms of the 20th Century: The Official Major League Baseball Guide*. New York: Sterling, 1991.

Orlando Evening-Star, 1968.

(Palm Springs, California) Desert-Sun, 1998.

Patterson, Ted. *The Golden Voices of Baseball*. Champaign, Ill.: Sports Publishing, 2000.

Philadelphia Inquirer, 1956.

Piersall, Jimmy, with Richard Whittingham. *The Truth Hurts*. Chicago: Contemporary Books, 1984.

Pittsburgh Post-Gazette, 1957–1969.

Pittsburgh Press, 1964–1969.

Poindexter, Ray. *Golden Throats and Silver Tongues: The Radio Announcers*. Conway, Ark.: River Road Press, 1978.

Rapaport, Ron, ed. *From Black Sox to Three-Peats: A Century of Chicago's Best Sportswriting*. Chicago: University of Chicago Press, 2013.

sabr.org/bioproject.

San Francisco Chronicle, 1996.

Santa Cruz (California) Sentinel, 1970.

Shea, Stuart. *Calling the Game: Baseball Broadcasting from 1920 to the Present*. Phoenix, Ariz.: Society for American Baseball Research, 2015.

(Sikeston, Missouri) Daily Standard, 1951.

Silvia, Tony. *Baseball over the Air: The National Pastime on the Radio and in the Imagination*. Jefferson, N.C.: McFarland, 2007.

———. *Fathers and Sons in Baseball Broadcasting: The Carays, Brennamans, Bucks, and Kalases*. Jefferson, N.C.: McFarland, 2009.

Smith, Curt. *Pull Up a Chair: The Vin Scully Story*. Washington, D.C.: Potomac Books, 2009.

———. *Voices of the Game: The First Full-Scale Overview of Baseball Broadcasting, 1920 to the Present*. South Bend, Ind.: Diamond Communications, 1987.

———. *Voices of Summer: Ranking Baseball's 101 All-Time Best Announcers*. New York: Carroll & Graf, 2005.

Snyder, John. *Cardinals Journal: Year by Year and Day by Day with the St. Louis Cardinals since 1882*. Cincinnati, Ohio: Emmis Books, 2006.

———. *Cubs Journal: Year by Year and Day by Day with the Chicago Cubs since 1876*. Cincinnati, Ohio: Clerisy Press, 2008.

———. *White Sox Journal: Year by Year and Day by Day with the Chicago White Sox since 1901*. Cincinnati, Ohio: Clerisy Press, 2009.

Sporting News, 1944–1998.

Sporting News Official Baseball Guide (1970–1982 editions). St. Louis: Sporting News.

Sports Illustrated, 1957–2014.

St. Louis Globe-Democrat, 1961.

St. Louis Post-Dispatch, 1945–2001, 1981–2016.

St. Louis Star-Times, 1943–1949.

Staats, Dewayne, with Dave Scheiber. *Position to Win: A Look at Baseball and Life from the Best Seat in the House*. St. Louis, Mo.: Advance Ink Publishing, 2015.

Stone, Steve, with Barry Rozner. *Where's Harry? Steve Stone Remembers His Years with Harry Caray*. Dallas, Tex.: Taylor, 1999.

Tampa Bay Times, 1956.

Terre Haute (Indiana) Tribune, 1961.

Thornley, Stew. *Holy Cow! The Life and Times of Halsey Hall*. Minneapolis, Minn.: Nodin Press, 1991.

USA Today, 2015.

Veeck, Bill, with Ed Linn. *Veeck—as in Wreck: The Chaotic Career of Baseball's Incorrigible Maverick*. New York: G. P. Putnam's Sons, 1962.

Vorwald, Bob. *Cubs Forever: Memories from the Men Who Lived Them*. Chicago: Triumph, 2008.

Walker, James R., and Robert V. Bellamy Jr. *Center Field Shot: A History of Baseball on Television*. Lincoln: University of Nebraska Press, 2008.

Washington Post, 1947–2017.

White, Bill, with Gordon Dillow. *Uppity: My Untold Stories about the Games People Play*. New York: Grand Central Publishing, 2011.

Wolfe, Rich, and George Castle. *I Remember Harry Caray*. Champaign, Ill.: Sports Publishing, 1998.

www.baseball-reference.com.

www.chicagonow.com.

www.forbes.com/mlb-valuations/list/#tab:overall.

www.hardballtimes.com.

www.retrosheet.org.

www.whitesoxinteractive.com.

INDEX

ABOUT THE AUTHOR

Don Zminda, a SABR member since 1979, retired in 2016 after two-plus decades with STATS LLC, where he served first as director of publications and then director of research for STATS-supported sports broadcasts, including the World Series, the Super Bowl, and the NCAA Final Four. Don has also written or edited more than a dozen sports books, notably the annual *STATS Baseball Scoreboard* (1990–2000) and the SABR publication *Go-Go to Glory: The 1959 Chicago White Sox*. A Chicago native, he lives in Los Angeles with his wife Sharon.